Sea Kayaking

Central and Northern California

Sea Kayaking

Central and Northern California

The Best Day Trips and Tours
from the Lost Coast to Pismo Beach

Second Edition

Roger Schumann and Jan Shriner

FALCONGUIDES

GUILFORD, CONNECTICUT
HELENA, MONTANA
AN IMPRINT OF GLOBE PEQUOT PRESS

FALCONGUIDES®

Copyright © 1999, 2013 by Roger Schumann

A previous edition was published as *Guide to Sea Kayaking Central & Northern California*.

FalconGuides is an imprint of Globe Pequot Press.
Falcon, FalconGuides, and Outfit Your Mind are registered trademarks of Morris Book Publishing, LLC.

Text design: Lisa Reneson
Layout artist: Casey Shain
Project editor: Ellen Urban
Maps by Melissa Baker and Daniel Lloyd © Morris Book Publishing, LLC

Library of Congress Cataloging-in-Publication Data

Schumann, Roger.
  [Guide to sea kayaking in Central and Northern California]
  Sea kayaking central and northern California : the best day trips and tours from the Lost coast to Pismo beach / Roger Schumann and Jan Shriner.
    pages cm
  Includes index.
  ISBN 978-0-7627-8280-2
  1. Sea kayaking—California—Guidebooks. 2. California—Guidebooks. I. Shriner, Jan. II. Title.
  GV788.5.S38 2013
  797.122'409794—dc23

                                                                                2012050291

Printed in the United States of America
10 9 8 7 6 5 4 3 2 1

To my mom, Lorraine Schumann, who now rests "at home in the sea," for her undying encouragement. And to my dad, Robert Schumann, who passes down his love for the sea as surely as his blue eyes, who taught me to catch waves on a boogie board practically since before I could walk, and who kept on "boogying," until catching his final wave, sometime in his eighties.

—ROGER SCHUMANN

To my family, especially my parents for nurturing my love of the water and the outdoors, my brothers for their camaraderie and acceptance of my adventures, and my grandparents, aunts, uncles, in-laws, cousins, nephews, and niece for sharing their exuberance and laughter.

—JAN SHRINER

Contents

Acknowledgments

The acknowledgements continue to pile up for a rewrite, but it didn't seem right to leave out those who made the first edition possible. In addition to Kate McLain and Tom Shores for sharing their local expertise of the Point Reyes area in the original version, I'm now also indebted to Laurie Manarik and Tressa Bronner of Point Reyes Outdoors who currently carry Kate's torch.

Thanks again to longtime colleagues and paddling buds Tom, Bryan, and Buck; and add in Gregg, Kim, Tim, Sean M., a number of recent Matts, and many others whose passion for paddling, playing, and pushing the envelope—and for sharing what they've learned in the process with their students—helps keep my own fires stoked.

Along with the original "A Team"—Alicia, Renie, Dan, Robert, Bill, and Lynda—for helping pioneer early exploratory adventures, I add all my students over the past twenty years at Eskape Sea Kayaking, new and old, who continue to seek out new skills and new adventures. Thanks, again, to Chris Cunningham at *Sea Kayaker* magazine for passing my name on to the original editor at Globe Pequot when she was looking for a guidebook author, and for his ongoing wit, charm, and friendship; and to my original co-author for her help in getting the book out in the first place.

Many of the photos for this edition were submitted by students and friends. My gratitude goes out to Kim Grandfield and Tim Andrews at Sunrise Mountain Sports, Peter Donohue of *California Kayaker* magazine, Cass Kalinski, Buck Johnson, Kim Patterson, Eric B. Norris, Ken Croy, and Susan DeQuattro, and to Jeff Laxier and Cate Hawthorne at Liquid Fusion Kayaking for both their photos and local expertise for trips in the Fort Bragg area.

Thanks also to siblings and family (you all know who you are) for a steady, lifelong stream of love and encouragement as I've navigated the uncharted seas of an alternative livelihood. And finally to my wife, Sandy, for her photos, encouragement, understanding and great patience, especially at those hectic times when deadlines loom large.

What's New in this Edition

Much has changed in the twelve years since the first edition (originally titled *Guide to Sea Kayaking in Central and Northern California*) was published. Roads, beach access, and campgrounds move or close, new ones open up, and co-authors move on to other careers.

In addition to simply updating information and maps for the original routes, however, I also wanted to make this guide even more useful. One way I've tried to do this is by extending many of the earlier routes so that even more of this spectacular coastline is covered.

Notably Cannery Row to Point Piños now rounds the entire Monterey Peninsula to Carmel, Golden Gate to Point Bonita now extends north all the way to Muir Beach, and routes out of Santa Cruz Harbor now cover from Davenport down and from the harbor to the Cement Ship. Similar route extensions have been made along the Mendocino and Big Sur coasts, and the Russian River estuary tour got stretched into a 16-mile camping trip from Guerneville to the sea.

Next, I added several new routes, including trips up the Navaro and Noyo Rivers and paddling out their mouths from Fort Bragg down to Caspar and from Navaro all the way to Elk. I've added an entire Bay Area Lakes section, covering seven popular freshwater paddles. And in San Luis Obispo County, the "mini Lost Coast" from Morro Bay to Port San Luis and the Dinosaur Caves to Pismo Beach are now included.

One of the biggest changes since the first edition is the sea of information now available online. To take advantage of this, routes now feature:

- links for weather and (where available) live webcams and online marine charts,
- addresses for launch sites (so you can plug them into your auto's GPS),
- GPS coordinates for many beaches and landmarks en route,
- and in my mind one of the coolest new features—links to aerial photos from the California Coastal Project website for the launch sites, so that geeks like me can easily do a virtual "fly by," scouting otherwise inaccessible sections of coastline for hidden landing beaches, surf spots and bailouts.

As with the first edition, I tried to keep in mind two overarching goals. First, to create a useful tool not only for my students and readers, but also for myself, focusing on key information we can all use when planning our next paddling adventures. Second, to remind ourselves of the marine treasure we are fortunate to have so close at hand, and to inspire you, as well as myself, to make time in our busy lives to get our boats out on the water to explore it.

Map Legend

Transportation

680	Interstate Highway
101	U.S. Highway
1	State Road
	Local/Forest Road
	Unpaved Road
	Trail
	Railroad Tracks
→	Main Route
·····>	Alternate Route

Hydrology

	Body of Water
	River/Stream
	Marsh
	Mud/Tidal Flats
	Visible Rocks
	Submerged Rocks
5 mph	Wakeless Speed Area

Symbols

	Boat Launch
	Bridge
1	Buoy Marker
▲	Campground
∩	Cave
ⅠⅠⅠⅠ	Cliffs
•–•	Gate
	Hills
⬟	House
	Launch Site
	Lighthouse
1	Mileage Marker
P	Parking
▲	Peak
■	Point of Interest
❶	Route Number
	Tower
○	Town

Paddling the Pacific Coast

Renowned for its world-class scenery, the coastline of Central and Northern California spans three of the nation's twelve National Marine Sanctuaries, two wilderness areas, and one National Seashore. It's no accident this area has received so much protection—it is among the most spectacular and wildlife-rich marine habitats on the planet—and it's no accident it is featured here. Although there are literally hundreds of lakes, rivers, and marshes to paddle farther inland, when originally asked to write a book of "best trips" in this region, my thoughts naturally drifted to the coast. By far the best paddling in the state is on salt water—from the quiet, bird-filled estuaries and protected bays to the exposed headlands of the open Pacific. In this new edition, however, I include new trips on several of the area's best lakes, especially as quick getaways for paddlers living inland, when they don't have the time to drive out to the coast.

The California coast, however, is still best known for the rugged beauty of its wave-sculpted cliffs, even though this may not be the sort of placid shoreline many paddlers typically think of when it comes to dropping their boats in the water. But tucked away along these craggy shores are pockets of glassy water where even new or timid paddlers shouldn't hesitate to explore. In addition to open-ocean adventurers, this book is also for paddlers who prefer protected waters, and whose thrills are more simple: drifting past shorebirds that stalk the mudflats of Morro Bay, sneaking through the maze of salt-marsh channels that fringe Elkhorn Slough, and camping on a deserted beach in the backwaters of Point Reyes National Seashore.

But after a taste of salt-sea air, don't be surprised if you get drawn like salmon smolt to the open sea. Vast horizons open up to any paddler willing to leave the security of the sloughs and harbors, and not all of them are limited to advanced rough-water kayakers. Many sheltered coves offer safe launching beaches with access to miles of intermediate paddling, and vistas expand exponentially to anyone prepared to practice surf landings. The amount of protected water is limited in our area, however, so advanced skills are the key to the best of the best: the remote "wilderness" beaches and sea caves that are inaccessible save by sea in a small boat seaworthy and maneuverable enough to negotiate surf zones and rock gardens.

This book is about both exploring the swimming-pool-calm backwaters as well as venturing out along the open coast. Routes described start with the famed Lost Coast of Mendocino County and sweep southward with the prevailing winds past the Point Reyes National Seashore, San Francisco Bay, the Monterey Bay National Marine Sanctuary and Big Sur coast, and on to Pismo Beach in San Luis Obispo County. Most of the forty-eight routes covered are day trips, giving options for beginner, intermediate, and advanced paddlers, so that well over a hundred route alternatives exist. Although camping is limited, places good for overnight trips are recommended. I also drop in my passion for kayak surfing and rock-garden play, mentioning many surfing and play spots.

Although specific paddling techniques are not covered, a section on trip planning and water safety as they pertain to local hazards is included. However, even the best book is no substitute for competent professional instruction. With some good training and a little time in the cockpit, much of this amazing watery wonderland can be yours to explore.

Trip Planning, Water Safety, and Sea Sense

The sea kayaking industry has done a great job of promoting the ease and accessibility of the sport—sometimes too good. It's true, practically anyone can enjoy kayaking. Modern boats are so user friendly that it's easy for people to hop on and go . . . and quickly get in over their heads. Making the boat go forward is the easy part. Picking a route that's compatible with your type of kayak, skill level, and conditions on the day you paddle takes experience and something called "sea sense." More art than science, sea sense takes time and experience to develop. Those with strong water backgrounds, sailors and surfers for example, may be ahead of the game, but they will still need to learn the limitations of this new craft. This is why we strongly recommend taking professional lessons at each level of your development and paddling with partners who know the area and are more skilled than you when exploring new places. The book *Deep Trouble,* a compilation of accident reports from *Sea Kayaker* magazine, is recommended as mandatory reading for every kayaker: There is much to be learned from the mistakes of others.

Water Safety Tips
- Don't paddle in water rougher than you've practiced rescues in.
- Check the weather before you launch, and tide books if appropriate.
- Paddle within your skills limits and the limits of your craft.
- Dress for immersion and wear your PFD: Hypothermia kills kayakers.
- Scout the route from land first, whenever possible, on open-coast trips to assess conditions on more exposed areas beyond the launch site.

Hypothermia—Dress for Immersion
Statistically speaking, hypothermia is a sea kayaker's number one threat, accounting for the vast majority of kayaking fatalities. And our area is no exception. Most routes in the book are considered cold-water paddling environments because water temperatures generally hover in the fifties year-round. Some estuaries, rivers, or reservoirs may warm up during the summer, but the open coast rarely does. The savvy paddler's catch phrase, "Dress for immersion," implies dressing for the water temperature not the air temperature. Assume you will end up in the water and dress accordingly—wear a wet or dry suit that will keep you warm if you get wet. If you get hot, it's easier to cool down around water than it is to warm back up if you get cold. For safety carry a spare change of warm clothes in a dry bag, and consider changing into a dry shirt when stopping for

lunch and the cool breeze starts to blow. A warm cap is especially helpful—it takes up little space, and you lose a lot of body heat from a bare head. Around cold water, it's said, "Cotton kills," so wear synthetics or wool. If not familiar with the stages and effects of hypothermia, do yourself a favor and find out.

Rescues and Reentries

The majority of kayaking accidents have a common theme: People start out in beginner areas, conditions change beyond their skill level, they capsize in bodies of water colder than sixty degrees (often without wet suit or life jacket); are unable to get back into their boats because they don't have the proper rescue gear or don't know how to use it, and then become hypothermic. People lose body heat five times faster when wet, but twenty-five times faster when submerged! So to combat hypothermia, practice rescues regularly. Instead of the term *rescue,* however, which connotes panic and being a victim, many prefer the more modern terms *reentry* or *recovery* because they're calmer, more in control: You've fallen out of your boat, so you don't need to call the Coast Guard, you just need to climb back aboard. The two most common reentries for closed-cockpit kayaks—the bread-and-butter minimum skills—are the "paddle float self-rescue" and the "T rescue." If you don't know what these two techniques are, don't venture farther from shore than you would wade until you've taken a lesson. Accident reports are full of those who thought they could simply climb back into their (now swamped and even less stable) kayaks or "just swim to shore." (Those on open-top kayaks should also be comfortable scrambling back aboard in a variety of conditions.) Then practice. Reentry skills get rusty quickly, so it's a good idea to practice every time you paddle, especially simulated rough-water reentries to get comfortable getting back into your boat in the type of choppy conditions in which you're likely to capsize. To practice this, find an impish friend who will enjoy trying to capsize you by bouncing on and twisting your bow while you're trying to reenter. This is an exercise in tough love, so show no mercy when you return the favor. Those with solid rescue skills rarely end up in accident reports, so remember the Golden Rule: Don't paddle in water that might get rougher than you've practiced rescues in.

Boats and Gear

Although many routes in the book are appropriate for a variety of boats—open-deck kayaks, recreational kayaks, whitewater kayaks, and even canoes and SUPs (stand-up paddleboards)—the more advanced routes are written with full-length, closed-deck sea-touring kayaks in mind, those in the 14- to 18-foot range and not more than 25 inches wide, with bulkheads and hatches fore and aft. These boats are the most efficient, seaworthy, and versatile. Open-deck kayaks will also work on most routes and have the advantage of being more affordable and more user-friendly for beginners. Most standard sit-on-tops, however, are less efficient, especially in wind, so overall mileage covered may be limited. The popular "recreational" kayaks (less than 13 feet long, wider than 25 inches and sans bulkheads) are not recommended beyond the "Beginner" segments of each route. Although these kayaks are generally quite stable and user friendly, they are typically designed only for calm-water locations near shore where you could easily swim to shore after a capsize. When capsized, their large, high-volume cockpits tend to flood with water, even if equipped with float bags, making them extremely difficult to do an assisted rescue on, and often impossible for solo reentry techniques.

Whatever your craft, the Coast Guard requires that each paddler carry a wearable PFD (personal flotation device or "life vest") on their boat; however, statistics show year after year that the vast majority of drownings involve people carrying PFDs instead of actually wearing them. The national Safe Boating Campaign (SafeBoatingCampaign.com), along with their partners at the US Coast Guard and the American Canoe Association, recommend all boaters to "Wear It!" Like wearing seat belts in your car, wearing life vests has been shown to save lives, and like a seat belt, you need to be wearing it before an accident happens.

The idea is to think ahead and be prepared with intentionally redundant safety items. The following list is considered the standard minimum safety equipment.

- Kayak with secure flotation (in both ends)
- Life vest (Coast Guard–approved Type III)
- Spray skirt (for closed-cockpit kayaks)
- Paddle and spare paddle (one per group, minimum)
- Appropriate clothing ("dress for immersion" wet suit, etc.)
- Spare warm clothing (preferably not cotton; in a dry bag)
- Paddle float self-rescue device (and the ability to use it)
- Bilge pump
- Water bottle (dehydration exacerbates hypothermia)
- Food (snacks you can reach while paddling)
- Tow line (one or more per group)
- First-aid kit
- Knowledge (of rescues, area to be paddled, weather forecast, etc.)
- Helmet (for any trip requiring surf launch/landing or paddling around rocks or caves)
- Additional safety gear (depending on the difficulty of the trip, this may include tide and current tables, charts and maps, compass, flares, waterproof flashlight, weather radio, boat repair kit, VHF marine radio or cell phone, survival kit, etc.)

Weather—The Pacific High, Northwest Winds, and Paddling in the Lee

For those who learn to work around the weather, our coast is blessed with a year-round paddling season. The main concept to understand about safely paddling this area is the prevailing northwesterly weather pattern and how it's affected by coastal topography. During most of the year (spring, summer, and fall), a stable high pressure system called the Pacific High parks off the California coast like a giant umbrella, sloughing storm systems north into Oregon and Washington. Largely responsible for the state's famous sunshine, the Pacific High also has a big effect on local winds. Because high pressure systems spin clockwise in the northern hemisphere, wind blows in off the ocean from out of the northwest, deflects off the coastal mountains, and follows the coastline southeastward. And since land heats faster than water—as the inland valleys heat up each day with the rising sun—hot air rising creates a giant vacuum, drawing the cool, dense coastal air southward and inland with increasing velocity as the day heats up. (This atmospheric suction is why some kayakers claim the wind doesn't blow on the coast, it sucks.) By afternoon 15- to 25-knot northwesterlies are commonplace, even on lakes and sloughs well inland.

The main problems with paddling in wind are that it slows progress if you're bucking it, it can push you where you don't want to go (into cliffs, rocks, or boat channels), and it creates choppy seas and waves. As whitecaps begin to form around 10 knots or so, a paddler heading into the wind will be slowed by about 1 knot (1 nautical mile per hour, approximately 1.2 mph). Because most paddlers cruise at 3 or 4 knots, that can mean a significant loss in progress. A 15-knot headwind can knock your speed in half, and only the strongest paddlers can make crawling progress against 20 to 25 knots. As you tire, the wind can blow you off course or into hazardous conditions, so consider wind strength and direction when planning a trip. Another problem with wind is that it forms waves. The longer and stronger it blows, and the longer the fetch—or expanse—of open water it blows across, the choppier the seas become. Even on a lake. Where wind opposes a tidal current, steep breaking seas can form. On the open coast, ocean waves break on beaches, greatly complicating launching and landing (see Swell and Surf, page 12).

Tips for Paddling in the Wind

So what's all this mean to a kayaker? There are a few good ways to deal with the wind, and the first thing you need to do is check the forecast. A portable weather radio (or VHF marine radio) is one of the best investments you can make for your comfort and safety. It broadcasts a continuous marine forecast from the National Weather Service, including wind and swell reports, that is updated every few hours. You can check the weather forecast before you launch and periodically throughout the day, although be aware that some cliffy areas of our coastline block reception, so you might need to listen as you drive to the put-in to discover where you lose the signal. These forecasts are also available online, and many paddlers find it easier to check their computers before leaving home or on their smart phones once they arrive, but understand that the same coastal cliffs that block radio reception often block cell phone signals as well. Two of my favorite phone apps are NOAA Buoy Data Reader and Surfline, and my favorite marine weather website is noted below.

An important key to using the marine forecasts is knowing the appropriate "zone forecast" to check of the several reported. See the sidebar on "Making Sense of Marine Weather Forecasts."

Once you've checked the forecast, one good way to avoid wind is to "time" your paddle: Leave early in the morning and get off the water before the wind starts blowing or try a short evening paddle after it has died. This is especially good advice for beginners. Note that when whitecaps begin to form (around 10 knots), they should act as warning flags to novice paddlers.

Another way to dodge the wind is to paddle in the lee, the protected downwind side of points of land. On this coast that generally means the windy side faces north and the lee faces south. Notice most routes begin in the lee of points.

Experienced kayakers typically paddle northward into the wind in the morning, so it's at their backs on the return; or they run a shuttle, leaving a vehicle at a landing site to the south and paddling downwind. Running a shuttle, however, creates logistical problems, the least of which are the time involved and remembering to bring your keys to the landing beach (don't laugh; it happens with embarrassing regularity), and the worst of which can include the inability to backtrack against the wind if conditions become too rough and finding yourself committed to completing a trip in dangerous conditions.

The final strategy is simply to plan to save some energy for the return trip, a common technique for paddling coastal rivers on which the last mile or so back to the launch site at the mouth often involves a slog into wind funneling upriver off the ocean. Using hills or banks as natural windbreaks can sometimes help in these situations.

Seasonal Weather Patterns

During wintertime the Pacific High weakens and drifts southward, allowing storm tracts to hit the coast. Because winds spin counterclockwise around low pressure systems, southerly winds typically precede a storm front and should be a warning sign to off-season paddlers. These storms often send large swells to batter the coastline, making coastal touring difficult. Between storms, however, calm, sunny days in the mid-fifties are not uncommon. With bird and gray whale migrations in full swing, paddling conditions are often quite good, even on the open coast, provided the swell is not up.

Spring is the unsettled season; the Pacific High battles with approaching storm fronts as it migrates northward and tries to reestablish itself. Gusty northwest winds are common as well as occasional late-season storms. It may be cool and breezy one day, sunny and calm the next, and stormy the day after. Coastal kayakers need to choose their days carefully to avoid large swells from storms passing to the north, but experienced kayak surfers often enjoy the year's best and most consistent surfing. Conditions tend to settle down as the season progresses.

Summer brings fog to the coast, which typically burns off about the time the afternoon winds kick up. For days and weeks on end a common coastal forecast will call for morning fog, afternoon winds to 15 knots, and swells of 4 to 6 feet. As inland valleys swelter, the coast keeps its cool, with temperatures in the high sixties to low seventies.

MAKING SENSE OF MARINE WEATHER FORECASTS

For the uninitiated, wading through the sea of information provided on a typical five- to ten-minute marine weather radio broadcast—or the endless options available online—can seem overwhelming. An important key is knowing which "zone forecast" to choose. Whether you're listening to the radio or surfing online, the National Weather Service forecasts are divided north to south into sections of about 50 to 100 miles of coastline, typically stretching between major points of land sticking out to sea.

These zones are then subdivided by their distance from shore: the "Coastal Waters Forecast," which goes out to 10 nautical miles from shore, is the one most kayakers use; and the zone "from 10 to 60 nautical miles" offshore, which most kayakers don't paddle in. It is also a good idea to pay attention to when the forecast was last updated. Theoretically this is done every three hours, but sometimes you might notice that you're listening to a stale broadcast that was last updated "as of 2:00 a.m." and you've just stopped on a beach for lunch, wondering whatever happened to the 8:00 a.m. update, much less the 11:00 a.m.

The eight Coastal Waters zones covered in the book are below (with links to their NWS forecast pages), and each route description tells you which zone or zones to use.

- Cape Mendocino to Point Arena (forecast.weather.gov/MapClick .php?zoneid=PZZ455)
- Point Arena to Point Reyes (forecast.weather.gov/MapClick .php?zoneid=PZZ540)
- Point Reyes to Pigeon Point (forecast.weather.gov/MapClick .php?zoneid=PZZ545)
- San Francisco/San Pablo/Suisun Bays and the West Delta (forecast .weather.gov/MapClick.php?zoneid=PZZ530)
- Pigeon Point to Point Piños (forecast.weather.gov/MapClick .php?zoneid=PZZ560)
- Monterey Bay (forecast.weather.gov/MapClick.php?zoneid=PZZ535)
- Point Piños to Point Piedras Blancas (forecast.weather.gov/MapClick .php?zoneid=PZZ565)
- Point Piedras Blancas to Point Arguello (forecast.weather.gov/ MapClick.php?zoneid=PZZ670)

One really handy feature of the web pages is the ability to obtain a "Point Forecast" within each zone. If you were planning a trip out of Santa Cruz Harbor, for example, you'd choose the Monterey Bay zone forecast, which includes a clickable Google map next to the text. By clicking on the map near the harbor, you can get a more precise forecast for that part of the bay. While the overall zone forecast might scare you off with predictions for northwest afternoon winds from 15 to 25 knots and seas to 8 feet, this would include exposed areas in the middle of the bay, miles from shore. The point forecast in the more protected waters near the harbor, on the other hand, might only be calling for winds from 5 to 10 knots with seas to 3 feet. While it is nice to be able to get a detailed "point forecast," it's still wise to tune in to the zone forecast to get a bigger picture view of what is going on with the weather.

To get a better sense of overall patterns, many coastal paddlers also like to check the forecasts for zones nearby (typically the one to the north where the weather is coming from during normal summer weather patterns), especially if paddling near a point that's on the border of two zones.

Another trick is to pay attention to the wind forecast for nearby coastal towns. This is especially handy in places where you can't get a point forecast off the Internet, like the Mendocino coast, which has generally good weather-radio reception but poor cell coverage. It's not uncommon for the coastal waters forecast to call for 20-knot winds while the forecast for the town of Mendocino is only 5 to 10 mph. In this case I've generally found that the town forecast is closer to what I experience when paddling close to shore. However, if the onshore winds are also forecasted to be 20, that's a different story.

Finally, savvy paddlers also tune in to the "three-hourly buoy reports." Updated more or less on the time scale mentioned, these are the actual wind and sea conditions being reported by the offshore buoys and onshore weather stations in a variety of locations up and down the coast. While the forecast might be predicting 15 knots, buoys nearby might already be reporting gusts to 25—or vice versa—so knowing which buoys are nearby is also handy. This information is also listed for each route. As with the forecast, it is also important to note the time of the update. Buoy reports can also be found online in a variety of places, such as lajollasurf.org/nocal.html.

Fall is the prime season, especially for coastal touring. Fog, wind, and swell often dwindle to naught, along with the summer beach traffic. Indian summer temperatures may soar into the seventies and eighties at the beach and the water temperature may reach the mid sixties.

Tides and Currents

Knowing how to read a tide book and then checking the tides before you paddle can be as important as checking the weather for many routes. Especially in estuaries, sloughs, and coastal rivers, knowing the tide height and direction of currents can make the difference between catching a free ride on the currents, becoming mired in a mile-wide mudflat, or even getting washed out to sea. Getting caught in strong, ocean-going currents at the mouths of rivers and estuaries during an ebb (falling) tide is a common cause of boating accidents; it has already contributed to at least one kayaking fatality in our area. On the open coast where small pocket beaches at the base of cliffs can be rare as jewels, currents are generally negligible, but a high tide can cover the only launch beach for miles under a wash of breaking waves, and a low tide could expose dangerous rocks in the surf zone at your landing site. Only the lake routes are exempt from tidal influences (but not from seasonal fluctuations in water level).

Our coast has two highs and two lows each day, so every six hours or so the tide rises to high, and six hours later falls to low. One of the highs is higher and one of the lows is lower, and height is measured from the mean level of the lower lows at 0.0 feet, and typically fluctuates within a 6-foot range of an average water level of around 3 feet. Lunar phases affect this range, with more extreme tides occurring every two weeks around the full and new moon. A small tide change for our area may only be from a 4- foot high to a 2-foot low, while larger changes typically range from more than 6 feet to minus tides of negative 1 foot.

The larger the tide range on a given day, the stronger the currents will be in narrow bodies of water during ebb (falling) and flood (rising) tides. San Francisco Bay is the only location in our area with actual current charts (widely available at kayak and sailing shops), showing direction and strength of currents. For other areas you'll need to extrapolate current strength from tide range and personal experience. We also suggest taking a "Tides and Currents" class to learn about hazards such as tide rips and skills such as eddy hopping as well as how to interpret tide and current logs.

Swell and Surf

Unlike many popular kayaking areas, such as the Pacific Northwest and much of the East Coast, which have literally hundreds of miles of protected inland passages, sheltered waters in our area are limited. This means that getting into the better paddling areas often means getting through the surf zone. Fortunately, there are many protected beaches and many days of small surf, so that given a little skills training, along with good site selection and timing, most paddlers can enjoy the ocean environment.

Since ocean swells, like the wind, typically approach our coast from the northwest, south-facing beaches in the lee of points tend to have the best protection. Therefore checking the marine weather forecast for the size and direction of the swell is an important part of any coastal tour. Expect swells approaching from the west or south to bring rougher conditions, and swells over 6 feet on exposed (west or northwest-facing) beaches to challenge even advanced paddlers.

Another important facet of waves is their period, the number of seconds between crests. The longer the period, the fatter and more powerful the wave. A typical summer forecast might be for 4-foot waves from the northwest at 8 to 10 seconds. But if a 15-second south swell is also forecast, even if only 2 feet high, that means that storms from the southern hemisphere are sending big, fat waves across the Pacific that can turn into large "sneaker" waves when they hit shore.

As swells reach the shallow bottom of a beach, they become breaking waves or surf, and handling a sea kayak in surf can be dangerous. Take at least one surf zone class before challenging the waves and always wear a helmet. Start small. A rule of thumb for novice surf launches: If the waves are over your head when you're sitting in your kayak, you are probably getting in over your head. Pick a different beach or a different day.

Be aware that some beaches, especially in the Santa Cruz area, do not allow kayaks or restrict their launch sites on busy days. Ask a local kayak store owner or lifeguard before unloading your boat. When landing or launching, it is important to stay well away from others in the water—swimmers, surfers, etc.—because an out-of-control kayak in the waves is a dangerous thing, and launch access could become further restricted if kayakers gain a reputation for running people over.

Once you gain good control in the surf, you may want to try kayak surfing. At first the best place to practice is well away from people, especially board surfers. Once a kayak broaches sideways on a wave and starts side-surfing toward shore, it becomes an out-of-control "surf mower," 15 feet wide and plowing over anything in its path. As you gain more control, and this probably means a reliable roll for closed-deck kayakers, you may want to tackle better-known surf breaks. If so, don't be a "Barney" or "kook": Please adhere to the longstanding rules of surf etiquette. To avoid collisions, catch waves with no one else on them, and especially don't "drop in" and catch a wave that is occupied. Even with expert surfing skills, I generally surf on the shoulders of the waves and well away from board surfers. Dropping in on or running over surfers in some spots will probably get you cussed out or even physically threatened. But most surfers are accepting when they see you understand the rules, are in control of your craft, and present no hazard.

Open-Coast Paddling

Once through the surf you'll find some of the finest paddling in our area—as well as some of the most challenging—along the open coast. Often a short paddle around a headland will leave the parking lot and people far behind as you enter a coastal wilderness of isolated beaches and rugged solitude. The siren call of the open coast can be very alluring. However, it can also be alarming, depending on the skills and experience of the group and the conditions that day. Coastal touring is often more akin to white-water river paddling than sea kayaking, sharing similar thrills and hazards, while requiring the same level of rough-water paddling expertise and water-reading skill.

Exposure is a key consideration: If something goes awry—if the fog comes in, or the wind or swell comes up, or you get tired or hurt, or you break a paddle—are you five minutes or 5 miles from the nearest landing beach? Does that beach have access to a road, or is it sheer cliffs? Is the beach even a twenty-four-hour beach, or is it awash with surf at high tide like many? A million things can go wrong at sea and the greater your exposure, the less room for error.

The open coast can be as unforgiving as it is awesome, so a conservative approach is wise for any who dare sample its wonders. Stay in protected areas unless you have strong surf and rough-water rescue skills. Wear a helmet. Take open-coast classes. Paddle with experienced partners. Always check the marine weather report and choose a day with conditions well within your limits. Know where "bail out" beaches are, and scout them from land first if possible. Stay outside of rock-garden surf zones and caves unless you have a reliable roll and advanced water-reading skills. (Remember, in many areas your paddling buddies will not be able to rescue you without endangering themselves.) And never, never underestimate the power of the sea—remember that waves breaking against rocks exert hundreds of pounds of pressure per square foot, and that kayakers in our area have already been injured or killed on the open coast. That some will ignore these warnings, no matter how emphatic, is regretful. For those who do heed this advice, we offer the best of luck, for there are no guarantees and no ways to eliminate the risks entirely.

Basic Kayak Navigation

With few islands, crossings, or confusing passages in this area, following the shoreline for 5 or 10 miles in a day and recognizing landmarks with or without a map often works just fine. Instead of marine charts, which in our area tend to cover too much territory to be useful to kayakers, topographic maps often provide better detail. The trick is to know what landmarks to look for while on the water, and what constitutes a major point versus another rock outcrop. The ability to navigate by chart and compass (and perhaps Global Positioning System [GPS]) can come in handy in the fog and could be essential on open-water crossings.

Minimum Impact

As relatively new kids on the block, sea kayakers are in somewhat the same boat as mountain bikers were when that sport began to boom. There were no regulations at first, until a few screw-ups started cutting new trail, zooming past hikers, and ruining it for the rest of us. Soon bikes were banned in many areas. To prevent this from happening to

WILDLIFE VIEWING TIPS

With a little sensitivity and a good pair of binoculars, viewing marine wildlife needn't disturb it. Keep your distance and act disinterested. Like humans, animals too have "comfort zones" and don't like anyone crowding their personal space. On the open coast where animals are not used to people, even the 100 yards recommended by the Marine Mammal Protection Act may not be sufficient. In areas with kayak rentals like Elkhorn Slough or Cannery Row where animals are used to kayaks, 50 feet (a good three or four kayak lengths) is about as close as you should get. If a marine mammal lifts its head to look at you, or if a bird defecates and stretches its wings to prepare for flight, that's a sign they're feeling nervous and about to flee. Move away quietly while turning and looking in the other direction. This is where the "act disinterested" part comes in. Animals can tell when they're being stalked; they don't understand that you're only brandishing a camera. Heading straight toward, or looking directly at an animal will generally be construed as a threat, regardless of your intentions. By approaching at a parallel angle and looking out of the corner of your eyes, you're less likely to spook them, and you'll enjoy better viewing. One final tip: Be quiet. If you drift silently and pretend not to notice them, animals tend to relax and let you view to your heart's content.

kayakers, it's important to establish a reputation as a responsible user group. Otherwise we may find NO KAYAKING signs at our favorite launch beaches.

"No Flee" Wildlife Viewing and the Marine Mammal Protection Act

A major concern resource managers have with kayakers is their effect on wildlife. Designed as a hunting boat, the kayak is so stealthy and efficient at approaching wildlife living in or near the water that it's easy to get too close. Scaring seabirds off nests exposes eggs and chicks to predators. Flushing seals off haul-outs disturbs their important "naps," when they are trying to warm up between hunting forays; it can also separate pups from mothers, and pups sometimes can get crushed in the stampede. We suggest adopting a "no flee" viewing ethic—that is, not getting close enough to cause animals to flee. Not only is this good wilderness etiquette, it's the law. In 1972 the Marine Mammal Protection Act was passed, prohibiting "harassment"—defined as any act causing animals to alter their natural behavior—and recommending that humans maintain a distance of 100 yards. Breaking this federal law carries a stiff penalty with fines up to $10,000. (Marine birds also enjoy protection under a different statute.) And in many areas, especially in state parks and wildlife refuges, rangers and visitors viewing animals from shore with high-powered binoculars will not hesitate to report an errant kayaker.

Pack It In, Pack It Out

This overused adage is obvious on the surface, but it applies to all our trash—even the "biodegradable." Beginning students sometimes ask if it's okay to toss an apple core on the launch beach at Elkhorn Slough, not realizing that maybe a hundred paddlers a week stop there, and that apple cores take weeks to break down. Besides the obvious aesthetic impact, introducing outside food sources attracts pests like wasps and ants. Human waste is also an issue. In general near salt water, the solution to pollution is dilution, so the best place to leave anything (from toothpaste spit to fire pits) is in the water or wet sand where the tides will "flush" it. Near fresh water, backcountry protocol recommends relieving yourself at least 100 feet from streams or lakes.

Other Access Issues

Respecting closed areas also avoids conflicts. Some areas are off-limits to protect sensitive wildlife habitat; others, to protect bathers at popular beaches or private property above the high-tide line. Kayakers need to be aware of these areas. During trip planning contact park rangers or local kayak shops to educate yourself. Learning about traffic patterns and etiquette before paddling around other boats also helps our reputation as competent boaters. Basically stay to the right, stay aware, and stay out of the way. "Sea lice" is a term other boaters use for kayakers whose lack of awareness makes them a navigational hazard. By educating themselves and minimizing their impact, kayakers can maximize their access and become a welcome addition to the marine environment.

How to Use This Book: Guide to Route Descriptions

The following is an explanation of the various sections of each route description. Especially important are the definitions of the rating system and the skills and types of boat expected at the Beginner, Intermediate, and Advanced levels.

Route Number/Title

This is the route number and area covered, followed by a description attempting to capture the essence of what makes the route unique.

Trip Highlights

An at-a-glance list of main attractions.

Trip Rating

Not intended to replace good judgment and experience, trip rating suggestions are meant only as a general guideline to the level of skill recommended and distance involved for each route (or portion). This assumes a typical summer weather forecast with prevailing wind (and swell, if applicable) coming out of the northwest and building in the afternoon. Paddlers may well need to adjust their plans during atypical conditions. Many normally protected coastal launch sites, for example, will lose some or all of that protection when swells approach from the south.

Rating routes is problematic because sea conditions often vary drastically from day to day. Some areas can change from dead calm to deadly in a matter of hours, especially on the open coast. Even the most protected inland routes can become extremely challenging on a blustery afternoon. On the other hand, some open-coast areas that generally require advanced skills will sometimes be appropriate for beginners or intermediates on very calm days; however, we only recommend paddling such areas (as noted in the text) when accompanied by a more experienced paddler with the water reading skills to choose a conservative route—and the rescue skills to get you back in your boat if you capsize anyway.

Beginner: This part of the route is for someone with basic boat handling skills who is comfortable maneuvering on flat water or light chop in winds to 10 knots. You've taken at least one class or have learned basic rescue techniques and are able to get back into your boat (or back on top of a sit-on-top) after a capsize. You understand the basics of local weather patterns and water safety, and you can read a tide book so that you don't get stuck in the mud. Most beginner sections are in enclosed estuaries, rivers, and lakes near shorelines, offering landing access in case conditions worsen. Surf is generally nonexistent or less than 1 foot, and currents are not more than 1 or 2 knots. In addition to touring kayaks and sit-on-tops, appropriate boats for this level may include recreational or compact kayaks and canoes, assuming you are close enough to shore to swim to it if you capsize.

Intermediate: Those with enough skill and experience to handle choppy water comfortably in wind to 15 knots. You've probably taken a surf zone class and can launch and land through small surf, using side surfing and timing, and you might even have started kayak surfing. You have good braces, but you also practice rescues in open water and can recover from a capsize within two minutes in "real-life" conditions; you may be working on a roll. Those paddling San Francisco Bay or other tidally influenced areas have a basic understanding of kayak navigation and tidal currents: ability to read charts, compasses, and tide logs, and to eddy hop. If paddling in coastal areas, you've done so with advanced paddlers to learn to avoid "boomers" and other hazards, and you have good sea sense, perhaps from your background in other ocean sports, like surfing or diving. Areas labeled intermediate may require launching through surf up to 3 feet, so helmets are assumed. You may encounter ocean swell of 3 to 6 feet or currents to 3 knots and expect increased exposure to shorelines where landing access is limited, with 1 mile or more between beaches. Boat recommendations: Touring kayaks are suggested for day and overnight trips, but sit-on-tops may be okay for shorter sections. Recreational or compact kayaks and canoes are generally not appropriate or seaworthy enough for the rougher conditions you'll encounter.

Advanced: Not only are you comfortable in rough water, you enjoy it, going out of your way to play around in surf, rock gardens, and tide rips. You have a roll and solid bracing and rough-water rescue skills. You have a firm grasp of navigation, strong water reading skills, and a well-developed sea sense. Several of the advanced sections are the intermediate sections during rough conditions: when waves on the beach are 3 to 6 feet or more and wind is above 15 to 20 knots. Other advanced sections are remote and exposed, with several miles or more between landing beaches, or with beaches that require running a gauntlet of rocks in the surf zone. We've kept advanced-level route descriptions intentionally vague: Advanced paddlers will need little more than directions to the parking lot, while those needing more details (such as what type of boat is appropriate) might consider going with more experienced paddlers.

Trip Duration

Tells whether the route typically takes a full day or only part, and if it has overnight camping possibilities.

Kayak Rentals

Lists shops offering kayak rentals at or near the put in, and indicates what types of kayaks they rent.

Navigation Aids

Gives the names of US Geologic Survey topographical maps (and scale in minutes of latitude, either 7.5 or 15) as well as any marine charts useful for the route.

Weather Information

Tells which zone forecast of the NWS marine weather radio forecast, or web page, to check, along with the closest buoys. (See Making Sense of Marine Weather Forecasts above on page 10.)

Tidal Information

Provides information regarding tide levels (such as "mudflats uncover at tides below 2 feet" or "beaches covered at high tide") and assumes you know how to read a tide book.

Cautions

A list of common hazards en route (e.g., "boat traffic at harbor mouth, offshore winds, submerged rocks"), also noted in the mile-by-mile route description.

Trip Planning

Tips to make the trip safer and easier; e.g., "paddle early to avoid the wind, and, on busy summer weekends, to find better parking."

Launch Site

Directions to the launch site, usually from Highway 1, now featuring an address (or approximate address) to plug into your auto's GPS; note that in many coastal areas this address is better used to "get you in the neighborhood" than to leave you at the front door. Facilities: Info on toilets, drinking water, etc., and if fees are charged. Alternate launch sites also listed. Aerial photo: Another new feature of this edition lists the "image number" to search on the California Coastal Records Project (Californiacoastline.org), an incredibly useful planning tool, with overlapping aerial photos of our entire coastline from about a 500-foot altitude. After entering the image number of the launch site, you can virtually "fly" down the coast, scouting out possible landing beaches in otherwise inaccessible areas.

Miles and Directions

A mile-by-mile route description listing prominent landmarks in bold type as noted on the maps, along with good landing beaches, interesting sites (now with GPS coordinates when applicable), cautions for hazards en route, and side-trip options.

Other Options

Gives information on other good trips in the same area.

Where to Eat and Where to Stay

Information on where to find food, lodging, and camping nearby.

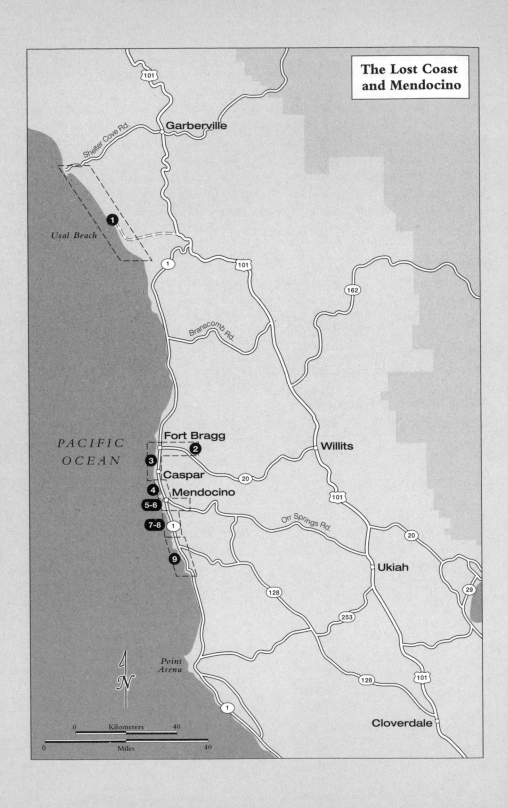

The Lost Coast
and Mendocino

PACIFIC
OCEAN

Usal Beach

Shelter Cove Rd.

Garberville

Branscomb Rd.

Fort Bragg

Caspar

Mendocino

Willits

Orr Springs Rd.

Ukiah

Point
Arena

Cloverdale

N

Kilometers
0   40

Miles
0   40

The Lost Coast and Mendocino

Route 1
Shelter Cove to Usal Beach

Dramatic vistas of steep cliffs plunging to the sea from a 2,000-foot ridgeline make the Lost Coast among the most scenic paddling areas on the West Coast. Here Cape Mendocino—the westernmost point of land in the "Lower 48"—plows into the Pacific, awash in sea spray, like the bow of a giant ship. In the 40-mile lee of this massive cape are a handful of remote beaches where, under the right conditions, a skilled and adventurous paddler might make landfall. Although intermediate kayakers with good sea sense may enjoy day trips around Shelter Cove, Bear Harbor, or Usal Beach, the rest of this route can challenge even the most advanced coastal paddlers. The rewards, however, are great, as this remains the wildest stretch of seashore in the state.

Trip highlights: World-class coastal scenery, solitude, and excellent rock gardens.

Trip rating:

Beginner: 1 mile around Shelter Cove or Usal Beach on days with no surf, little wind, and an experienced paddler in the lead.

Intermediate: 1 mile around Shelter Cove or Bear Harbor and 1 to 8 miles around Usal Beach in surf to 3 feet, wind to 15 knots, for those with previous coastal paddling experience, and 1- to 8-mile (round-trip) day trips north from Usal, Bear, or Shelter if led by experienced paddlers; however, joining multiday tours isn't recommended because conditions can worsen overnight, leaving you stranded due to the extreme exposure: If anything goes wrong, the fog comes in, or the wind comes up, you can be a long way from a landable beach and even farther from an actual take out.

Advanced: 19 miles one-way; shorter day or overnight trips possible from launch sites at either end. Strong coastal skills are required: rough-water and surf paddling and rescue skills, water reading, and navigation. Advanced surf landings in loaded boats through rocks and onto steep beaches may be necessary. Extremely challenging in swells above 6 to 8 feet or winds above 20 to 25 knots.

Trip duration: Part day, full day, or overnight.

Navigation aids: *Trails of the Lost Coast: A Recreation Guide to King Range National Conservation Area and Sinkyone Wilderness State Park,* designed for hikers, shows beaches and campsites but not the numerous offshore rocks. Map 39123-E1-TB-100: Covelo provides a good overview. It does an excellent job of showing and naming offshore reefs, rocks, and sea stacks, but it misses the first couple miles around Shelter Cove, shows no campsites, and the 1:100,000 scale is a bit small on detail. USGS: Shelter Cove, Bear Harbor,

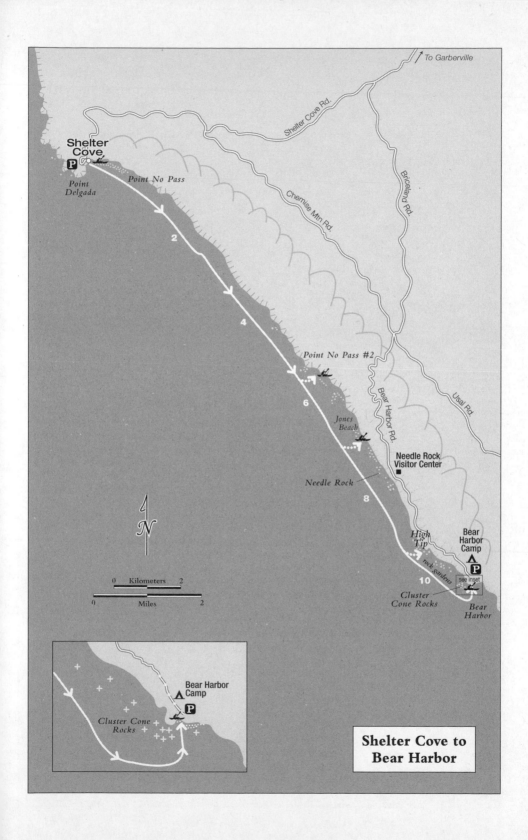

To Garberville

Shelter Cove Rd.

Shelter
Cove

Point Delgada

Point No Pass

Chemise Mtn Rd.

Briceland Rd.

2

4

Point No Pass #2

6

Bear Harbor Rd.

Usal Rd.

Jones Beach

Needle Rock
Visitor Center

Needle Rock

8

High Tip

Bear
Harbor
Camp

rock gardens

see inset

10

Cluster
Cone Rocks

Bear
Harbor

N

0   Kilometers   2
0   Miles   2

Cluster Cone
Rocks

Bear Harbor
Camp

**Shelter Cove to
Bear Harbor**

Bear Harbor to Usal Beach

To Shelter Cove

Priceland Rd.

High Tip

To Shelter Cove

10

P

Bear Harbor

11

Jackass Ridge

Usal Rd.

12

13

Wheeler Camp

Jackass Creek

14

Anderson Cliffs

Little Jackass Creek Camp

15

Mistake Point

Cave

16

Anderson Gulch

Timber Point

Timber Ridge

Usal Rd.

17

18

County Rd. 431

P

Usal Camp

Usal Beach

To 1 (6 miles)

PACIFIC OCEAN

To Hardy Creek (10 miles)

N

0 Kilometers 2

0 Miles 2

A long way from nowhere, near High Top point BUCK JOHNSON

Mistake Point and Hales Grove (7.5 minute) and NOAA chart 18620 (charts. noaa.gov/OnLineViewer/18620.shtml).

Weather information: Zone forecast: "Coastal waters from Cape Mendocino to Point Arena" (forecast.weather.gov/MapClick.php?zoneid=PZZ455); buoys: Cape Mendocino and Point Arena. Web cam: Looking north from Shelter Cove toward Cape Mendocino (northcoastaviation.com/shelter_cove/shelter_cove_lost_coast_inn_headlands.htm).

Tidal information: More landings possible on cliff-front beaches at lower tides.

Cautions: This coast is well known for fog, strong afternoon winds, and rough seas that can arrive suddenly, so advanced seamanship is necessary to paddle safely here. The area is extremely exposed, with numerous offshore rocks and boomers but few good landing beaches. If camping en route, worsening sea conditions overnight could leave you stranded, facing a long, steep hike out without your boat. A weather radio is a must; unlike most cliffy coastal areas in the state, reception here is good throughout.

Trip planning: The best advice is to be either very conservative in paddling within the protection of Shelter Cove or very good at open-coast kayaking. Once you leave Shelter Cove, beaches are few, and the prevailing winds will be in your face if you need to turn around. You can try to avoid wind by paddling early in the day, but fog could be a problem. Small swell and low tide will be required to land on most beaches along the cliffs.

Although you could paddle the 19 miles from Shelter Cove to Usal in a long day, I prefer 2 to 4 days, allowing time for exploring rock gardens, layovers, and weather days. Bring extra food in case you get weathered in, and have strong paddling skills and lots of experience—then get lucky with the weather.

This challenging trip has shuttle logistics to match. If you don't want to bother, Lost Coast Shuttle (lostcoastshuttle.com; 707-986-7437) offers a shuttle service, or you can skip the shuttle and paddle north out of Usal to Bear Harbor (or Little Jackass Creek) and back. Otherwise, be prepared to spend 2 hours on small, serpentine roads (not to mention the 1-hour round-trip on a one-lane dirt road to Usal) after dropping off a car at Usal Beach. If planning to camp, don't forget to self-register and pay your fees at either Usal Beach or Needle Rock Visitor Center. Links: Sinkyone Wilderness State Park: (parks.ca.gov/?page_id=429).

Launch site: To reach the Shelter Cove boat ramp (492 Machi Rd., Shelter Cove, is an approximate address) from Highway 101 in Garberville, take the Redway exit and follow signs to Shelter Cove on Shelter Cove Road, a very scenic and twisting 1-hour drive. In Shelter Cove, follow signs to the boat ramp off Machi Road, a couple hundred yards down a steep, unnamed road, to a protected beach. Facilities: Water and restrooms at Marios on Machi Road. No fee. Aerial photo: Launch ramp beach with Shelter Cove in the background (californiacoastline.org, image 200902220).

Landing site: Usal Beach is on Usal Road (a steep, dusty, 6-mile, one-lane dirt road not recommended for RVs), which angles northwest off Highway 1 at mile marker 90.88 (13 miles north of Rockport and 17 miles south of Leggett). Park your shuttle car in the overnight lot at the backpacker trailhead, remembering to put your camping tag on your dash. Backcountry camping fees are $5 per person per night. Facilities: Pit toilets, no water. Aerial photo: Landing beach at mouth of Usal Creek (californiacoastline.org, image 200502816).

The landing site/alternate launch site at Bear Harbor can be reached directly from Shelter Cove Road via Briceland Road/Bear Harbor Road, or from Shelter Cove by following Chemise Mountain Road/Usal Road south to Briceland/Bear Harbor Road.

Miles and Directions

0.0   Launch in the shelter of the stone jetty (N40 01.43 W124 03.97) and head east and south along the coastline.

1.0   Point No Pass marks the end of the walking-accessible beach and probably the end of the road for less-experienced paddlers. Caution: For the next 4 miles, a near-constant wall of cliffs prevents landings except on occasional low-tide beaches with steep shores and dumping surf. A profusion of nondescript points and countless offshore rocks makes navigation challenging, and it's difficult to tell where you are on the map, especially in the fog.

Cover girl Patty Andrews contemplates what lies beyond the gap. R. SCHUMANN

5.5 In the lee of (the second) Point No Pass (N39 58.33 W123 59.71), there are a few slightly larger and better-protected beaches, making this area among the best midway stopping points if you're ready to stretch your legs.

7.0 Jones Beach, an inviting mile-long stretch of sand at the foot of a coastal bench, is one of the longest beaches on this coast. A good place to land on calm days, it has less protection from surf than the beaches at Point No Pass. The marine terrace behind the beach is the first obvious landmark (but it could be difficult to spot in the fog). Look for the Needle Rock Visitor Center by a cluster of pines on the bluff about a mile farther down the coast.

9.5 High Tip (N39 55.40 W123 57.23), an obvious and aptly named landmark, is the 113-foot, cone-shaped spire at the end of the bluffs, where the coastline steepens again. Expert paddlers will find the scattering of sea stacks for the next 1 mile below the point among the more interesting and challenging rock gardens so far.

11.0 To reach the beach at Bear Harbor (N39 54.77 W123 56.28), swing wide around the reef off the point at Cluster Cone Rocks and approach from the south, winding your way carefully between the submerged rocks and surf breaks to a fairly protected sand beach.

Continue south from Bear Harbor Camp along more thousand-foot cliffs with no landings. Caution: Before leaving the road access at Bear Harbor, check your weather radio (and your luck). Landing sites to the south are few, and the beaches are steep and more exposed.

13.5 A brief break in the cliffs, the beach at the mouth of Jackass Creek makes a better landmark than a landing. It's steep and exposed, and the closest campsites are a good half-mile schlep from the beach to Wheeler Camp.

14.0 Where Anderson Cliffs begin, the precipice steepens noticeably (assuming there's no fog) just when you thought the landscape couldn't get any more vertical.

15.4 Little Jackass Creek Camp (N39 51.59 W123 54.13), tucked in a cove in the meager lee of Mistake Point, has excellent creek-side camping on the beach and an outhouse 0.25 mile up the trail. The hike along the edge of Anderson Cliffs gives an awesome overview of the coastline just paddled. Caution: Slightly more protected on the left, the beach's steep dumping shore break can get vicious in a swell. Side trips: If conditions are calm, the narrow arch in Mistake Point is runnable but risky, with no room for mistakes.

17.0 The next 1 mile or so to Timber Point is the best of the best—more steep cliffs, sea stacks, tiny coves, and runnable rock gardens, climaxing in a long, narrow, T-shaped cave with three openings near Anderson Gulch. Caution: These rock gardens are as challenging as any on the West Coast and more remote than most.

LOST COAST

Coast Route 1 is renowned as much for its scenic beauty as for being an engineering marvel. It winds steadily up the California coastline for hundreds of miles, hairpin curves clinging stubbornly to impossible cliffs, overlooking some of the finest ocean vistas on the planet. Then suddenly, somewhere below Cape Mendocino, it loses its way. The famous highway runs into 100 miles of shoreline so steep and rugged, it turns tail and scampers miles inland. This is the Lost Coast, a region of dizzying verticality and supreme isolation. It's well known among savvy backpackers who've discovered what road builders long ago conceded, the region is best traversed on foot. Or is it? The Lost Coast Trail through Sinkyone Wilderness yo-yos up and down over a series of thousand-foot ridges, rigorous as it is beautiful. The route by sea is definitely shorter, but it is no less demanding. Beaches along the cliffs are few, steep and exposed, and tough to land on. There are just no easy ways around the Lost Coast, no shortcuts. Therein, for some, lies the attraction.

19.0   Usal Beach (N39 49.89 W123 51.09) is the next break in the cliffs. With only moderate protection from prevailing seas, the beach is at least wide and sandy and not as steep as those before it. The left side of the beach near the end of the road is the best place to land with the shortest carry to your car.

Other options: The most conservative way to attempt kayak camping on the Lost Coast is to paddle 4 miles north from Usal Beach to Little Jackass and back as an overnighter, during a calm-weather window. The next 10 miles south of Usal to Hardy Creek, where Highway 1 rejoins the coast, are not quite as scenic—the coastal mountains fade back to their usual size and steepness—but the paddling terrain is some of the best. Several miles of incredible sea-stack rock gardens cover the lower half. Unfortunately there are only a few low-tide beaches on the route and no legal campsites, except at Rockport Bay, which is a private campground not open to the public. Also, Rockport Rocks and Cape Vizcaino Rocks are both now designated as Seasonal Special Closure zones as part of the Marine Life Protection Act (dfg.ca.gov/mlpa) where it is prohibited to approach within 300 feet between March 1 and August 31 in order to protect nesting seabirds.

Where to Eat and Where to Stay

Restaurants: Shelter Cove Deli (707-986-7474), featuring fresh-caught fish and chips, burgers, and sandwiches, is part of the Shelter Cove RV Park and Campground (see below). **Lodging:** Shelter Cove Beachcomber Inn (800-718-4789 is one of the more rustic and economical options, and Inn of the Lost Coast (innofthelostcoast.com; 707-986-7521) with ocean-front rooms perched on the bluffs is among the many fancier alternatives. **Camping:** Shelter Cove RV Park and Campground (707-986-7474) near the boat launch makes a convenient staging ground for a trip, although its closely packed sites are nothing special. Overnight parking is $5 per day if you plan to head down the coast.

Route 2
Noyo River Estuary

Noyo River Estuary gives kayakers the chance to experience the mellower mood of the Mendocino coast, by turning their backs on the sea to cruise in the opposite direction of the caves and waves and excitement for which the area is famous. A few minutes' paddle upriver from the launch ramp you'll leave the marinas, boats, and people behind and enter a tranquil backwater bursting with birdlife. A great blue heron stalking the shallows, a mother merganser leading her string of ducklings, an osprey circling overhead clutching a fish in its talons, glimpses of songbirds flitting in through the streamside trees—are all common sights here. Farther upstream the forest and the solitude thickens as the redwoods close in around you. The river gradually narrows and gets shallower until even the kayaks can't continue; then it's time to change direction with the tide and ride the ebb back out toward the sea.

Trip highlights: Birding, calm-water serenity, redwoods.

Trip rating:

Beginner: 1 to 6+ miles round-trip upriver.

Trip duration: Part to full day.

Kayak rentals: Liquid Fusion Kayaking (liquidfusionkayak.com; 707-962-1623) rents single and double closed-deck sea kayaks and sit-on-tops from their site at Dolphin Isle Marina.

Navigation aids: USGS: Fort Bragg (7.5 minute) and NOAA chart 18626 (charts .noaa.gov/OnLineViewer/18626.shtml).

Weather information: Zone forecast: "Coastal waters from Cape Mendocino to Point Arena" (forecast.weather.gov/MapClick.php?zoneid=PZZ455); buoys: Cape Mendocino and Point Arena.

Tidal information: The estuary is tidally influenced for several miles, so a rising tide will give you more water, especially beyond Dolphin Isle where the river gets shallow. To reach the railroad trestle or beyond, a high tide of at least 4.2 feet is necessary, although you can paddle beyond Dolphin Isle with only 2 feet if you are willing to portage the occasional gravel bar.

Cautions: Watch for shallow sand bars and snags as you head upriver, and for boat traffic around the marinas.

Trip planning: For paddling upriver, the more water the better. Ideally you can pick a day when you can ride the rising tide upriver and return with the ebb.

Launch site: Noyo boat ramp in the upper harbor on Basin Street (32400 Basin St., Fort Bragg, approximate). From Highway 1 take Highway 20 east to South Harbor Drive, and turn left and take the first right onto Basin. The boat ramp

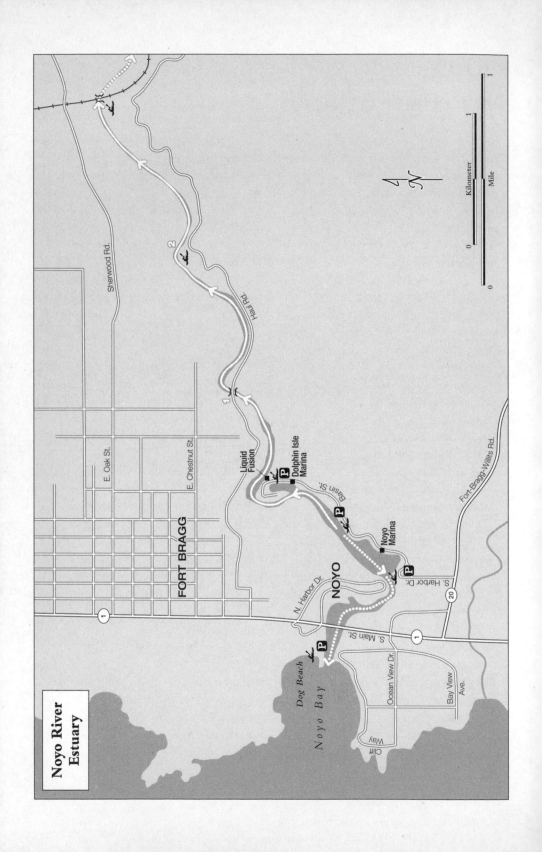

Noyo River Estuary

Noyo River Estuary

Sherwood Rd.

Haul Rd.

E. Oak St.

E. Chestnut St.

FORT BRAGG

Liquid Fusion

Dolphin Isle Marina

Basin St.

N. Harbor Dr.

NOYO

Noyo Marina

S. Harbor Dr.

20

Dog Beach

Noyo Bay

S. Main St.

Ocean View Dr.

Cliff Way

Bay View Ave.

Fort-Bragg-Willits Rd.

1

1

Kilometer

Mile

N

Heading up the Noyo River CATE HAWTHORNE

is 0.5 mile upriver on the left, just between the Noyo Basin and Dolphin Cove marinas. Facilities: Porta-potties, no water. Parking fee $3. Aerial photo: Shows jetties at mouth of Noyo Harbor and the beach to the north (californiacoastine.org, image 200503217).

Alternate launch sites: The main launch ramp at Noyo Harbor (19101 South Harbor Dr., Fort Bragg) is straight ahead as you approach the harbor on South Harbor Drive, so it is easier to find but more crowded than the Basin Street ramp. Facilities: Restrooms and water. Fee parking. Dolphin Isle Marina is a free launch option if there is parking available, either off the dock inside the marina or from the beach behind Liquid Fusion Kayaking. Check in at the deli to see where/if parking is available.

Miles and Directions

0.0   From the Basin Street ramp (N39 25.60 W123 47.92) head upriver past Dolphin Isle Marina. Side trip: Head downstream 1.0 mile past the marina to the harbor mouth, and if it is very calm, out into Noyo Bay (see Route 3) to land on Dog Beach. Caution: Watch for boat traffic.

0.5	As the river bends north and east, up and around Dolphin Isle, and you start to head southeast, the alternate launch site at the kayak rental shop is on your right. Keep an eye out for river otters and harbor seals in the water and egrets and scads of other birdlife in the bushes and trees.
1.0	Bridge at Haul Road (N39 26.02 W123 47.23); depending on the water height, you can land to stretch your legs on the beach on your right where the river bends to the right.
1.9	Another small beach (N39 26.25 W123 46.52) on the inside of the right-hand bend. The river enters a steeper canyon, narrows, and begins to feel wilder as the forest starts to press in around you. Look for turtles resting on the banks.
3.0	Railroad bridge crosses the river. This makes a good rest stop on the beach just before the bridge. There is a small riffle here that may be difficult to paddle up. Land on the beach and make the short portage to the other side if you want to continue upriver.

Side trip: With a high tide you can continue another mile or so upriver.

Where to Eat and Where to Stay

Restaurants: Heron's by the Sea (707-962-0680), rustic fishing ambiance overlooking the harbor mouth with excellent happy hour menu; North Coast Brewing Co. (northcoastbrewing.com; 707-964-3400), taproom and grill. **Lodging:** Harbor Lite Lodge (harborlitelodge.com; 800-643-2700) overlooks the harbor with private balconies. Many other options in Fort Bragg. **Camping:** Van Damme, Russian Gulch, and MacKerricher State Parks (reserveamerica.com; 800-444-7275) all book up to seven months in advance. If they're full, try Caspar Beach RV Park and Campground (casparbeachrvpark .com; 707-964-3306) and Albion River Campground (albionrivercampground.com; 707-937-0606).

Route 3
Noyo Bay to Caspar Beach

With its generally well-protected semicircle of cliffs sheltering the entrance to the marina, Noyo Bay is a good place for adventurous beginners and aspiring intermediates to gain some exposure to ocean conditions with safe harbor nearby. Beyond the shelter of the bay, experienced paddlers will find lots of chutes and channels, and fun, technical rock gardens to play around on. Although the caving possibilities here are not on par with what's found further south around Mendocino, there are a couple of challenging tunnel complexes to explore in the cliffs before Soldier Point that make a trip here worth the effort. On calm days the exposed, 5-mile maze of rocks and stacks down to Caspar is a fun challenge for experienced rock-garden paddlers.

Trip highlights: Good protection inside the cove and fun rock garden play outside of it.

Trip rating:

Beginner: 1 to 3+ miles round-trip out to the #3 buoy in Noyo Bay, good for adventurous beginners able to handle boat traffic and ready to gain some experience with ocean paddling in a generally protected area.

Intermediate: 1 to 4+ miles round-trip to Soldier Point; previous coastal experience or an experienced leader recommended past the #3 buoy in seas between 3 to 5 feet and wind to 15 knots.

Advanced: 1 to 4+ miles round-trip to Soldier Point, or the 6.5-mile one-way trip to Caspar is fun for play in 4- to 6-foot swells; because of the west exposure, things start to wash out much above 6 feet.

Trip duration: Part to full day.

Kayak rentals: Liquid Fusion (liquidfusionkayak.com; 707-962-1623) rents closed-deck sea kayaks and sit-ons, and also runs an introductory rock garden tour out toward Soldier Point for adventurous beginners (no experience required).

Navigation aids: USGS: Fort Bragg (7.5 minute) and NOAA chart 18626 (charts. noaa.gov/OnLineViewer/18626.shtml).

Weather information: Zone forecast: "Coastal waters from Cape Mendocino to Point Arena" (forecast.weather.gov/MapClick.php?zoneid=PZZ455); buoys: Cape Mendocino and Point Arena. Mendocino web cam: Caspar Beach Web Cam, 5 miles south of the launch beach (casparbeachrvpark.com/webcam).

Tidal information: Lower tides give better protection from outer reefs and more beach access.

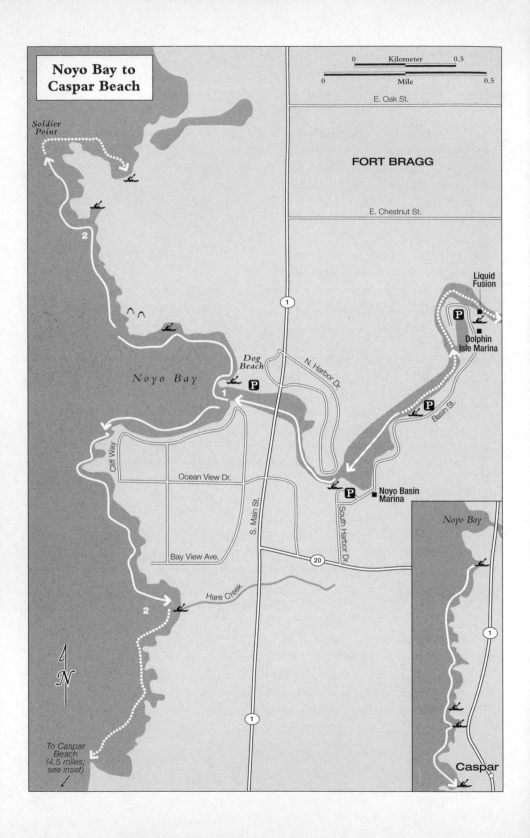

Noyo Bay to Caspar Beach

Soldier Point

2

Noyo Bay

FORT BRAGG

E. Oak St.

E. Chestnut St.

Kilometer

Mile

1

Liquid Fusion

Dolphin Isle Marina

Basin St.

N. Harbor Dr.

Dog Beach

1

Cliff Way

Ocean View Dr.

S. Main St.

Bay View Ave.

Hare Creek

Noyo Basin Marina

South Harbor Dr.

20

1

2

To Caspar Beach (4.5 miles; see inset)

N

Noyo Bay

1

Caspar

Cautions: Boat traffic around the harbor mouth, waves, submerged rocks, wind, and fog.

Trip planning: Noyo Dog Beach generally has little or no surf in swells below 6 to 8 feet if the swell direction is from the west. During northwest or south swells, it is still protected in swells over 10 feet. Best protection in the rock gardens with lower tide and swell.

Launch site: Boat ramp in the upper harbor on Basin Street (32400 Basin St., Fort Bragg is approximate address). From Highway 1 take Highway 20 east to South Harbor Drive, and turn left, and take the first right onto Basin. The boat ramp is 0.5 mile upriver on the left, just between the Noyo Basin and Dolphin Isle marinas.

Alternate launch sites: The main launch ramp at Noyo Harbor (19101 South Harbor Dr., Fort Bragg) is straight ahead as you approach the harbor on South Harbor Drive, so it is easier to find and closer to the ocean than the Basin Street ramp, but not as easy to launch and park. Noyo Beach (Dog Beach), under the Highway 1 bridge (701 North Harbor Dr., Fort Bragg) next to the north jetty at the harbor mouth, gives direct access to the ocean. Aerial photo: Shows jetties at mouth of Noyo Harbor, the beach to the north, and beginning of rock-garden section to the south (californiacoastine.org, image 200503217).

Miles and Directions

0.0   From the Basin Street ramp (N39 25.60 W123 47.92) head toward the ocean past Noyo Basin Marina. Caution: Boat traffic around the marinas and harbor mouth.

0.4   Alternate launch site in main harbor.

1.0   Harbor mouth, depending on the conditions, can be calm or crazy. This is a good place to reassess sea conditions.

1.1   Noyo Beach (Dog Beach) is an easy landing spot most days, with little surf reaching the beach.

1.5   Contour north around the bay past a couple possible landings on pocket beaches to the point across from the #3 buoy. Some of the better advanced play spots are located in this area, including some nice pourovers and a challenging complex of intersecting tunnels, neither of which are particularly protected or forgiving. Caution: Conditions beyond the buoy get rough quickly, with many shallow rocks and breaking waves.

2.0   Weave your way through the rocks along the cliffs to a pocket beach landing possibility (N39 26.19 W123 49.08).

2.3   Continue out to Soldier Point or round it to access a couple of exposed, north-facing beaches in the cove beyond.

Paddling toward the light near Noyo Bay FRANK LUCIAN

Other options: Head south out of the bay and slalom your way through a mile-long maze of excellent slots and channels to a fairly protected cove with a sandy beach at the mouth of Hare Creek. This play maze is exposed, shallow, and prone to surf, so you'll need a calm day or strong skills. Or continue your way another 4.5 miles down to Caspar Beach along a similarly exposed, west-facing and rock-strewn coastline, with possible landings at Jug Handle and a couple pocket coves a mile north.

Where to Eat and Where to Stay

Restaurants: Heron's by the Sea (707-962-0680), rustic fishing ambiance overlooking the harbor mouth with excellent happy hour menu; North Coast Brewing Co. (northcoastbrewing.com; 707-964-3400), taproom and grill. **Lodging:** Harbor Lite Lodge (harborlitelodge.com; 800-643-2700) overlooks the harbor with private balconies. Many other options in Fort Bragg. **Camping:** Van Damme, Russian Gulch, and MacKerricher State Parks (reserveamerica.com; 800-444-7275) all book up to seven months in advance. If they're full, try Caspar Beach RV Park and Campground (casparbeachrvpark .com; 707-964-3306) and Albion River Campground (albionrivercampground.com; 707-937-0606).

Route 4
Russian Gulch to Caspar Beach and Beyond

Russian Gulch is an excellent alternative for experienced coastal kayakers who've already done the more popular, and more protected, Van Damme (see Route 7 for an introduction to paddling the area's caves), and who are looking for some new caves to explore. The stretch between Russian Gulch and Point Cabrillo is among the top rock garden and cave play spots in the region for advanced paddlers. Limited options for less-experienced paddlers also exist.

Trip highlights: World-class sea caves and rock gardens, seabirds, seals, and solitude.

Trip rating:

Beginner: Although the launch site is accessible to beginners on calm days with no surf on the beach, there is only a half mile of protection before the open ocean. Inside the cove stay well away from rocks and caves unless you have expert guidance, in which case you might be able to access the first set of coves and caves a half mile north in seas below 3 feet and wind to 10 knots. The cove to the south is generally more protected, although shallow and rocky and without caves.

Intermediate: 1 to 4 miles, round-trip, for those with previous coastal paddling experience and good sea sense in swells below 4 feet and winds to 15 knots; the guidance of an experienced cave paddler is highly recommended.

Advanced: 1 to 9+ miles round-trip (or 4.5 miles one-way from Caspar to Russian Gulch), with miles of rock garden heaven awaiting experienced paddlers with strong open-coast skills. Seas above 6 feet limit access to most caves and rock gardens.

Trip duration: Part to full day.

Navigation aids: USGS: Mendocino (7.5 minute) and NOAA charts 18628 (charts.noaa.gov/OnLineViewer/18628.shtml) and 18626 (charts.noaa.gov/OnLineViewer/18626.shtml).

Weather information: Zone forecast: "Coastal waters from Cape Mendocino to Point Arena" (forecast.weather.gov/MapClick.php?zoneid=PZZ455); buoys: Cape Mendocino and Point Arena. Mendocino web cam: Looking south from Mendocino, 3 miles south of the launch (weather.mcn.org), and at Caspar Beach, 4 miles north (casparbeachrvpark.com/webcam).

Tidal information: Lower tides give better protection from outer reefs, more beach access, and more headroom in caves.

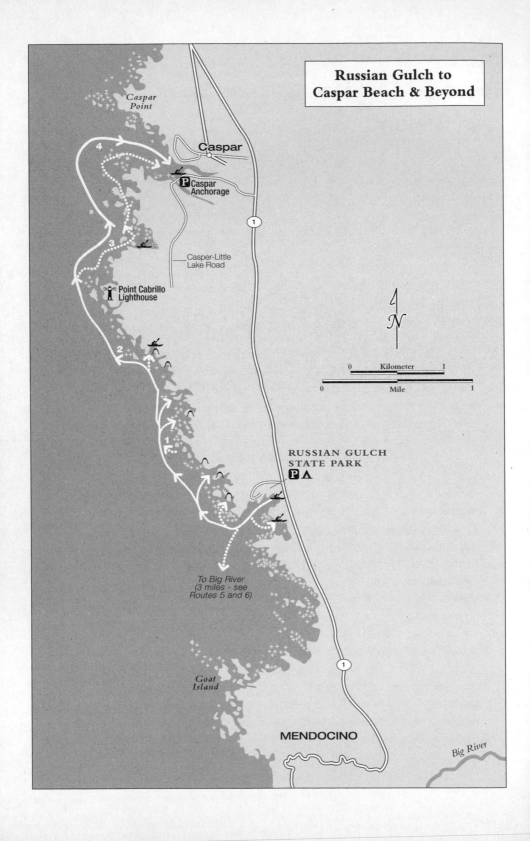

Caspar Point

Caspar

4

3

P **Caspar Anchorage**

1

Casper-Little
Lake Road

2

Point Cabrillo
Lighthouse

N

0   Kilometer   1

0   Mile   1

1

**RUSSIAN GULCH
STATE PARK**
P A

*To Big River
(3 miles - see
Routes 5 and 6)*

*Goat
Island*

1

MENDOCINO

Big River

Cautions: Waves, submerged rocks, clapotis, wind, and fog.

Trip planning: Best protection with lower tide and swell. Although it's possible to paddle outside the reef in swells of 8 feet or more, that's missing the point: To access the caves and rock gardens inside the reef, the calmer the better (only experts recommended in swells above 6 feet). Paddle north early in the day and return with the wind. Be very careful and skilled.

Launch site: Russian Gulch State Park (Brest Road and Point Cabrillo Drive, Mendocino) is 2 miles north of Mendocino on Highway 1: Turn west on Brest, and left on Point Cabrillo Drive into the park, and follow signs to the beach. Facilities: Porta-potties and cold outdoor showers. $8 day use fee. Aerial photo: Launch cove and beginning of rock garden section to the north (californiacoastine.org, image 200503401).

Alternate launch site: Caspar Beach (14441 Point Cabrillo Dr., Mendocino) 3 miles north. From Highway 1, head west on Caspar Little Lake Road/County Road 409 and wind your way 0.75 mile down to the beach.

Miles and Directions

0.0 From the beach (N39 19.74 W123 48.30), contour along the cliffs to the north, exploring a few small caves and arches before leaving the protection of the gulch. Caution: The dangers of submerged rocks, waves, and caves persist along this entire route.

0.5 Exposure increases immediately as you round the point and head north. Side trips: On a calm day, less-experienced paddlers can access the small, secluded beach inside the southern arm of the cove for some solitude.

0.6 Work your way inside the reef, if possible, into a complex of coves that feature some of the area's finest caves, arches, chutes, and rock gardens, as well as a few small, hidden beaches. Caution: Watch for seal haul outs.

1.0 As you round the next minor point (where the Point Cabrillo Lighthouse comes into view), exposure increases, so either cut back inside the reef for more excellent coves, caves, beaches, and rock gardens for the next mile or so or turn around if it's too rough. Caution: The farther north you paddle up this coast, the more exposed it becomes.

2.0 Protected beach (N39 20.66 W123 49.25) at the back of a long, south-facing cove is one of the better landing options, and it features an intricate cave system in the adjacent headland.

2.5 Point Cabrillo makes a good spot to turn around as conditions get generally rougher beyond.

3.5 Beyond the point, a few small beaches, channels, and coves may be accessible on uncommonly calm days, but this area is exposed to the north.

Looking for light at the end of the tunnel, exiting Rainbow Mist Cave north of Russian Gulch
KIM GRANDFIELD

4.5 Caspar Beach (N39 21.66 W123 49.07) is semi-protected, shallow, and sandy, so it's a reasonably straightforward surf landing in most conditions.

Other options: Run a shuttle and do a one-way trip from Caspar down to Russian Gulch or from Russian Gulch down to Mendocino or Van Damme.

Where to Eat and Where to Stay

Restaurants: Among many fine options are Mendocino Cafe (mendocinocafe.com; 707-937-2422), Bayview Cafe (bayviewcafe.com; 707-937-4197) overlooking Mendocino cove, and Moodys Organic Coffee Bar (moodyscoffeebar.com; 707-937-4843). **Lodging:** In addition to lodging, Sweetwater Gardens (sweetwaterspa.com; 707-937-4140) has hot tubs whether or not you're staying there. **Camping:** Van Damme, Russian Gulch, and MacKerricher State Parks all book up to seven months in advance (reserveamerica .com; 800-444-7275). If the state parks are full, try Caspar Beach RV Park and Campground (casparbeachrvpark.com; 707-964-3306) and Albion River Campground (albionrivercampground.com; 707-937-0606).

PADDLING IN CAVES:
THRILLS, THREATS, TIPS, AND TERMS

A hundred feet into the cave's deepening shadows, our kayaks bob on half-lit, stained-glass seas. Switching on our headlamps, we paddle around a corner into darkness, the cave twisting and turning like the inside of a giant seashell. Our lights reveal a narrowing fissure, its walls glossed with coralline algae that glistens conch-pink below the barnacles where the tide has fallen. Since before Odysseus stumbled bewitched into Circe's lair, the damp musk of an unexplored sea cave has cast an irresistible lure. But caution is advised. Sea caves provide one of the great thrills and greatest dangers of ocean kayaking. Although Mendo's caves are sometimes quite calm, any swells entering can become compressed laterally and surge toward the ceiling. This can be exciting if there is enough headroom and paddling skill, or it can be dangerous. Unwary paddlers have fractured neck vertebrae after large waves bounced their heads off the ceiling. Consider the waves that carved the caves and stay out when there's "cave making in progress." Before entering any cave, no matter how calm it looks, watch for several minutes to see how rough the waves are inside when a large set rumbles through. When unsure of the conditions, paddle backward into caves to facilitate a hasty retreat. If you don't have a reliable roll, consider how difficult it will be to perform a rescue in a dark, sloshing cave. Caves with two openings are safer to run heading into the direction of the swell, if possible, to decrease the chance of getting surfed out of control into the rocks. But our best tip: Don't try to learn how to paddle in caves by reading a book. Take lessons from a knowledgeable professional, and gain experience with skilled paddlers around. Know your limits, and respect the ocean's power. Here's some caving lingo, for the curious: A cave that passes through a piece of land and comes out the other side is, technically speaking, a *tunnel,* unless of course it's higher than it is long, and then it's an *arch.* The term *cave* is used loosely to describe all three.

Route 5
Big River Estuary

This peaceful, emerald green estuary wandering through forested and undeveloped lands makes a great trip for novices or a sane alternative for all paddlers on those days when the sea beyond is raging. Because of turn-of-the-century logging, the redwoods now begin 2 miles upstream and remnants of the logging operations act as landmarks along the banks. Few fishing boats or powerboats venture here, leaving only those in human-powered craft to absorb the quiet, engulfed by serene lushness. When the ocean is calm, the mouth of the Big River offers excellent access to the area's outstanding coves and sea caves for those comfortable launching through surf.

Trip highlights: Calm water, solitude, redwoods; access to surf and coastal touring with excellent caves.

Trip rating:

Beginner: 1 to 16 miles round-trip on very protected estuary.

Intermediate: 1 to 16 miles round-trip with access to open-coast side trips and surfing options when waves are below 3 feet and winds to 15 knots for those with previous coastal touring experience or an advanced paddler leading.

Advanced: 1 to 16 miles with access to coastal side trips and surfing options in waves to 6+ feet and winds to 25 knots; excellent rock gardens and caves (see Route 6).

Trip duration: Part to full day.

Kayak rentals: Catch a Canoe and Bicycles, Too! (catchacanoe.com; 707-937-0273) rents a variety of single and double, sit-on and sit-inside kayaks as well as canoes and bikes, from their shop near the mouth of the Big River, Mendocino.

Navigation aids: Big River map is available from Catch a Canoe boat rentals (707-937-0273) on south side of Big River bridge. USGS: Mendocino (7.5 minute) and NOAA chart 18628 (charts.noaa.gov/OnLineViewer/18628.shtml).

Weather information: Zone forecast; "Coastal waters from Cape Mendocino to Point Arena" (forecast.weather.gov/MapClick.php?zoneid=PZZ455); buoys: Cape Mendocino and Point Arena. Web cam: Looking south over Mendocino Bay, about 1 mile west of the launch (weather.mcn.org).

Tidal information: The river is tidally influenced for 8 miles. (We've seen a harbor seal 4 miles upstream.)

Cautions: Strong ocean-going currents under Highway 1 bridge at the river mouth during ebb tide. Near the launch site, afternoon winds blowing upriver are common during summer. Potential for flooding during winter.

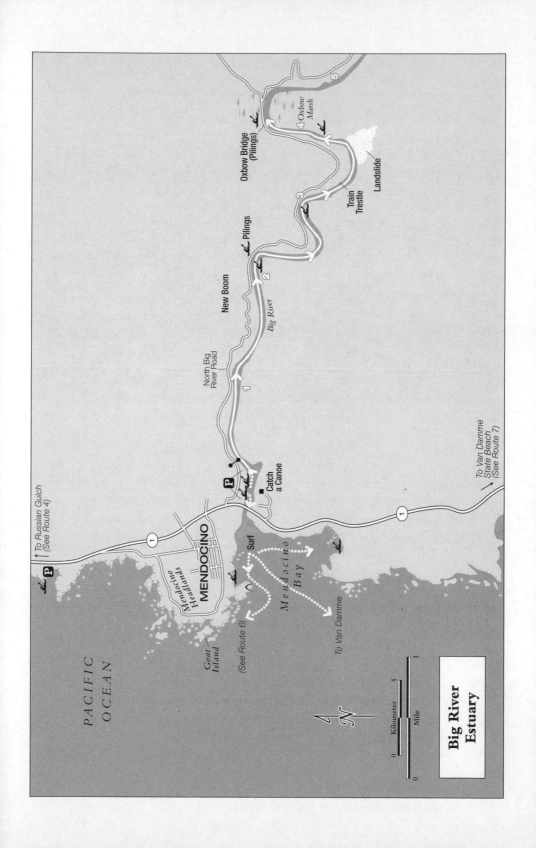

Big River Estuary

Up the creek with two paddles, on Mendocino's Big River CATE HAWTHORNE

Trip planning: Ride the flood tide on your way in and the ebb on your way out for an easier time. Save some energy to fight the upriver winds on the last mile or so of the return.

Launch site: The launch beach on the northeast side of the Big River bridge (North Big River Road, Mendocino) is immediately north of the bridge on Highway 1. Turn inland onto North Big River Road, leading to the broad dirt pullout on the flood plain beside the bridge. Facilities: Porta-potties; no fees. Aerial photo: Mendocino Cove, looking up the Big River (californiacoastline .org, image 11621).

Miles and Directions

0.0 Head upriver from the beach (N39 18.14 W123 47.45), along conifer- and rhododendron-lined banks. Caution: During a falling tide, potentially hazardous currents sweep seaward into the surf. Side trips: On calm days, surf-savvy paddlers can play in the waves or explore the cliffs and caves in Mendocino Bay (see "Other options").

2.0 Large pilings and small landing beaches on either side of the river mark New Boom, remnants of a dam that gathered logs to be floated downriver to mill. Beyond here the alder and willow woodlands give way to redwoods, and the river becomes more narrow and convoluted.

3.0 Short pilings, the remains of logging train tracks, parallel the left bank.

3.5 Just beyond the large landslide on the right bank is a sandy beach with a grassy area that can be a nice place to take a break, but it can be a bit of a steep scramble for 5 or 6 feet. Side trip: Continue through more beautiful forest another mile or so to Oxbow Marsh until eventually the kayaking will be restricted by lack of water, approximately 6 to 8 miles from the mouth, depending on the tide height.

Caution: The final 1 mile of the return to the launch site can be against the coastal winds that funnel into the mouth of the river and under the bridge. Use the banks as windbreaks when possible.

Other options: On calm days, intermediates can launch through small surf and explore up to a mile in the protection of the cliffs on the north side of Mendocino Bay, paddling around sea stacks and into one of the area's best-known caves, to find isolated beaches beneath the bluffs. Experienced open-coast kayakers can leave the bay and explore the rock gardens up to Goat Island and beyond, or do one-way coastal tours down to Van Damme or down from Russian Gulch.

Where to Eat and Where to Stay

Restaurants: Among many fine options are Mendocino Cafe (mendocinocafe.com; 707-937-2422), Bayview Cafe (bayviewcafe.com; 707-937-4197) overlooking Mendocino cove, and Moodys Organic Coffee Bar (moodyscoffeebar.com; 707-937-4843). **Lodging:** In addition to lodging, Sweetwater Gardens (sweetwaterspa.com; 707-937-4140) has hot tubs whether or not you're staying there. **Camping:** Van Damme, Russian Gulch, and MacKerricher State Parks all book up to seven months in advance (reserveamerica .com; 800-444-7275). If the state parks are full, try Caspar Beach RV Park and Campground (casparbeachrvpark.com; 707-964-3306) and Albion River Campground (albionrivercampground.com; 707-937-0606).

Route 6
Mendocino Headlands and Beyond

When the sea is calm, the mouth of the Big River offers excellent access to some of Mendocino's better coves and caves for paddlers comfortable launching through surf. Reasonably protected rock gardens inside the cove's northern edge give intermediates the opportunity to explore on their own, featuring "Hole in the Head" cave, one of the area's larger and longer tunnels. Rounding the bay's northern point to Goat Island, experienced paddlers will find one of Mendo's best playgrounds, riddled with caves, waves, chutes, channels, secret passageways, and hidden coves. Although several calm-water labyrinths are tucked away behind offshore islets, getting to them requires advanced water-reading skills, running complex channels from the open sea. Short but sweet, the Headlands is one of Mendocino's top trips.

Trip highlights: World-class sea caves and rock gardens, seabirds, and surf.

Trip rating:

Beginner: 1- to 2-mile round-trip to Hole-in-the-Head point for adventurous beginners on days with less than 1-foot surf and 10-knot wind; or up Big River 6 miles (see Route 5).

Intermediate: 1- to 4+-mile round-trip with kayak surfing options when waves are below 3 feet and winds to 15 knots for those with previous coastal touring experience or an experienced paddler leading, especially beyond Hole-in-the-Head point.

Advanced: 1- to 4+-mile round-trip with surfing options in waves to 6 feet and winds to 20 knots.

Trip duration: Part to full day.

Navigation aids: USGS: Mendocino (7.5 minute) and NOAA chart 18628 (charts .noaa.gov/OnLineViewer/18628.shtml).

Weather information: Zone forecast: "Coastal waters from Cape Mendocino to Point Arena" (forecast.weather.gov/MapClick.php?zoneid=PZZ455); buoys: Cape Mendocino and Point Arena. Mendocino Web Cam: Looking south over Mendocino Bay (weather.mcn.org); Caspar Beach Web Cam, 5 miles north of the launch beach (casparbeachrvpark.com/webcam).

Tidal information: More access to small beaches below cliffs at lower tides.

Cautions: Strong ocean-going currents under Highway 1 bridge at the river mouth during ebb tide. Surf break with board surfers on the sand bar at the river mouth. Submerged rocks, sneaker waves, exposure. The area around Goat Island can get dicey during large northwest swells. Avoid disturbing seal haul outs and sea-bird nesting sites on the islets.

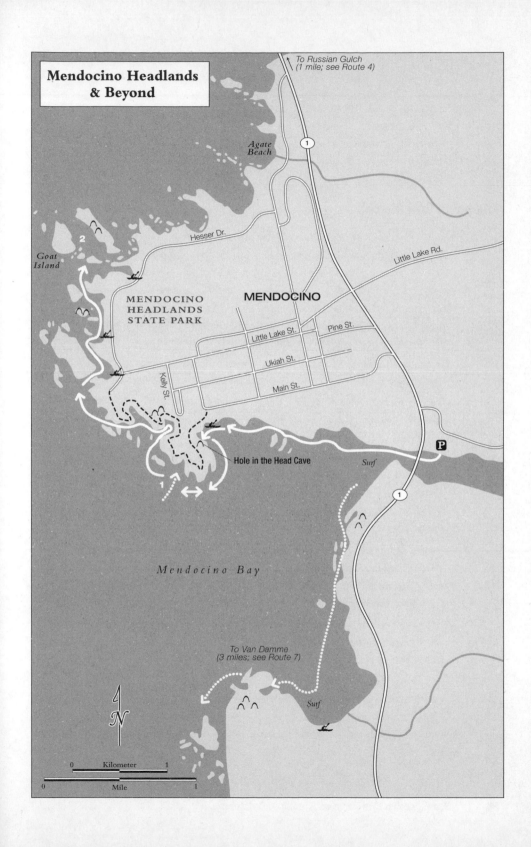

Mendocino Headlands & Beyond

To Russian Gulch
(1 mile; see Route 4)

1

Agate Beach

Hesser Dr.

Little Lake Rd.

Goat Island

2

MENDOCINO HEADLANDS STATE PARK

MENDOCINO

Little Lake St.

Pine St.

Ukiah St.

Kelly St.

Main St.

1

Hole in the Head Cave

Surf

P

1

Mendocino Bay

To Van Damme
(3 miles; see Route 7)

Surf

N

0   Kilometer   1

0   Mile   1

Trip planning: If you can't get through the surf break easily, don't go out. Before launching, take some time to scout the exposed coves around Goat Island from pullouts along Hesser Drive.

Launch site: Launch beach on northeast side of Big River bridge (North Big River Road, Mendocino) is immediately north of the Highway 1 bridge. Turn inland onto North Big River Road, leading to the broad dirt pullout on the flood plain beside the bridge. Facilities: Porta-potties; no fees. Aerial photo: Mendocino Cove, looking up the Big River (californiacoastline.org, image 11621).

Miles and Directions

0.0   From the beach (N39 18.14 W123 47.45), head out the river mouth into the cliff-lined cove to the north, passing several sea stacks and small beaches sometimes accessible at low tide. Caution: Give plenty of room to any board surfers in the area. During an ebb tide, currents sweep seaward into the surf. If you capsize and swim, you could get washed out to sea. Option: You can also find a few nice cave mazes along the cliffs to the south and the southern point of Mendocino Bay, but this exposed shoreline is only accessible on calm days.

0.7   Beach (N39 18.19 W123 48.24) at the far end of the cove is a good landing site in all tide heights.

0.8   If you contour along the cliffs past the beach, you'll find the entrance to Hole in the Head cave, a 100-yard tunnel with a cave-in skylight (the hole) at the end. This cave is generally protected, but watch for surf breaking in the shallow entrance.

1.0   As you round the southern point of the headlands the coastline becomes much more exposed and challenging. Caution: This is no place for inexperienced paddlers. Accessing the caves and coves beyond requires challenging runs through shallow channels. Avoid disturbing resting seals and seabirds along this entire stretch.

1.25   If seas are calm enough to navigate around the point and through the minefield of submerged rocks back into the next cove, several protected caves await— including Cloverleaf Cave, where two tunnels intersect in the middle of a small promontory—and a small beach at the base of the cliffs.

1.6   Access a protected beach (N39 18.34 W123 48.58) by making another out-and-around maneuver through another tricky slot. From here to Goat Island you can remain in the semi-protected passageway behind the many offshore islets, featuring a maze of caves.

2.0   Another good beach in the back of a small cove (N39 18.61 W123 48.50) is hiding in the convolutions by Goat Island. Caution: Caves in Goat Island and the surrounding islets can get rough, and are covered with nesting seabirds.

Paddlers exploring among Mendocino's many sea caves **TIM ANDREWS**

Other options: Paddling to Big River from Russian Gulch, about 3 miles, makes a nice one-way trip for advanced paddlers. The 3-mile trip down to Van Damme also has some good caves and rock gardens, but they are very exposed and difficult to access in seas above 4 to 5 feet.

Where to Eat and Where to Stay

Restaurants: Among many fine options are Mendocino Cafe (mendocinocafe.com; 707-937-2422), Bayview Cafe (bayviewcafe.com; 707-937-4197) overlooking Mendocino cove, and Moodys Organic Coffee Bar (moodyscoffeebar.com; 707-937-4843). **Lodging:** In addition to lodging, Sweetwater Gardens (sweetwaterspa.com; 707-937-4140) has hot tubs whether or not you're staying there. **Camping:** Van Damme, Russian Gulch, and MacKerricher State Parks all book up to seven months in advance (reserveamerica .com; 800-444-7275). If the state parks are full, try Caspar Beach RV Park and Campground (casparbeachrvpark.com; 707-964-3306) and Albion River Campground (albionrivercampground.com; 707-937-0606).

Route 7
Van Damme State Beach to Albion

Although the craggy Mendocino coast is among the more scenic shorelines in a state famous for its beautiful shores, what puts Mendo on the map as one of the planet's premier paddling destinations is the number and complexity of its sea caves. Many are short and straight, little more than arches, while others tunnel 100 yards from one hidden cove to the next. A few caves are big and simple as barns; still others snake and divide into multiple passages so dark we use waterproof headlamps to find our way to the back. The easiest and safest place to get into a sea cave here is probably from Van Damme State Beach. Its sandy, south-facing launch beach together with its nearby parking lot makes it the region's most accessible and protected sea-caving area. In addition to its caves, there is an excellent variety of marine life—from seabirds and seals to a rich intertidal zone. For experienced paddlers, the one-way trip to Albion is one of the area's classic advanced trips.

Trip highlights: Great location for an introduction to sea-cave paddling, with good protection and world-class sea caves and rock gardens, seabirds, seals, and excellent tide pools.

Trip rating:

Beginner: 1- to 3-mile round-trips are possible on days with swells below 4 feet and winds below 10 knots, but it is recommended that you steer clear of rocks and caves without expert guidance (Kayak Mendocino [kayakmendocino.com; 707-937-0700] runs 2-hour tours on sit-on-tops from Van Damme, which would give you a basic introduction to the area). Helmets recommended for paddling anywhere near rocks.

Intermediate: 1 to 5 miles round-trip (or one-way to Albion) for those with previous coastal paddling experience and good sea sense on days with swells below 4 feet and winds below 15 knots; the guidance of an experienced cave paddler is recommended, especially beyond the protection of the cove at Van Damme.

Advanced: 5+ miles one-way of rock garden heaven await experienced paddlers with strong open-coast skills. Seas above 6 feet limit access to most caves and rock gardens.

Trip duration: Part to full day.

Navigation aids: USGS: Mendocino and Albion (7.5 minute) and NOAA chart 18628 (charts.noaa.gov/OnLineViewer/18628.shtml).

Weather information: Zone forecast: "Coastal waters from Cape Mendocino to Point Arena" (forecast.weather.gov/MapClick.php?zoneid=PZZ455); buoys:

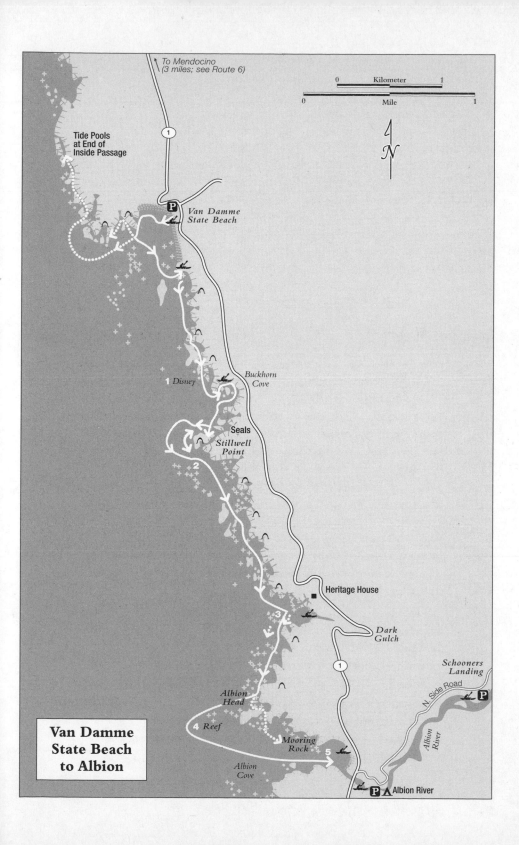

To Mendocino
(3 miles; see Route 6)

Kilometer
0   1

0   Mile   1

N

Tide Pools
at End of
Inside Passage

P Van Damme
State Beach

1 Disney   Buckhorn
                   Cove

            Seals
            Stillwell
            Point
      2

                   Heritage House

            3   Dark
                            Gulch

                      1   Schooners
                                                 Landing

                                        N. Side Road   P

Albion
Head
                                              Albion
4 Reef   River

            Mooring
            Rock
Albion   5
Cove

                      P Albion River

Van Damme
State Beach
to Albion

Cape Mendocino and Point Arena. Web cam: Looking south over Mendocino Bay, 3 miles to the north (weather.mcn.org).

Tidal information: Lower tides give better protection from outer reefs, more beach access, and more headroom in caves.

Cautions: Waves, submerged rocks, clapotis, wind, and fog.

Trip planning: Best protection is with lower tide and swell. Paddle north early in the day and return with the wind. Although it's possible to paddle outside the reef in swells of 8 feet or more, that's missing the point: to access the caves and rock gardens inside the reef, the calmer the better. Heading south of the blowhole island in swells above 6 feet (or when a south swell is running) is only recommended for experienced paddlers. Be very careful and skilled.

Launch site: Van Damme State Beach (7332 Shoreline Hwy., Little River) is located on Highway 1, 3 miles south of Mendocino. Free parking, outhouse, and cold outdoor showers. Aerial photo: View of cove and launch beach (californiacoastline.org, image 200503517).

Miles and Directions

0.0 Launch from Van Damme State Beach (N39 16.38 W123 47.50), heading south toward "Blowhole Island." Caution: The dangers of submerged rocks and waves persist along this entire route. Side trip: On rough days beginners will find more protection by contouring along the cliffs to the north past rock gardens and a couple of relatively protected caves. After 0.5 mile you reach the west end of the cove, where it's possible on calm days to turn north up the coast for another 0.5 mile and explore mazelike channels, caves, and hidden coves of the "inside passage," a semiprotected route between the offshore rocks and the cliffs. At the end of the inside passage, the channel gradually narrows to naught; either turn around and retrace your route, or, if the tide is high and you are nimble, scramble out of your kayak onto the rocks and explore the great tide pool on the left side of the passage. Caution: On rough days it's better to turn around and skip the inside passage, which becomes increasingly more exposed to the north, unless you have a skilled paddler leading.

0.3 Protected beach in small, secluded cove adjacent the blowhole island. This makes a good turn-around point for less-experienced paddlers or on rough days. Side trip: Check out the blowhole on the northeast side of the island. Caution: Exposure increases to the south, and you'll have to fight any afternoon winds on your return.

0.8 Continue exploring down the cave-riddled coastline to a slot where it's usually possible to cut into the swimming-pool calm of the large cove behind several islets and access a small beach. Caution: When seas are rough, this slot becomes a washing machine: challenging to paddle in and especially to attempt a rescue if someone capsizes. Also, watch for seal haul outs.

Punching his E-ticket, Tom Shores gets vertical on Disney. **KIM PATTERSON**

1.0   Behind the islets is a playground maze of chutes, tunnels, and other features, including "Disney," a large but generally forgiving pourover (see "Running Disney" below).

1.2   Round the point into Buckhorn Cove to find a small, pocket beach (N 39 15.60 W123 47.11) hidden along its north side.

1.7   A large double tunnel in the island off Stillwell Point makes a great photo op, but avoid spooking the large colony of seals on the islets inside the south cove.

Caution: Waves rebounding off Stillwell Point often make for confused seas and a rough rounding, so this is generally a good turn-around point for many paddlers. Recommended for advanced paddlers beyond Stillwell: Exposure increases the farther south you paddle, and the assumption is that if you've come this far, you're planning to paddle all the way to Albion rather than try to return against the wind. Unless you feel very comfortable in the bumpy seas off Stillwell, don't continue; Albion Head (and many spots in between) will be much worse. And if it's foggy, groping your way around Albion Head safely can be extremely difficult.

3.0   The next mile down to a brief respite in Dark Gulch features dynamic water—big boomers, rock gardens, and rebound waves abound—along with several of the

RUNNING DISNEY:
A POUROVER PRIMER

"Should we see if Disney's going off?" Tom asks. Bryan and I nod and lead our class through a small arch to the seaward side of a 4-foot ridge of kelp-covered reef that sticks out of the sea like a brick wall. Chasing a swell, I sprint toward the wall on an apparent kamikaze collision course. But a V-shaped gap forms a low spot, where the wave gets funneled, and just before pitoning into the rock my kayak is lifted several feet up over the wall and splashed down into the calm pool behind. The effect is like hopping the neighbor's fence and landing on a waterslide into their backyard swimming pool. Bryan grins, gives me a thumbs up—*yep, Disney's going off!* He turns to the students and launches into an explanation about how pourovers work—how it takes "just the right combination of tide height, swell size, and rock angle." Basically, if the tide or swell is too low, there's not enough water to carry a kayak over the rock. If the tide's too high, the water simply flows over the reef without first mounding up into a big bubble on the ocean side, so the waterslide effect is lost. Finally, if the rock is irregular or at an angle to the swell, the surge of water tends to wash into the rock instead of cleanly over it. Symmetrical, funnel-shaped pourovers like this one, that run perpendicular to the swell direction, are a rarity. Because it's so perfectly angled to funnel the swell into a big bubble, with safe, deep water on either side—and because its rocky slot was even well padded with kelp—we started referring to it as "Disney," Tom explains. "Because if Disney were to design a pourover ride for sea kayakers," exciting but with little actual danger, "it would look pretty much like this." After coaching several students over the waterfall, Tom sees a big one coming, and takes off. Most of us are already sitting in the calm pool watching and taking photos. We gawk wide-eyed as Tom rises up and up, teeters, and plunges bow-first over an 8-foot wall of water. Then our jaws drop when, as the rest of the wave cascades over the ledge and onto his stern, his 15-foot kayak gets squirted totally vertical by the force. He balances on a high brace for a full second, in a move later dubbed the "Mendo-Endo," before slowly splashing down. When he rolls up to cheers after his E-ticket ride, he asks what any kayaker would in his situation: "So did anyone get a picture?"

area's deeper, darker, and more challenging tunnels. A sandy, protected beach in the back of Dark Gulch makes an easy landing, but road access is blocked by private property.

4.0 Exposure maxes out on the final mile around Albion Head. Even on relatively calm days, running the gauntlet of rocks along the cliffs creates an interesting route-finding challenge for skilled rock gardeners. Side trip: Albion Head is actually an island, so it is possible to run the channel behind it into Albion Cove. Caution: On big days it's often necessary to remain a quarter mile or more to seaward of this minefield of rocks and boomers and from the shallow, dangerous reef that extends well beyond the head.

5.0 Albion River Bridge and the launch ramp (N 39 13.56 W123 46.11) just beyond on the left.

Where to Eat and Where to Stay

Restaurants: Among many fine options are Mendocino Cafe (mendocinocafe.com; 707-937-2422), Bayview Cafe (bayviewcafe.com; 707-937-4197) overlooking Mendocino cove, and Moodys Organic Coffee Bar (moodyscoffeebar.com; 707-937-4843). **Lodging:** In addition to lodging, Sweetwater Gardens (sweetwaterspa.com; 707-937-4140) has hot tubs whether or not you're staying there. **Camping:** Van Damme, Russian Gulch, and MacKerricher State Parks all book up to seven months in advance (reserveamerica .com; 800-444-7275). If the state parks are full, try Caspar Beach RV Park and Campground (casparbeachrvpark.com; 707-964-3306) and Albion River Campground (albionrivercampground.com; 707-937-0606).

Route 8
Albion River to Dark Gulch and Beyond

For novice and intermediate paddlers, the narrow gorge of Albion Cove, with its dramatic and scenic cliffs, offers even better protection than the more popular Van Damme (see Route 7); unfortunately, there are no sea caves until you leave this protection and round Albion Head. Calm-water paddlers can enjoy the shelter of the cove or explore several miles upriver along the quiet, tree-lined banks of the Albion River. Advanced paddlers will find this rugged stretch to the north of Albion Head riddled with some of Mendo's best caves and rock gardens—and most challenging conditions.

Trip highlights: Access to both quiet water and world-class sea caves and rock gardens.

Trip rating:
Beginner: 1- to 8-mile flat-water round-trip upriver, or 1 mile of good protection on calm days to Albion Head.
Intermediate: 1 to 4 miles for those with previous coastal paddling experience and good sea sense in swells below 4 feet and winds to 15 knots; not recommended beyond Albion Head without experienced paddler leading.
Advanced: 5+ miles of rock garden heaven await experienced paddlers with strong open-coast skills. Seas above 6 feet limit access to most caves and rock gardens.

Trip duration: Part to full day.

Kayak rentals: Albion River Campground (albionrivercampground.com, 707-937-0606) has single and double sit-on-tops.

Navigation aids: USGS: Albion (7.5 minute) and NOAA charts 18628 (charts.noaa.gov/OnLineViewer/18628.shtml) and 18626 (charts.noaa.gov/OnLineViewer/18626.shtml).

Weather information: Zone forecast: "Coastal waters from Cape Mendocino to Point Arena" (forecast.weather.gov/MapClick.php?zoneid=PZZ455); buoys: Cape Mendocino and Point Arena. Web cam looking south from town of Mendocino, about 6 miles north (weather.mcn.org).

Tidal information: Lower tides give better protection from outer reefs, more beach access, and more headroom in caves. If heading upriver, do so on a rising tide.

Cautions: Waves, submerged rocks, clapotis, wind, and fog.

Trip planning: Best protection with lower tide and swell. Although it's possible to paddle outside the reef in swells of 8 feet or more, that's missing the point: To access the caves and rock gardens inside the reef, the calmer the sea the better are your chances (only experts recommended in swells above 6 feet).

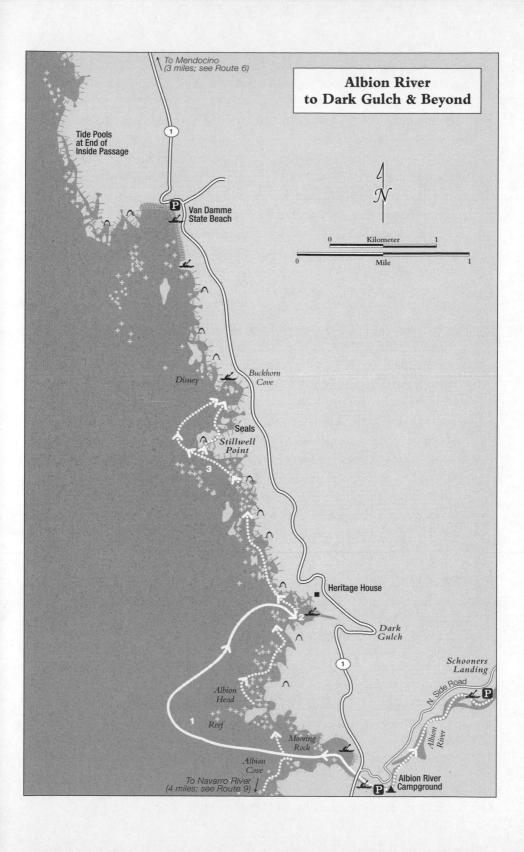

**Albion River
to Dark Gulch & Beyond**

To Mendocino
(3 miles; see Route 6)

1

Tide Pools
at End of
Inside Passage

0   Kilometer   1

0   Mile   1

N

P Van Damme
State Beach

Disney

Buckhorn
Cove

Seals
*Stillwell
Point*

3

Heritage House

2

*Dark
Gulch*

1

*Schooners
Landing*

P

N. Side Road

*Albion
Head*

1   *Reef*

*Albion
River*

*Mooring
Rock*

*Albion
Cove*

To Navarro River
(4 miles; see Route 9)

P ▲ Albion River
Campground

THE CAVE

The cliffs continue to tower overhead as the five of us round another sharp point. "Cave," someone calls out, but none of us paddles toward it. We only note the western exposure of its small, seaward opening, a narrow throat of jagged rock and crashing surf that foams at the mouth as it swallows a set of four 6-foot waves. "Ain't no place for kayakers," I think. In the lee of the point, however, maybe 100 feet from the mouth, we notice a better-protected side entry from the south, a single-wide garage door leading into darkness and the sloshing guts of midcave. As a set boils through, I paddle closer to gawk, certain the ceiling's too low to be passable. During the ensuing lull, however, I'm drawn toward the cave, a moth to the flame. Paddling backward to facilitate a hasty retreat, I duck through the narrow opening and discover a vaulted ceiling with plenty of headroom and steep, deep walls. My favorite cave type: lots of bounce and bluster but little real danger. I slosh around inside for awhile, tensing up as the next set pours in down the throat, like an avalanche, frothing off the sides and ceiling, cutting off light, only to reach the wider midcave section to reform as a swell that bobs me gently up toward the ceiling, then sloshes off the sides, creating a confusion of chop but also a pillow of safety that keeps my kayak from washing into the black walls. I beckon the others with a raised paddle—"it's not as bad as it looks," I yell—but only Billy shares my twisted idea of a good time. We bounce around together through another set, bracing and hooting and laughing in the din. And Billy's had enough. He flees out the side, and I eye the back opening, a narrow slot between rocks, but a short enough sprint to run between waves. Digging hard into black water, the freight train echo of the next wave hard on my heels, I burst out into sunlight, giddy with adrenaline.

Paddle north early in the day and return with the wind. Be very careful and skilled beyond Albion Head. If you're planning to land at Dark Gulch, scout conditions beforehand from the overlook at Heritage House.

Launch site: To reach the launch ramp at Albion River Campground (34500 Hwy. 1, Albion) from Highway 1, turn east on North Side Road, just north of the Albion River bridge, and follow it down to the water. There is a $5 launch fee per kayak. Restrooms available.

Alternate launch site: Schooners Landing, 0.5 mile farther on North Side Road. The charge here is $10 day-use fee per vehicle to launch. Facilities: Water and restrooms available. Aerial photo: Albion Cove and river bridge (californiacoastline.org, image 200503580).

Freshwater rinse in Waterfall Cave north of Albion R. SCHUMANN

Miles and Directions

0.0 From the launch ramp (N 39 13.56 W123 46.11), paddle out the river mouth into Albion Cove. Caution: Stay out of the way of fishing boats in this narrow channel. Side trip: Wind up to 4 miles upriver with a rising tide into second-growth redwood forest; several small beaches provide an opportunity to stop and rest.

0.2 After leaving the river mouth, contour along the steep cliffs to the north, passing the first of two wide sandy beaches in the inner cove. Side trip: A gentle surf break sometimes forms off the point on the south side just beyond the mouth when swell and tide are right. Caution: The dangers of submerged rocks, waves, and caves persist along this entire route, especially beyond Mooring Rock.

0.4 Navigational marker atop Mooring Rock at the end of the "inner cove" is a good place for beginners to turn around if not accompanied by an experienced paddler. Beyond this point are a couple small beaches in hidden coves on the north side of Albion Cove that can be landable if swell and tide are down. Caution: When seas are up, the outer cove can get quite rough.

1.0   Albion Head (a large sea stack that only appears to be an attached headland) is a good place to reassess conditions or turn around. Caution: Advanced coastal touring skills are required beyond Albion Head. It can be one of the roughest roundings in this area, and it will only get rougher as wind and seas rise during the day. Swing wide to round the rocks that extend well out to sea off the point. Side trip: On calm days skilled paddlers can try running the shortcut gap between Albion Head and shore, but it is long and rocky and can be quite dangerous if waves are breaking through it.

2.0   Good caves and rock gardens along this exposed stretch to the sandy, well-protected beach at Dark Gulch. Caution: When the swell is up, waves breaking on submerged rocks at the entrance to the cove can make getting into the cove difficult to dangerous. Side trip: Continue north past more caves and sea stacks for another 1.5 miles to the fine landing beaches in Buckhorn Cove.

Other options: Run a shuttle and do a one-way trip 5 miles south from Van Damme (see Route 7) or head down the very exposed cliffs south of Albion 4 miles to the mouth of the Navarro River (see Route 9). Options abound in this area for advanced paddlers.

Where to Eat and Where to Stay

Restaurants: Albion River Inn (albionriverinn.com; 800-479-7944) across Highway 1 features "luxury dining" on fresh local seafood; many more options 7 miles north in Mendocino (see Route 7). **Lodging:** Albion River Inn (albionriverinn.com) has ocean-view rooms. Many more options 7 miles north in Mendocino (see Route 6). **Camping:** Albion River Campground (albionrivercampground.com; 707-937-0606) and Schooners Landing (schoonersrvpark.com; 707-937-5707) are more crowded and less attractive than state parks in the area, but don't book up as early. Van Damme, Russian Gulch, and MacKerricher State Parks all book up to seven months in advance (reserveamerica.com; 800-444-7275).

Route 9

Navarro River Beach and Albion to Elk

The beach at the mouth of the Navarro River offers easy access to either a calm-water paddle upriver or an optional launch site for coastal kayakers looking to explore beyond the area's more popular destinations. Upriver a shallow estuary with lots of birdlife—osprey, herons, shorebirds, and waterfowl—heads into a narrow river valley overarched with redwoods. On the sea, those with surf skills can launch off the fairly exposed ocean beach and head 4 miles north along the cliffs to Albion or run a shuttle and head 5 miles downwind to Elk.

Trip highlights: Access to both quiet water with lots of birdlife and coastal paddling.

Trip rating:

Beginner: 1- to 8-mile flat-water round-trip upriver, or 1 mile to the cove north of the river mouth on days with no surf on the beach.

Intermediate–Advanced: 1 to 5+ miles for those with previous coastal paddling experience.

Trip duration: Part to full day.

Navigation aids: USGS: Albion (7.5 minute) and NOAA chart 18626 (charts.noaa .gov/OnLineViewer/18626.shtml).

Weather information: Zone forecast: "Coastal waters from Cape Mendocino to Point Arena" (forecast.weather.gov/MapClick.php?zoneid=PZZ455); buoys: Cape Mendocino and Point Arena.

Tidal information: Tides generally have little effect on river levels upstream in summer after the river mouth has closed. Lower tides give more beach options for coastal paddlers.

Cautions: Shallow sand bars, upriver wind. In winter and spring, strong currents after rains.

Trip planning: Paddle early to avoid upriver afternoon winds on your return. Paddlers heading to Elk should bring kayak wheels for the long uphill carry to the highway.

Launch site: Navarro Beach Campground (Navarro Beach Road, Albion) is off Highway 1 on the south shore of the Navarro River. Facilities: 10 first-come, first-served, primitive campsites, pit toilets only. Day use fee $8 (parks.ca.gov/?page_id=435). Aerial photo: Looking upriver from the beach (californiacoastline.org, image 200904073).

Other options: Albion River Campground (34500 Hwy. 1, Albion) and beach trail across the street from Elk Store (6101 S. Hwy. 1, Elk).

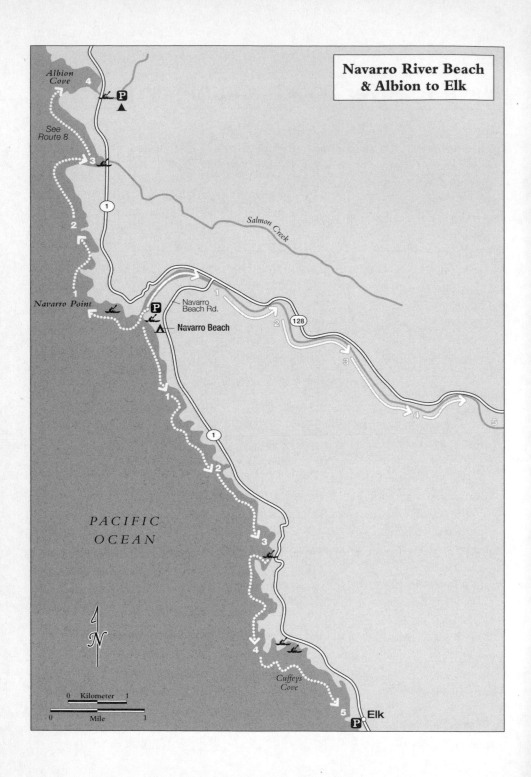

Navarro River Beach
& Albion to Elk

Albion
Cove

4

See
Route 8

3

1

2

1

Salmon Creek

Navarro Point

P

Navarro
Beach Rd.

1

2

128

Navarro Beach

3

4

5

1

2

3

4

PACIFIC
OCEAN

5

N

0   Kilometer   1

0   Mile   1

Cuffeys
Cove

5   Elk

P

Miles and Directions

0.0   From the beach (N39 11.55 W123 45.57), head upriver, across the wide, shallow estuary, skirting around several midstream islets.

1.0   After passing under the Highway 1 bridge, the river continues to narrow and enters the forest.

2.0   The river bends away from Highway 128, becoming narrower, shallower, and more wooded, as it winds deeper into the redwoods. Depending on the time of year, in the next mile or two, you will likely begin to encounter shallow gravel bars. Most are short and easy to portage, with stretches of deeper water just upstream. The farther upstream you go, the bars get longer and the deep water sections get shorter. You should be able to get another 2 to 4 miles upriver, depending how much portaging you're willing to do. A scattering of small beaches offers many opportunities to stop and rest.

Other options: On days with little or no surf, adventurous calm-water paddlers can paddle north 0.5 mile around the first point into the protected and very scenic cove and land on a secluded beach at the base of towering cliffs. Those with ocean skills can explore the many rock gardens and coves, and a few caves, either 4 miles north to Albion (with good landing in a protected cove 2.5 miles north at Salmon Creek and not much else), or 5 miles south to Elk (little in the way of landings until the west-facing cove at mile 3, and then many well-protected coves, and the best paddling on the route, in the last mile or so in Cuffeys Cove).

Where to Eat and Where to Stay

Restaurants: Nearest food at the Albion River Inn (albionriverinn.com; 800-479-7944) 4 miles north, with many more options in Mendocino, 10 miles north (see Route 7). **Lodging:** Albion River Inn (albionriverinn.com) has ocean-view rooms; many more options 7 miles north in Mendocino (see Route 7). **Camping:** Sites at Navarro Beach Campground are first-come, first-served and primitive (pit toilets, no water); arrive early on Friday on busy summer weekends to get a spot; Van Damme and Russian Gulch take reservations (reserveamerica.com; 800-444-7275) but often fill months in advance (see Route 7).

Quick Trip Tips: Other Launch Sites along the Mendocino Coast

Westport Union-Landing State Beach (Advanced)
This exposed coastline at the south end of the Lost Coast, 3 miles north of Westport, offers challenging launches below rugged bluffs.

A dog's life on the Navarro River CATE HAWTHORNE

Point Arena (Beginner–Intermediate to Advanced)

Good protection in Arena Cove for all skill levels when conditions are calm. But once beyond the cove, you immediately enter an exposed shoreline of cliffs, reefs, and rocks, 4 miles north to the lighthouse.

Gualala River (Beginner to Advanced)

Paddle several miles upriver into the redwoods or explore the rocky open coast beyond the mouth. Rentals available through Adventure Rents (adventurerents.com; 707-884-4386).

Point Reyes National Seashore and Vicinity

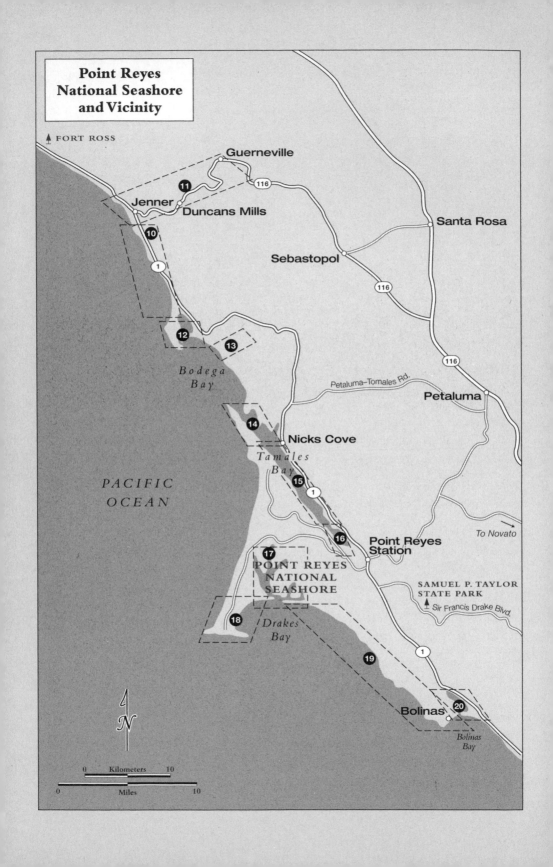

Point Reyes National Seashore and Vicinity

FORT ROSS

Guerneville

11

116

Jenner
Duncans Mills

Santa Rosa

10

Sebastopol

1

116

12

13

Bodega Bay

116

Petaluma–Tomales Rd.

Petaluma

14

Nicks Cove

Tamales Bay

PACIFIC OCEAN

15

1

16

Point Reyes Station

To Novato

17

POINT REYES NATIONAL SEASHORE

SAMUEL P. TAYLOR STATE PARK

Sir Francis Drake Blvd.

18

Drakes Bay

19

1

N

Bolinas

20

Bolinas Bay

0   Kilometers   10

0   Miles   10

Route 10
Russian River Estuary to Duncans Mills and Beyond

Winding past hills covered in coastal scrub at the mouth, this peaceful ribbon of water meanders through willow thickets and dense evergreen stands as you continue inland. The relative solitude, scenery, and wildlife along this stretch make it an excellent choice for an easy day trip, despite the proximity of Highway 116, which runs the length of the river. A variety of birds—from cormorants and ducks to shorebirds and osprey—are commonly seen along with harbor seals and the occasional river otter. Upriver, currents are generally easy to paddle against and helpful when returning against the afternoon winds. Kayak camping here is easily accessible to beginners at a few campsites upstream. For skilled and adventurous paddlers, the coastline beyond the river mouth is thick with skyscraper cliffs, sea stacks, and surf.

Trip highlights: Good protection, wildlife, warm(er) water to practice rescue skills, with easy access to kayak camping and coastal touring.

Trip rating:
Beginner: 1 to 13+ miles of well-protected river.
Intermediate–Advanced: 1 to 20+ miles with access to coastal touring, rock gardens, and surf in waves to 3 to 6 feet and winds to 15 to 20 knots.

Trip duration: Part day, full day, or overnight(s).

Kayak rentals: Water Treks (watertreks.com; 707-865-2249) in Jenner rents touring kayaks and SOTs and offers a shuttle service; Casini Ranch Family Campground (casiniranch.com; 800-451-8400) in Duncans Mills rents sit-on-tops.

Navigation aids: USGS: Duncans Mills (7.5 minute).

Weather information: Zone forecast: "Coastal waters from Point Arena to Point Reyes" (forecast.weather.gov/MapClick.php?zoneid=PZZ540); buoys: Point Arena and Bodega Bay.

Tidal information: Currents at mouth but little effect on water levels.

Cautions: At river mouth, avoid spooking resting seals, strong currents sweeping you out to sea when the river mouth is open, and strong afternoon winds blowing upriver. Currents upriver are generally weak in summer, but swift and dangerous with runoff after winter storms.

Trip planning: Expect strong afternoon wind blowing upriver within a few miles of the mouth, so paddle early to avoid returning against it or save some energy. Although downstream current is generally weak, you might make better

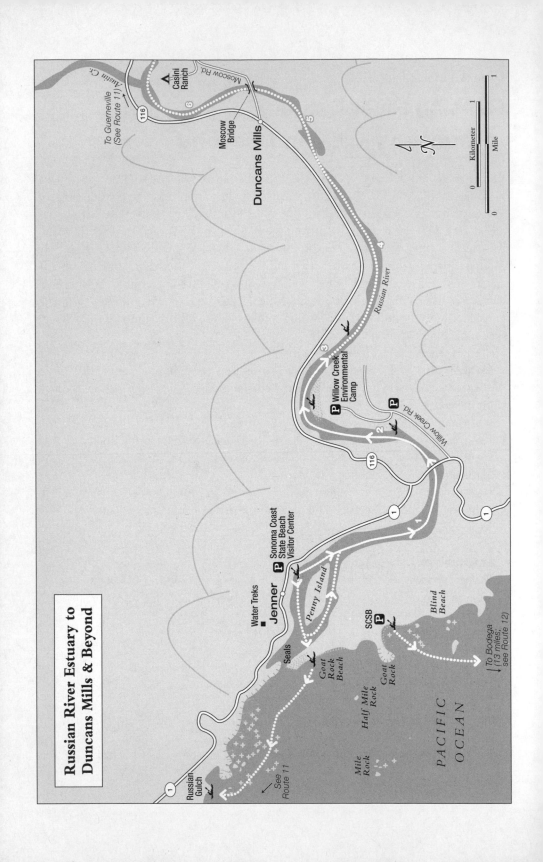

Russian River Estuary to Duncans Mills & Beyond

Canoes and kayaks: coexisting on the Russian River CASS KALINSKI

progress upriver by staying near the banks and out of the main flow. Securing a good campsite at Willow Creek Environmental Camp can take some doing, especially on busy weekends. There are only 11 first-come, first-served sites, not all of which have direct river access. Note: Willow Creek Environmental Camp was temporarily closed in 2012 due to budget cuts, so check first to see if it has reopened (707-875-3483, parks.ca.gov/?page_id=451).

Launch site: Sonoma Coast State Beach Visitor Center (10439 Hwy. 1, Jenner) is just past the post office, first building on the left as you enter town from the south. Facilities: Outhouses, boat ramp, water, and parking; no fee. Aerial photo: Russian River mouth and Penny Island (californiacoastline.org, image 200905).

Alternate launch sites: Willow Creek Road (N38 26.33 W123 05.78) is on the south bank where the Highway 1 bridge crosses the river; head east on Willow Creek Road (past Sizzling Tandoor restaurant) for 0.5 mile and look for a small pullout on your left. The left turn for Willow Creek Environmental Camp is another 0.25 mile up the road.

Casini Ranch Family Campground (22855 Moscow Rd., Duncans Mills) is 5 miles upriver from Jenner on Highway 116; turn right onto Moscow Road, cross the river, and continue 0.75 mile to entrance on left.

Miles and Directions

0.0   Head upstream from the boat launch (N38 26.95 W123 06.95) past Penny Island toward the Highway 1 bridge. Side trip: Head downstream to circumnavigate Penny Island (where some landings are possible, but much of the island is muddy or overgrown) or continue along the sandspit to see the seals near the river mouth; land near pilings to portage to Goat Rock Beach (instead of paddling past seals) to launch through surf and access rock gardens. Caution: Be alert for seals, surf, and ocean-going currents.

2.0   Alternate launch at mouth of Willow Creek (N38 26.33 W123 05.78) is on right, 0.5 mile past Highway 1 bridge.

3.0   Willow Creek Environmental Camp (N38 26.65 W123 05.14) is hidden in the willow thicket behind the long, sand-and-gravel beach on the right. Caution: Avoid shallow water on the extensive gravel bar on your right and harbor seals resting on logs along the left bank. The two campsites with the best river access are 50 yards upriver from the long beach and up a steep bank from a small beach with room for five or six boats. (See note in "Trip planning" about possible campground closure.)

5.5   Large beach on the left as you pass under Moscow Road Bridge makes a good stretch break after winding up the river valley, past forested banks on your right and views of the coastal hills on your left.

6.5   The river makes a big right-hand U turn at Casini Ranch beach and boat launch (N38 27.89 W123 02.95) on your right, across the river from the confluence with Austin Creek. Take out here or continue another 3.5 miles to Monte Rio.

Other options: Skilled coastal paddlers can head north past sea stacks and cliffs for 2 miles to the beach at Russian Gulch, tackle the 7-mile stretch from Goat Rock to Salmon Creek, or continue down the full 13 miles around Bodega Head (see Route 12).

Where to Eat and Where to Stay

Restaurants: Sea Gull Gifts and Deli (707-865-2594) has made-to-order sandwiches, and the Sizzling Tandoor (707-865-0625) features Indian cuisine. **Lodging:** Jenner Inn and Cottages (jennerinn.com; 707-865-2377) and the River's End Resort (ilovesunsets .com; 707-865-2484) overlook the bluffs of Jenner. **Camping:** Casini Ranch Family Campground (casiniranch.com; 800-451-8400); Willow Creek Environmental Camp (707-865-2391 for information on reservations and current closure status).

Route 11
Russian River Camping Trip from Guerneville to the Sea

With its variety of launch and take-out options, this ambitious, 15-mile paddle to the sea through dense stands of redwood forest can easily be broken up into shorter sections. It's also popular as an easy overnighter and can be extended into a 30-mile, multiday adventure by launching as far upriver as Healdsburg. The farther you get from the coast in the summer, the more both water and air temperatures begin to rise as you leave the sea fog behind, along with immersion gear like wetsuits and paddle jackets. Rather than the coastal kayaker's usual preoccupation with hypothermia, you might find yourself slipping out of your boat and into the water in little more than your bathing suit, just to cool off.

Trip highlights: Calm, warm water on sunny, summer days. Paddling through redwoods and lots of birdlife.

Trip rating:
  Beginner: 1 to 15+ miles of well-protected water if your timing is good.
  Intermediate: 1 to 15+ miles with potentially swift currents and strong winds depending on time of year and time of day.

Trip duration: Part day, full day, or overnight(s).

Kayak rentals: Water Treks (watertreks.com; 707-865-2249) in Jenner rents touring kayaks and SOTs and offers a shuttle service; Johnson's Beach in Guerneville, Monte Rio Community Beach in Monte Rio, and Casini Ranch in Duncans Mills rent mostly sit-on-tops for day trips to and from their locations (see "Launch sites" below).

Navigation aids: USGS: Duncans Mills (7.5 minute).

Weather information: Zone forecast: "Coastal waters from Point Arena to Point Reyes" (forecast.weather.gov/MapClick.php?zoneid=PZZ540); buoys: none. Web cams: View of river from Guerneville (stumptown.com), including current weather info.

Cautions: Overheating in summer. Strong currents in winter. This is a late spring to autumn run only, unless you are a skilled, whitewater paddler. Currents upriver are generally weak in summer, but swift and dangerous with runoff after winter storms. Not recommended at flows above 500 CFS at the Hacienda Bridge gauge (americanwhitewater.org/content/Gauge2/detail/id/42633). Finding a landing site on some stretches can be difficult or impossible due to steep, overgrown banks; also, be aware that some beaches

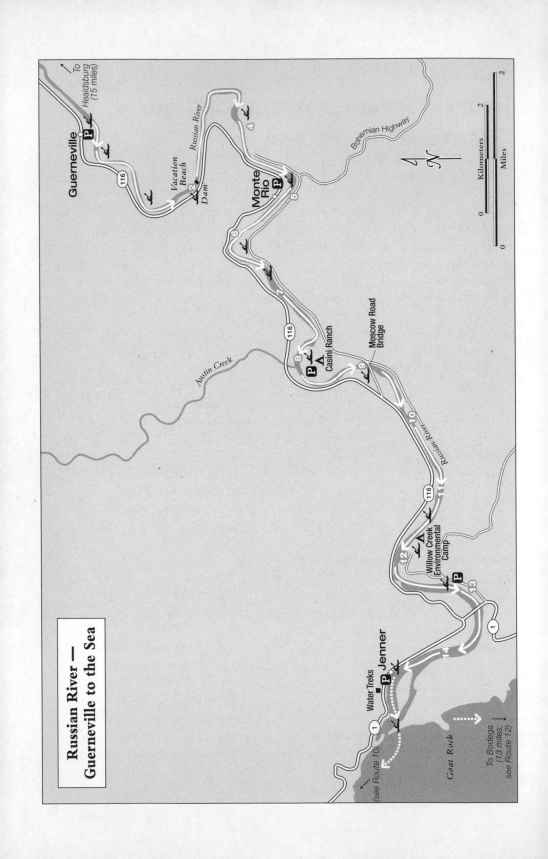

Russian River —
Guerneville to the Sea

are private—if it looks like someone's backyard, it probably is. Beware of currents sweeping you seaward at the mouth, and upriver afternoon winds. And no matter how warm it might be at the put in upriver, if you're heading to the coast, bring warm clothes. It might be high nineties inland and foggy in the fifties at the beach.

Trip planning: A typical overnight itinerary would be to camp at Casini Ranch near the halfway point in Duncans Mills, then paddle the rest of the way to the mouth the following morning before the upriver wind comes up. Easy day trips up- or downriver from put ins at Duncans Mills, Monte Rio, or Guerneville are possible, either round-trip or one-way. If you don't want to run a shuttle yourself, Water Treks in Jenner (see rentals) offers a shuttle service. To avoid wind, paddle early in the day and plan to be heading upriver with the prevailing ocean breezes in the afternoon, which can be especially strong the closer you get to the mouth. However, even well upriver, up-canyon winds can be strong for stretches, depending on what direction the river bends happen to be facing.

If you prefer solitude, try paddling midweek. On busy summer weekends expect stretches of redwood serenity to be shattered by a party ambiance as you pass beaches crowded with sunbathers, swimmers, and revelers, and share the waterways with people paddling everything from kayaks and canoes to duckies and inner tubes. Note: Willow Creek Environmental Camp was temporarily closed in 2012 due to budget cuts, so check first to see if it has reopened (707-875-3483, parks.ca.gov/?page_id=451).

Launch sites: Each of the first 3 sites has toilet facilities, water, and parking fees.

Johnson's Beach (16241 First St., Guerneville; johnsonsbeach.com/Johnsonswebsite/beach.html) is 14 miles up Highway 116 from Jenner, on the right, one block down First Street.

Monte Rio Community Beach (20488 Hwy. 116, Monte Rio; mrrpd.org/monteriobeach.html#andpanel1-1) is 10 miles up Highway 116 from Jenner on the right at the corner of Church Street.

Casini Ranch Family Campground (22855 Moscow Rd., Duncans Mills, casiniranch.com), is 5 miles upriver from Jenner on Highway 116.

Willow Creek Road (N38 26.33 W123 05.78) is on the south bank where the Highway 1 bridge crosses the river. Head east on Willow Creek Road (past Sizzling Tandoor restaurant) for 0.5 mile and look for a small pullout on your left. Facilities/fees: None.

Sonoma Coast State Beach Visitor Center in Jenner on Highway 1 is just past the post office, the first building on the left as you enter Jenner from the south. Facilities: Outhouses, boat ramp, water, and parking; no fee.

Miles and Directions

0.0 Head downstream from Johnson's Beach (N38 29.99 W122 59.88) into the outskirts of town, passing multiple landing beach options on either side.

2.1 A seasonal dam is typically installed at Vacation Beach by Memorial Day weekend to create deeper water for swimmers upstream. It is easily portaged, and there are a few more beach options downriver, but more widely spaced than before.

5.0 The popular Monte Rio Community Beach (N 38 27.97 W123 00.63) is on the north bank beneath the big bridge over the river.

8.0 The river valley begins to open up as you approach Casini Ranch beach and boat launch (N38 27.89 W123 02.95), located on the flood plain on the south side on the inside of a big U bend in the river, across from the confluence with Austin Creek.

9.1 Bridge at Moscow Road.

11.5 Forest gradually gives way to grass-covered hills along the north bank as you approach Willow Creek Environmental Camp (N38 26.65 W123 05.14), which is hidden in the willow thicket along the left bank, just after passing the long sandy beach on the right. The two campsites with the best river access are 50 yards upriver from the long beach and up a steep bank from a small beach with room for five or six boats. (See note in "Trip planning" about possible campground closure.)

12.5 The small launch site at Willow Creek Road (N38 26.33 W123 05.78) is on the southeast bank, about 0.5 mile before you reach the Highway 1 bridge.

14.6 The launch ramp at Sonoma Coast State Beach Visitor Center in Jenner (N38 26.95 W123 06.95) is on the north bank, where the first buildings in town begin. You can take out there or paddle the final 0.5 mile to the sea. (See Route 6 for more information on paddling this area.)

Other options: The Russian River is navigable for 30 miles or so, all the way from Healdsburg. Alternate launch sites upriver from Guerneville include Steelhead Beach Park (9000 River Rd., Forestville; sonoma-county.org/parks/pk_stlhd.htm) 8 miles upstream, and Healdsburg Memorial Beach (13839 Healdsburg Ave., Healdsburg; sonoma-county.org/parks/pk_hvet.htm) 15 miles up.

Where to Eat and Where to Stay

Restaurants: Sea Gull Gifts and Deli (707-865-2594) has made-to-order sandwiches, and the Sizzling Tandoor (707-865-0625) features Indian cuisine. **Lodging:** Jenner Inn and Cottages (jennerinn.com; 707-865-2377) and the River's End Resort (ilovesunsets .com; 707-865-2484) overlook the bluffs of Jenner. **Camping:** Casini Ranch Family Campground (casiniranch.com; 800-451-8400); Willow Creek Environmental Camp (707-865-2391 for information on reservations and current closure status).

Route 12
Bodega Harbor and
Goat Rock to Doran Beach

Alfred Hitchcock's *The Birds* was filmed in nearby Bodega, and birds still flock to Bodega Bay to feed on the rich mudflats in the harbor. A boat channel bisects the harbor's tide flats; small marinas, restaurants, and homes line the north shore; and parks, dunes, and grassy headlands complete the harbor's circumference. Beginners and intermediates can enjoy a 4-mile flat-water loop inside the harbor, practice reentries and other skills, or play in the surf on a well-protected stretch of sandy ocean beach. Experienced paddlers can access miles of rugged open coast—especially interesting is the 13-mile stretch south from Goat Rock to Bodega Head.

Trip highlights: Protection from swell, birding, a good place to practice beginning skills and watch the small local fishing fleet come and go.

Trip rating:

Beginner: 1 to 5 miles round-trip in protected harbor in winds below 10 to 15 knots.

Intermediate: 1 to 5+ miles round-trip with surf zone practice on Doran Beach in waves to 3 feet, and wind to 15 knots.

Advanced: 1 to 6+ miles round-trip with surfing at Doran Beach and open-coast rock gardens at Bodega Head or 13 miles one-way from Goat Rock in swell to 6 feet, winds to 20 knots.

Trip duration: Part to full day.

Kayak rentals: Bodega Bay Kayak (bodegabaykayak.com; 707-875-8899) rents single and double kayaks as well as offering tours of the area.

Navigation aids: USGS: Bodega Head (7.5 minute) and NOAA chart 18643 (charts.noaa.gov/OnLineViewer/18643.shtml).

Weather information: Zone forecast: "Coastal waters from Point Arena to Point Reyes" (forecast.weather.gov/MapClick.php?zoneid=PZZ540); buoys: Bodega Bay. Web cams: Looking toward the mouth from Spud Point Marina, in the back of the bay (sonoma-county.org/parks/spptcam.htm). Coastal conditions in Horseshoe Cove about 2 miles north of Bodega Head at the UC Davis Marine Lab (bml.ucdavis.edu/about/webcams).

Tidal information: Extensive mudflats and shallows begin to uncover at tide heights below 3 feet.

Cautions: Mudflats, traffic in boat channel, currents at harbor mouth during ebb tide, and fog; waves and offshore winds on Doran Beach. Standard coastal hazards around Bodega Head: rocks, waves, cliffs, and wind.

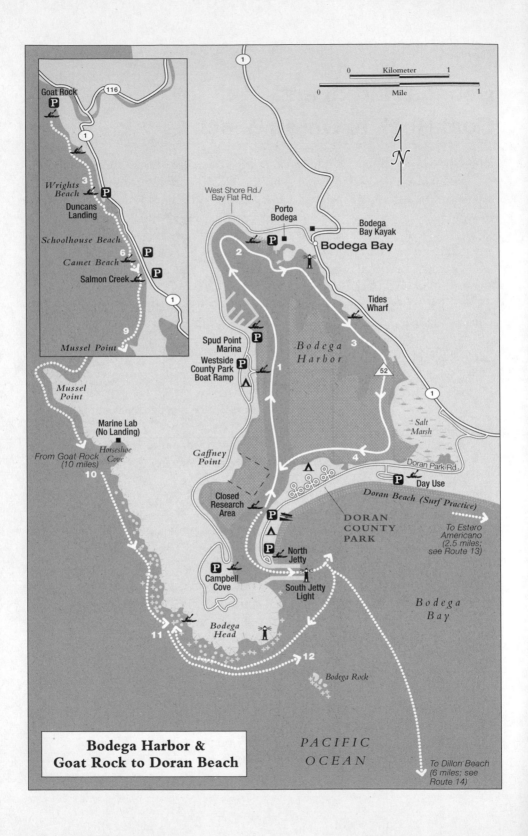

**Bodega Harbor &
Goat Rock to Doran Beach**

Goat Rock

116

1

Wrights
Beach 3

Duncans
Landing

Schoolhouse Beach

Camet Beach 6

Salmon Creek

1

9

Mussel Point

1

West Shore Rd./
Bay Flat Rd.

Porto
Bodega

Bodega
Bay Kayak

Bodega Bay

2

Tides
Wharf

Spud Point
Marina

Westside
County Park
Boat Ramp

1

Bodega
Harbor

3

52

Kilometer

Mile

N

Mussel
Point

Marine Lab
(No Landing)

Horseshoe
Cove

Gaffney
Point

From Goat Rock
(10 miles)

10

Closed
Research
Area

Salt
Marsh

Doran Park Rd.

Day Use

Doran Beach (Surf Practice)

4

DORAN
COUNTY
PARK

To Estero
Americano
(2.5 miles;
see Route 13)

Campbell
Cove

North
Jetty

South Jetty
Light

Bodega
Bay

11

Bodega
Head

12

Bodega Rock

PACIFIC
OCEAN

To Dillon Beach
(6 miles; see
Route 14)

Trip planning: Make a clockwise loop, heading north into the harbor before the wind kicks up (leave an hour or two before high tide to ride the incoming current) and have the wind at your back on the return. Although it's possible to paddle here at any tide height if you stay in the boat channel, 3 feet or more of tide is necessary to cross the mudflats at the end of the channel and complete the loop. On a falling tide, you might try crossing the mudflats first and riding the ebb current in the boat channel in a counterclockwise loop. When camping at Doran County Park, choose a campsite you can launch from.

Launch site: To reach the boat ramp at Doran County Park (201 Doran Beach Rd., Bodega Bay; sonoma-county.org/parks/pk_doran.htm) from Highway 1, take Doran Beach Road just south of the town of Bodega Bay and head west out the sandspit; pass the Doran Beach day-use parking and the campgrounds and look for the boat ramp on the right after you pass the Coast Guard dock. Launch from the beach to left of ramp to avoid traffic. Facilities: Restrooms, water, and showers. Parking fee: $7. Aerial photo: Looking north over Doran Beach with harbor in background (californiacoastline.org, image 12607).

Alternate launch sites: Westside County Park boat ramp has restrooms and water, and $7 parking, but there are several free launch sites possible from pullouts along West Shore Road, as well as from Porto Bodega Fishermans' (sic) Marina or at Campbell Cove.

Open-coast launch sites are at Goat Rock (Highway 1 and Goat Rock Road, Jenner), about 1 mile south of Jenner; Wrights Beach 3 miles south of Goat Rock on Highway 1; and North Salmon Creek, another 3.5 miles south of Wrights.

Miles and Directions

0.0   Head north from Doran County Park boat ramp (N38 18.62 W123 03.22), skirting the well-marked boat channel to stay out of traffic. Caution: Stay out of the posted "Ecological Research Area" adjacent to Gaffney Point. Side trip: Experienced paddlers may head left out the mouth of the harbor (see "Other options").

0.9   A well-marked side channel leads to the landing beach, campground, and alternative launch site at Westside County Park (N38 19.38 W123 03.28).

1.5   Spud Point Marina has a small beach where the breakwater meets the shore at the Bosco Keene Promenade. Caution: Commercial fishing boat traffic at the mouth of marina. Side trip: Circumnavigate the shoreline of the marina except at extreme high or low tides when passage beneath gangplanks may not be possible.

2.0   Beach and launch ramp at Porto Bodega marina.

In a foot of water, Patty Andrews reflects on a rising tide over the mudflats of Bodega Harbor.
R. SCHUMANN

3.0   Tides Wharf, the large, white building along the water, has a dinghy dock you can land on to stop for lunch at their snack bar, which has outdoor tables and sells fish and chips and sandwiches.

3.3   Channel Marker #52 marks the end of the boat channel and the beginning of the mudflats. With 3 feet of tide or more, you can cross the mudflats and skirt the salt marsh for some of the harbor's better birding. If the mudflats are exposed, retrace your path along the boat channel.

4.7   Pass camping area and return to launch site.

Other options: On calm days intermediates may paddle out the harbor mouth and land through small surf along Doran Beach. Caution: Scout the beach from shore first and be careful of currents at the harbor mouth during ebb tide and offshore winds off Doran Beach that can push you out to sea. Two launch sites on Doran Beach, at the north jetty and the day-use parking area, give more direct access to 2 miles of sandy ocean beach. This semisheltered, south-facing beach generally has small surf that gets gradually larger as you head east, making it a good place for surf zone practice and an introductory coastal tour to the mouth of Estero Americano (2.5 miles each way), provided you stay close to shore and the offshore winds don't kick up. Advanced ocean kayakers can run a shuttle south to Lawson's Landing or Nicks Cove (see Route 14) and paddle across 6 miles of open ocean to Tomales Bay, or head north along the cliffs of Bodega Head for some challenging rock gardens.

Goat Rock to Doran: A popular trip among skilled north-coast kayakers is the 7-mile stretch from Goat Rock to Salmon Creek, or the full 13 miles around Bodega Head to Doran Beach. From the reasonably protected but steep-beach surf launch at Goat Rock you'll find a handful of challenging pocket coves where landing may be possible through the rocks until you reach the alternate launch site at Wrights Beach (mile 3.5), a sandy, but exposed, west-facing beach. Duncans Landing (mile 4.5) is the most-protected beach on the route. Portuguese (mile 5.0), Schoolhouse (mile 5.5), and Camet Beaches (mile 6) are all sandy with decent access up the bluffs to Highway 1, so might make good alternatives to landing at the more-exposed Salmon Creek. Exposure intensifies continuing to Bodega; the long, northwest-facing, surf beach at Salmon Creek extends over 2 miles to Mussel Point (mile 9.4), where the wave-pounded cliffs of the Bodega Headlands begin. The well-protected beach at Horseshoe Cove (mile 10.0) is unfortunately closed to landing, but you might be able to stop at a few pocket coves after mile 11.0, and seas should begin to calm somewhat as you start to round the southern point at mile 12.0. Land at the west end of Doran or inside the harbor at the boat ramp.

Where to Eat and Where to Stay

Restaurants: Many choices in Bodega Bay, especially for seafood, including Lucas Wharf Restaurant and Bar (lucaswharfrestaurant.com; 707-875-3522), for finer dining, or the Dog House (doghousebodegabay.com; 707-875-2441) and 3 Daughters Deli (707-875-8881) for food without frills. **Lodging:** Bodega Bay Lodge (bodegabaylodge .com; 888-875-2250), Inn at the Tides (innatthetides.com; 800-541-7788), or contact the chamber of commerce (bodegabayca.org; 707-347-9645). **Camping:** Sites on bay at Doran County Park or Westside County Park (sonoma-county.org/parks/camping/ camp_reservations.htm; 707-565-2267), or 4 miles north at Bodega Dunes State Park (parks.ca.gov/?page_id=451, reserveamerica.com; 800-444-7275). RV parking available at Porto Bodega Fishermans' Marina (portobodega.com; 707-875-2354).

Route 13
Estero Americano

From its humble beginnings in a cow pasture (some local paddlers refer to the launch site as "the muddy ditch"), Estero Americano winds 6 miles to the sea, the scenery improving constantly with each turn downstream. Within a mile of the Holsteins at the put in, the narrow channel slips between grassy, golden hills and widens into salt marsh. In addition to ducks and shorebirds, this riparian corridor is an excellent place to view raptors, including peregrine falcons, golden eagles, and a variety of hawks, soaring over the ridge tops. Near the ocean, the hills become steeper and wilder still, now cloaked in coastal scrub and traversed by deer and elk. When the estero exits a gap in the steep ocean cliffs, the vista is about as far from a cow pasture as you can get. Beyond the cliffs and sea stacks stretches the entire sweep of Bodega Bay, from Bodega Head in the north to Tomales Point in the south; on clear days you can even see Point Reyes headland, 20 miles in the distance. You can hunker out of the wind behind the low dunes at the mouth for lunch and even camp overnight, if you don't mind sharing the view with a house high on the bluff.

Trip highlights: Flat water, solitude, and wildlife: raptors, elk, and deer.
Trip rating:
Beginner: 1- to 12-mile round-trip of flat water to ocean and back for energetic beginners.
Intermediate: 12 miles round-trip to ocean. Surf practice is possible on calm days with waves to 3 feet, and winds to 15 knots.
Advanced: 12 miles round-trip to ocean with rock gardens, coastal touring, and difficult surf (with waves above 6 feet and winds above 20 knots).
Trip duration: Part day, full day, or overnight.
Navigation aids: USGS Valley Ford (7.5 minute), tide book.
Weather information: Zone forecast: "Coastal waters from Point Arena to Point Reyes" (forecast.weather.gov/MapClick.php?zoneid=PZZ540); buoys: Bodega Bay.
Tidal information: Check tides when the mouth is open to the sea—to get past the shallow area midway requires at least 2 feet, and more is better; currents are fairly weak except at the mouth when it is open to the sea.
Cautions: Mud, afternoon wind, and steep beach at mouth with channel to ocean sometimes open with swift seaward currents. Shores of the estero are private property until you reach the ocean beach.
Trip planning: Paddle to mouth in morning to beat wind coming off the ocean; enjoy the tail wind on return—this is a great place for a sail rig.

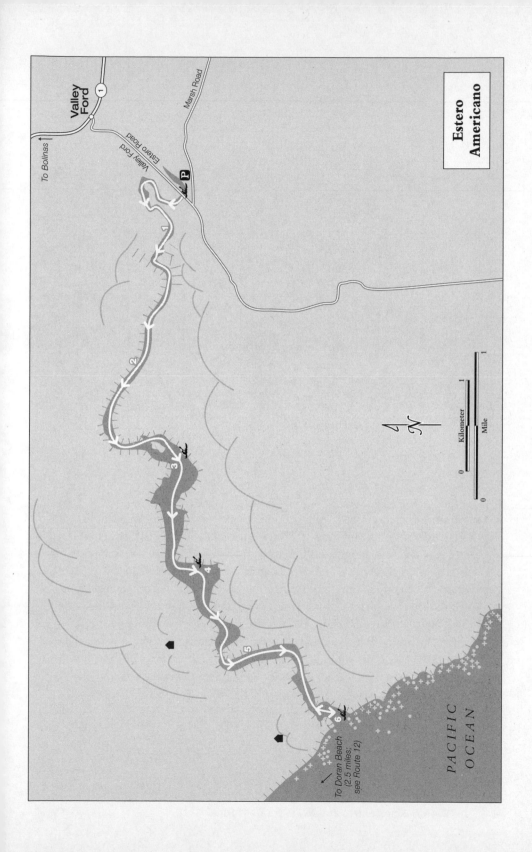

Estero Americano

Down the channel into Estero Americano R. SCHUMANN

Launch site: Off Marsh Road in Valley Ford (corner of Marsh and Valley Ford Estero Roads). From Highway 101 in Petaluma, take the East Washington Street exit and follow signs through town toward Bodega Bay; Washington turns into Bodega Avenue and then Highway 1. In Valley Ford, take a left at Dinucci's Italian Restaurant onto Valley Ford Estero Road. Cross the bridge over the estero at Marin County Line, take the next left onto Marsh Road, and an immediate left on the short, bumpy driveway to the launch beach near the base of the bridge. Boating etiquette dictates unloading gear at the beach then parking the car on the shoulder of the road. No facilities. Free, but limited parking (overnight okay). Aerial photo: Looking up the estuary from the mouth (californiacoastline.org; image 200504849).

Miles and Directions

0.0 Head west under the bridge (N38 18.57 W122 56.13), while bearing left along the bank. Not only will the route be obvious, but also why some refer to this stretch as the muddy ditch: The mud-bank channel is only as wide as your kayak is long. Have faith, the scenery soon improves. If the area at the put in is flooded (as it can be after heavy rains), the muddy ditch will be a broad pond, and the route will be ambiguous for the first 0.25 mile. Bear left and head for the dense copse of oaks 0.5 mile away on the left bank; the way will become clear as it narrows and winds between hills.

3.0 The channel widens and becomes shallower and often windier as it bends right back to the west, rounding a small islet (inundated at very high water). Look for landing spots along left bank (N38 18.58 W122 58.10). If you land, don't hike up from the water's edge: the banks of the estero are private property. This makes a good turnaround if it's too windy, you're tired, or the tide is too low. Caution: You'll need at least 2 feet of tide to make it past this broad, shallow area. When in doubt, stay left for the next mile or so to find deeper water.

3.5 During high water, you may angle left into a wide, shallow bay and find a landing site. There is an old fishing boat left high and dry on the left bank near here.

4.8 The channel bends sharply south and narrows into a steep valley, now covered in coastal scrub, the best scenery so far.

6.0 There are dunes and sandbar at the estero mouth (N38 17.73 W123 00.10). This beach is the only public access point beyond the launch. Caution: If the mouth is open, stay well left and land to avoid being swept out to sea.

Where to Eat and Where to Stay

Restaurants: Dinucci's Italian Restaurant (dinuccisrestaurant.com; 707-876-3260) in Valley Ford serves hearty, family-style meals. **Lodging:** The historic Valley Ford Hotel (vfordhotel .com; 707-876-3600). **Camping:** Doran County Park or Westside County Park (sonoma -county.org/parks/camping/camp_reservations.htm, 707-565-2267), Bodega Dunes State Park (parks.ca.gov/?page_id=451, reserveamerica.com; 800-444-7275). (See also Routes 12 and 14.)

Route 14

North Tomales Bay—Nicks Cove to Tomales Point and Beyond

With its proximity to Point Reyes National Seashore, Nicks Cove provides access to some of the finest paddling in the greater San Francisco Bay Area. A mile or so across the water from Nicks, Tomales Point jabs a rocky finger 14 miles up into the Pacific—a giant, natural breakwater 500 feet high, forming Tomales Bay, the longest, most uninhabited stretch of protected salt water on this coast. From behind its bluffs and beaches rise deserted windswept hills, quilted golden green with coastal scrub, and grassy meadows laced with wildflowers. In addition to numerous day-trip options—with access to a range of conditions from calm to coastal touring and surf beyond the mouth of the bay—this area is known for its excellent kayak camping opportunities. However, since it does require a potentially challenging bay crossing to access campsites, those looking to try overnight touring for the first time often prefer launching from more protected sites on the other side of the bay (see Route 15).

Trip highlights: Wildlife, scenery, and kayak camping.

Trip rating:

Beginner: 4-mile round-trip along shore to Toms Point or up Walker Creek. Basic tide and current knowledge is essential. Avoid afternoon winds and crossing the bay unless you are accompanied by an experienced trip leader and are comfortable paddling in 10- to 15-knot winds and 1- to 2-foot chop.

Intermediate: 9+ miles round-trip with bay crossing. Great place to get your feet wet kayak camping. Open-water rescue skills and tow rope highly recommended. Surf zone practice at mouth of bay not recommended during ebb tide or when waves are bigger than 3 feet and winds above 15 knots.

Advanced: 15+ miles with open-coast side trip. Surfing and tide rips play at mouth of the bay. Access to rock gardens. Combat roll recommended. Begins to get dicey in swells greater than 6 feet and winds above 20 knots.

Trip duration: Part day, full day, overnight, and multiday.

Kayak rentals: Blue Waters Kayaking (bwkayak.com; 415-669-2600) rents a variety of open-top and sit-inside kayaks from their locations in Inverness and Marshall.

Navigation aids: USGS: Tomales (7.5 minute), Point Reyes National Seashore map from Bear Valley Visitor Center, and NOAA chart 18643 (charts.noaa.gov/OnLineViewer/18643.shtml).

Weather information: Zone forecast: "Coastal waters from Point Arena to Point

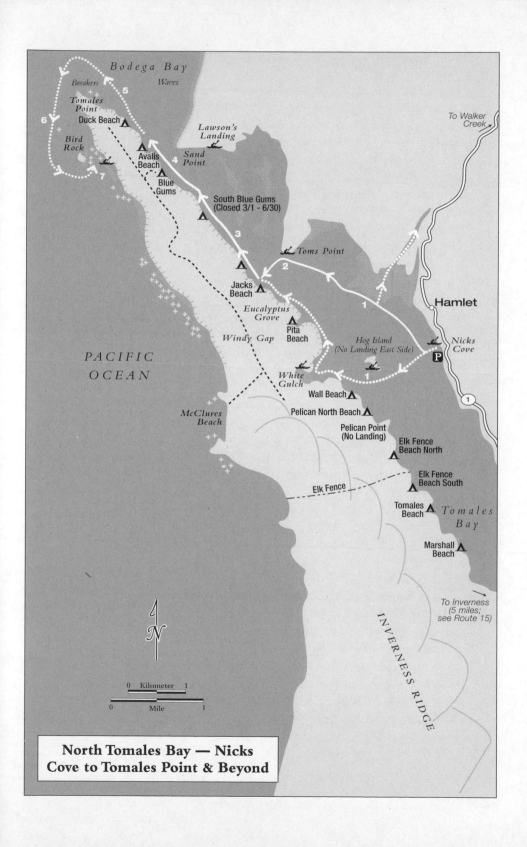

Bodega Bay

Breakers

Waves

5

Tomales Point

6

Duck Beach

Bird Rock

7

Avalis Beach

4

Blue Gums

Sand Point

Lawson's Landing

South Blue Gums (Closed 3/1 - 6/30)

3

Toms Point

2

Jacks Beach

Eucalyptus Grove

Pita Beach

Windy Gap

1

Hog Island (No Landing East Side)

Hamlet

Nicks Cove

P

PACIFIC OCEAN

White Gulch

1

McClures Beach

Wall Beach

Pelican North Beach

Pelican Point (No Landing)

Elk Fence Beach North

Elk Fence Beach South

Elk Fence

Tomales Beach

Tomales Bay

Marshall Beach

To Walker Creek

1

To Inverness (5 miles; see Route 15)

INVERNESS RIDGE

N

0   Kilometer   1

0   Mile   1

North Tomales Bay — Nicks Cove to Tomales Point & Beyond

Reyes" (forecast.weather.gov/MapClick.php?zoneid=PZZ540); buoys: Bodega Bay and Point Reyes.

Tidal information: Tides above 2 to 3 feet necessary to explore shallow areas over mudflats along the shallow eastern half of the bay. Currents of 3 knots or more are possible during tide changes of 4 feet or more.

Cautions: Dangerous waves and ocean-going currents around Sand Point at the mouth of the bay, especially during ebb tide; the bay's northwest orientation funnels afternoon winds, often 15 to 25 knots, which can quickly whip the bay into a froth of whitecaps and 1- to 2-foot chop in exposed areas, with waves becoming especially steep in shallow areas. Avoid disturbing seal haul outs and resting birds. The east side of Hog Island and all of its neighbor Duck Island are off limits for landing year-round, as is Pelican Point. South Blue Gums Beach is closed from March 1 to June 30.

Trip planning: To take advantage of tidal currents, choose a day with a morning ebb tide and afternoon flood, which should put both wind and currents at your back on the return trip. Less-experienced paddlers can paddle before the winds kick up, cross the bay only at narrow points, or avoid crossings entirely. Mild fall weather tends to provide the best paddling conditions, but calm or stormy weather is possible any time of year. To experience the solitude of Tomales Bay, midweek and off-season are best. On summer weekends, fishing skiffs ply the shore, zipping back and forth to check crab pots and occasionally stopping to picnic on the beaches; by sunset, however, the bay is generally quiet and deserted. As the popularity of kayak camping increases, so does competition for the bay's campsites; although permits are required (see "Camping"), sites are first-come, first-served. Consider setting up early and sharing popular beaches with other campers on busy summer weekends. Links: National Park Service information for kayaking around Point Reyes National Seashore (nps.gov/pore/planyourvisit/kayak.htm).

Launch site: To reach Nicks Cove/Miller Boat Launch (23240 Hwy. 1, Marshall) from Highway 101 near San Rafael, head west on Sir Francis Drake Boulevard to Highway 1 North. About 10 miles north of Point Reyes Station you'll hit Nicks Cove/Miller Landing County Park Boat Launch (marincountyparks .org/Depts/PK/Divisions/Parks/Miller-Boat-Launch). Turn left into Nicks and continue past the boat ramp on your left for an easier launch off the kayakers' beach at the far northern end of the parking lot. Park there for day trips, being careful not to block the boat-trailer turnaround at the end of the road; for overnights, use the upper lot. Parking fees are $5 per day, $10 per overnight. Nicks has outhouses but no drinking water. If traveling from north of Petaluma on Highway 101, take the East Washington Street exit and head west to Bodega Avenue, which becomes Tomales/Petaluma Road; head south on Highway 1 for 4 miles and look for Nicks on your right.

Ridgetop view of Tomales Bay, looking southeast from Tomales Point SUSAN DEQUATTRO

Alternate launch site: Lawson's Landing (lawsonslanding.com) in Dillon Beach: $5 per day, or $12 overnight. Aerial photo: Looking from the sea over Tomales Point and across the mouth of the bay in the background (californiacoastline .org, image 200905503).

Miles and Directions

0.0 From Nicks Cove (N38 12.07 W122 55.30) the most conservative route for beginners is to head northwest, hugging the shore toward Walker Creek. Side trip: On calm days, experienced paddlers may opt to make the more direct, albeit longer and more exposed, crossings (1.2 to 1.5 miles) past Hog Island to reach campsites at Pita, White Gulch, Wall, and Pelican North Beaches (see map). Caution: The east side of Hog Island and its tiny neighbor to the south, Duck Island, are closed to landing. Also, heading too far south from Nicks is asking for trouble on the return if the prevailing northwesterlies kick up, but you may want to run a shuttle down to Chicken Ranch Beach in Inverness (see Route 15) for a one-way ride.

0.7 Continuing north from Nicks, the mudflat at the mouth of Walker Creek is among the bay's prime birding spots, especially for shorebirds and white pelicans. Caution: At low tide (less than around 3 feet), stay 0.5 mile off shore to avoid running aground on this extensive mudflat, keeping to the west of the white stakes that mark the oyster beds. Head toward Toms Point (bearing 280° MN), which provides protection from both wind and incoming currents. Side trip: On blustery days, you can meander 2 to 3 miles up Walker Creek, with fair protection from the wind, but a high, incoming tide of at least 3 to 4 feet is recommended.

2.0 Toms Point (N38 12.88 W122 57.14) makes a good lunch stop at higher tides when the mudflats are covered, and is also the narrowest place to cross the bay (just under 0.5 mile), offering less-experienced paddlers a good spot to reassess sea conditions before committing to a crossing. To avoid traffic, cross the boat channel (bearing 225° MN) without delay and hug the far shoreline; because much of the bay is barely 6 feet deep, powerboats limit themselves to the narrow channel that skirts the bay's western shore.

2.5 Jacks Beach (aka Ropeswing), straight across from Toms, offers some good wind protection among the large eucalyptus and cypress by the rope swing, making it popular and typically among the first to fill on busy weekends. Several beach camps lie within 1 or 2 miles of Jacks. A mile to the south is Pita Beach at the head of a small marsh area, and White Gulch, another mile from there. Several small beaches at the base of the bluffs in this area, generally awash at high tide, make good rest stops. Side trips: Hog Island, a picturesque speck of land covered in cypress trees a few hundred yards across, is worth the visit. Overnight camping is not allowed on the island, and signs now limit landing to the western shore to protect wildlife. Mudflats in the shallow backwaters of White Gulch attract hundreds of shorebirds at low tide.

3.4 South Blue Gums, a small, sandy beach with little wind protection, is closed seasonally from March 1 to June 30 to protect harbor seals breeding there.

4.0 The small sand beach at Blue Gums (N38 13.60 W122 58.62) gives moderate protection for several tents and hiking access to the ridge trail running past stock ponds where elk sightings are common. Whether or not you see elk, the vistas of the Point Reyes Peninsula and the open sea from the ridge crest are outstanding, especially at sunset. Caution: When paddling near the mouth of Tomales Bay, be extremely wary of tide rips on outgoing tides and surf. In recent years, two fishing skiffs have been swept out the mouth and into heavy surf, resulting in several drownings—a fate that could easily befall an unprepared paddler, as it did in 1996 to a kayaker at the mouth of nearby Drakes Estero.

4.5 Avalis Beach has great views of Bodega Bay, the most room for camping, and good hiking access, but little wind protection.

NATIVE TULE ELK

In 1978, seventeen native tule elk were reintroduced on Tomales Point. The herd now numbers nearly five hundred, making it one of the largest of the twenty-two herds in the state. The herd is thriving so well that wildlife managers are currently experimenting with elk contraception and transplanting herd members to other areas of the park in order to maintain an ecological balance. July through September promises the most exciting time for elk watching, as males are actively bugling, locking horns, and rutting.

5.5 A side trip to Tomales Point offers excellent ocean views for intermediates with coastal touring experience in calm conditions. Caution: Ocean swells, breaking waves, winds, strong currents, and no landing options the last mile to the point make this area unsuitable for inexperienced paddlers.

7.0 Caution: The side trip around Tomales Point to Bird Rock is for advanced coastal kayakers only. Once around the point, prevailing winds can make return difficult. Boomers, cliffs, and large surf make landing difficult unless you have the skills to pick your way through the rock garden to the small beach in the lee of Bird Rock.

Where to Eat and Where to Stay

Restaurants: Nick's Cove (nickscove.com; 415-663-1033) next door to the launch site or the Station House Cafe (stationhousecafe.com; 415-663-1515) in Point Reyes Station both serve fresh seafood and local oysters. **Lodging:** Numerous options, from the Point Reyes Youth Hostel (norcalhostels.org/reyes; 415-663-8811) to the elegant Point Reyes Seashore Lodge (pointreyesseashore.com; 415-663-9000). **Camping:** Kayak camping on Tomales Point is primitive with no facilities. Backcountry permits are required from the National Seashore (nps.gov/pore/planyourvisit/camping.htm; 877-444-6777), as is packing out all human waste; you can purchase portable "wag bags" from Point Reyes Outdoors (pointreyesoutdoors.com; 415-663-8192) in Point Reyes Station. Campgrounds nearby include Samuel P. Taylor State Park (reserveamerica.com; 800-444-7275), Olema Ranch Campground (olemaranch.com; 415-663-8106) and Lawson's Landing (lawsonslanding .com; 707-878-2443).

Route 15
Central Tomales Bay—
Inverness to Hog Island

With its access to numerous flat-water day trips as well as overnight camping on the Point Reyes National Seashore, Central Tomales Bay is a favorite choice of local paddlers. For less experienced kayakers, this area is less exposed to wind and currents than the previous route from Nicks Cove, and it is possible to access camping beaches without having to make any open-water crossings. As you paddle from Inverness toward the more exposed northern part of the bay, conditions become gradually more challenging. The first 3 miles to Indian Beach are well protected and scenic, following high bluffs that are cloaked in a forest of Bishop pines and punctuated every half mile or so by a sandy beach. Around Marshall Beach, the pine forest gives way to the brushy grasslands and the steep, rolling hills of Tomales Point. From here on the bay begins to widen slightly and campsites become available.

Trip highlights: Excellent birding, protected water, scenery, and camping.

Trip rating:

Beginner: 1- to 15-mile round-trips. On calm days with winds to 10 knots, energetic beginners might make it all the way to Hog Island. On rougher days, the 6-mile round-trip to Indian Beach makes a good day trip. Bay crossings not recommended unless accompanied by intermediate paddlers in winds below 15 knots.

Intermediate: 6 to 15+ miles possible in winds 15 to 20 knots. Bay crossings not recommended unless experienced performing open-water rescues.

Trip duration: Part day, full day, overnight, or multiday.

Kayak rentals: Blue Waters Kayaking (bwkayak.com; 415-669-2600) rents a variety of open-top and sit-inside kayaks from their locations in Inverness and Marshall.

Navigation aids: USGS: Point Reyes National Seashore and Vicinity (15 minute) and Tomales Quadrangle (7.5 minute), Point Reyes National Seashore map from Bear Valley Visitor Center, and NOAA chart 18643 (charts.noaa.gov/OnLineViewer/18643.shtml).

Weather information: Zone forecast: "Coastal waters from Point Arena to Point Reyes" (forecast.weather.gov/MapClick.php?zoneid=PZZ540); buoys: Bodega Bay and Point Reyes.

Tidal information: More landing options if not high tide; currents become progressively stronger farther north, especially beyond Hog Island. If the tide

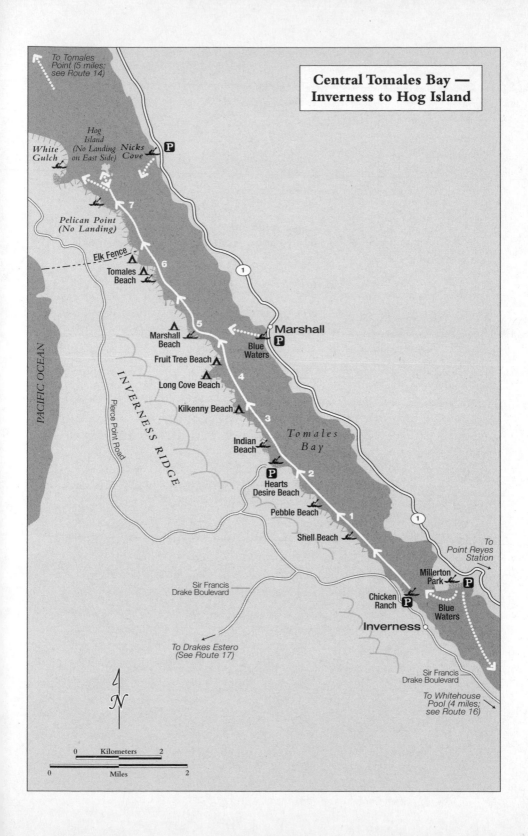

Central Tomales Bay —
Inverness to Hog Island

To Tomales Point (5 miles; see Route 14)

Hog Island (No Landing on East Side)

White Gulch

Nicks Cove

P

Pelican Point (No Landing)

7

Elk Fence

Tomales Beach

6

PACIFIC OCEAN

INVERNESS RIDGE

Pierce Point Road

1

Marshall

P

Blue Waters

5

Marshall Beach

Fruit Tree Beach

Long Cove Beach

4

Kilkenny Beach

3

Tomales Bay

Indian Beach

2

P

Hearts Desire Beach

Pebble Beach

1

Shell Beach

To Point Reyes Station

Millerton Park

P

P

Chicken Ranch

Blue Waters

Sir Francis Drake Boulevard

Inverness

1

To Drakes Estero (See Route 17)

Sir Francis Drake Boulevard

To Whitehouse Pool (4 miles; see Route 16)

N

0   Kilometers   2

0   Miles   2

drops below about 2 feet some beaches—particularly around Inverness and the launch at Chicken Ranch—can get pretty mucky. You'll still be able to launch and land at any tide height at Chicken Ranch, it just depends on how much mud you are willing to slog through.

Cautions: Mudflats, currents, afternoon wind, restricted swimming areas, and private beaches.

Trip planning: Paddle north with a morning outgoing tide and return with the incoming tide and the wind at your back. Stay close to shore for better wind protection, contouring your route behind points of land to take advantage of wind shadows. If planning to camp, see launch sites (following) for those that allow overnight parking. As the popularity of kayak camping increases, so does competition for the bay's campsites; although permits are required (see Camping), sites are first-come, first-served. Tomales Beach and Marshall beach are the only sites with pit toilets, so camp there if you don't want to deal with packing out your wastes (required at all other beaches). Consider setting up early and sharing popular beaches with other campers on busy summer weekends. Midweek and non-summer weekends are generally fairly quiet. Links: National Park Service information for kayaking around Point Reyes National Seashore (nps.gov/pore/planyourvisit/kayak.htm).

Launch site: To reach Chicken Ranch Beach (12944 Sir Francis Drake Blvd., Inverness) from Highway 101 in San Rafael, head west on Sir Francis Drake Boulevard (5 miles north of Golden Gate Bridge) and turn right where it joins Highway 1 North in Olema. Just south of Point Reyes Station, turn left off Highway 1 to stay on Sir Francis Drake where it heads west again at the sign for Tomales Bay State Park. In Inverness, just after Tomales Bay Resort (formerly Golden Hinde Inn and Marina) and Blue Waters Kayaking on the right, you will see a large pullout and an outhouse across from Pine Hill Drive. This is the Chicken Ranch launch site. No fee, outhouse, overnight parking okay. Aerial photo: Chicken Ranch beach on right and Golden Hinde Marina/Blue Waters beach on left (californiacoastline.org, image 200500787).

Alternate launch sites: Hearts Desire Beach in Tomales Bay State Park (no overnight parking, $8 day-use fee, fresh water); to reach it follow signs through Inverness to Tomales Bay State Park, turn right on Pierce Point Road, and right again into the state park at Hearts Desire Beach. Easier to get to is Tomales Bay Resort/Golden Hinde Inn and Marina, but they charge $10 for parking and $5 per boat to use their launch ramp. Across the bay on Highway 1, you can park overnight at Marshall (not Marshall Beach) or Nicks Cove (see Route 14).

Campers enjoy a calm morning on Tomales Beach. TIM ANDREWS

Miles and Directions

0.0   From Chicken Ranch Beach (N38 06.54 W122 51.88), head north along the bluffs. Caution: During summer stay outside of swimming areas marked by buoys, and don't land on private docks or beaches. Among the several small beaches for the next 3 miles, landings are permitted only on those with brown state park signs.

0.8   Shell Beach (N38 07.04 W122 52.40) is a small sand beach inside the state park with landings permitted outside the swim area.

1.8   Pebble Beach (N38 07.71 W122 53.19) is also part of the state park and allows landings.

2.5   Hearts Desire Beach (N38 07.96 W122 53.56) makes a good alternate launch site to access the beaches farther north, but no overnight parking is permitted; launching and landing allowed on south side of swimming beach.

2.7   When you spot the kotcas, the Miwok bark dwellings that look like wooden teepees, you'll know you've found Indian Beach. As the site of an original village, the beach makes an interesting rest stop. In addition to the recreated dwellings,

COASTAL MIWOK:
THE FIRST LOCAL PADDLERS

The name Tomales has nothing to do with Mexican food. In the tongue of the original Miwok inhabitants, *tamal* means *bays.* Early settlers added the word *bay* to Tomales. So essentially the name Tomales Bay translates to "bays bay." These bay people took full advantage of their fertile waterfront location, harvesting a bounty of waterfowl, fish, and shellfish. The Miwok were also the area's first paddlers, fishing and hunting from kayaklike boats called *saka,* made from bundles of reeds lashed together at the ends. When these disposable boats became waterlogged, the Miwok simply gathered up another bundle of reeds and whipped up a new one.

the beach has a self-guided natural history trail that winds through the forest to the south, and the lagoon behind the beach has good birding. This makes a good turn-around spot on windy days as exposure to wind and currents increases beyond. If you continue around the point, look for Pelican Point and Hog Island in the distance.

5.0 Marshall Beach (N38 09.76 W122 54.90) is popular with kayakers and other boaters because it is one of only two campsites on the bay with pit toilets and trash cans, so you won't have to pack out your waste. Just beyond Indian Beach, you cross from state park property to the national seashore. Shoreline camping is allowed on this stretch at Kilkenny, Long Cove, and Fruit Tree Beaches, and landings are permitted just about any place you can find a beach.

6.0 Tomales Beach (N38 10.42 W122 55.39) is the other campsite with pit toilets. A near continuous mile of sandy beach to the north allows good landing options except at high tide.

6.5 The fence coming down the hill at Elk Fence North Beach marks the boundary of the Tule Elk Preserve.

7.0 Pelican Point (N38 11.26 W122 55.89) makes a good landmark but landing is strictly prohibited to protect sensitive seabird habitat.

8.0 Hog Island (N38 11.81 W122 56.15) only permits landings on the west side, and tiny Duck Island just to the south is closed. Three camping beaches—Pelican North Beach, Wall, and White Gulch—are along the shore adjacent to Hog Island.

Side trip: Ambitious paddlers can continue another 5 miles to Tomales Point (see Route 14).

Where to Eat and Where to Stay

Restaurants: Station House Cafe (stationhousecafe.com; 415-663-1515) in Point Reyes Station serves fresh seafood and local oysters, and don't miss local favorite Bovine Bakery (thebovinebakery.wordpress.com). **Lodging:** Numerous options, from the Point Reyes Youth Hostel (norcalhostels.org/reyes; 415-663-8811) to the elegant Point Reyes Seashore Lodge (pointreyesseashore.com; 415-663-9000). **Camping:** Kayak camping on Tomales Point is primitive with no facilities (except at Tomales and Marshall Beaches). Backcountry permits are required from the National Seashore (nps.gov/pore/planyourvisit/camping.htm; 877-444-6777), as is packing out all human waste; you can purchase portable "wag bags" from Point Reyes Outdoors (pointreyesoutdoors.com; 415-663-8192) in Point Reyes Station. Campgrounds nearby include Samuel P. Taylor State Park (reserveamerica.com; 800-444-7275) and Olema Ranch Campground (olemaranch.com; 415-663-8106).

Catching some rays on a casual exploration around Duck Beach cove SUSAN DEQUATTRO

Route 16

South Tomales Bay—
Whitehouse Pool to Millerton Park

The well-protected first section of this trip winds along a creek at the northern edge of Olema Marsh, a dense alder-willow thicket providing one of the most diverse bird habitats in the area, where the range of migrant land birds overlaps that of waterfowl. Gradually the creek's tree-lined banks open up to reeds, then salt marsh, and finally into the broad expanse of south Tomales Bay, offering nice views of pine-forested Inverness Ridge along the left and rolling coastal hills on the right. Birding is good along the entire route. Ducks, geese, and shorebirds abound in the marsh, and Millerton Park harbors an osprey nesting site.

Trip highlights: Excellent birding and protected water.

Trip rating:

Beginner: 1- to 8-mile round-trip to Millerton Park on days with high tide (3 to 4 feet) and low wind (less than 10 knots); ability to read a tide book essential.

Intermediate: 8-mile round-trip to Millerton can get choppy in strong wind.

Trip duration: Part to full day.

Kayak rentals: Blue Waters Kayaking (bwkayak.com; 415-669-2600) rents a variety of open-top and sit-inside kayaks from locations in Inverness and Marshall.

Navigation aids: USGS: Point Reyes National Seashore and Vicinity (15 minute), Point Reyes National Seashore map from Bear Valley Visitor Center, and NOAA chart 18643 (charts.noaa.gov/OnLineViewer/18643.shtml).

Weather information: Zone forecast: "Coastal waters from Point Arena to Point Reyes" (forecast.weather.gov/MapClick.php?zoneid=PZZ540); buoys: Bodega Bay and Point Reyes.

Tidal information: When tides are below 3 to 4 feet, mud blocks access to Tomales Bay within 1 to 2 miles of the launch site, and the creek may be too shallow to paddle.

Cautions: Mud, wind, and confusing channels.

Trip planning: Pick a day with a high, rising tide, and paddle early before the wind picks up (or do a shuttle and one-way trip). Be sure to return before the tide drops. Links: National Park Service information for kayaking around Point Reyes National Seashore (nps.gov/pore/planyourvisit/kayak.htm). Marin County Parks (marincountyparks.org/Depts/PK/Divisions/Parks/Whitehouse-Pool).

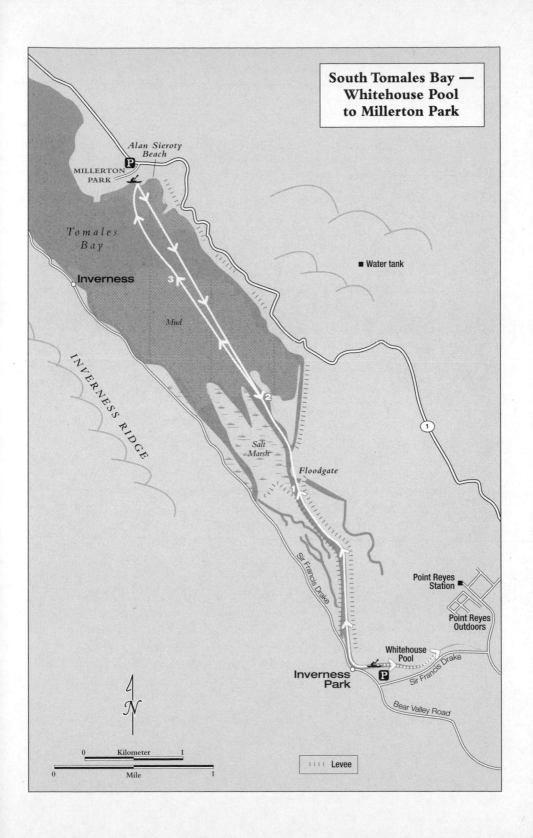

**South Tomales Bay —
Whitehouse Pool
to Millerton Park**

*Alan Sieroty
Beach*

**MILLERTON
PARK**

P

*Tomales
Bay*

Inverness

■ Water tank

Mud

3

INVERNESS RIDGE

2

*Salt
Marsh*

Floodgate

Sir Francis Drake

Point Reyes
Station ■

Point Reyes
Outdoors

**Whitehouse
Pool**

**Inverness
Park**

P

Sir Francis Drake

Bear Valley Road

N

0   Kilometer   1

0   Mile   1

│││ **Levee**

Single kayak on Marshal Beach, Tomales Bay TIM ANDREWS

Launch site: The parking for Whitehouse Pool (approximately 12349 Sir Francis Drake Blvd., Point Reyes Station) is 100 yards east of the junction of Bear Valley Road. From Highway 101 in San Rafael, head west on Sir Francis Drake (5 miles north of Golden Gate Bridge) and turn right where it joins Highway 1 North in Olema. Just south of Point Reyes Station, turn left off Highway 1 to stay on Sir Francis Drake for 0.7 mile, where it heads west again at the sign for Tomales Bay State Park. Take the first right into parking lot for Whitehouse Pool (unsigned until you turn into the lot). Facilities: Pit toilets; no fee.

Alternative launch sites: Alan Sieroty Beach on the south side of Millerton Park on Highway 1, 4 miles north of Point Reyes Station; free parking, outhouses. Aerial photo: Looking south across Olema Marsh toward Whitehouse Pool (californiacoastline.org, image 200505131).

Miles and Directions

0.0   The mud bank at the put in at Whitehouse Pool (N38 03.77 W122 49.02), which can be a little awkward, is one of the more challenging aspects of this easy first section. Head left along the narrow, tree-lined channel. Side trip: With a rising tide of 3 to 4 feet or more, you can paddle up Lagunitas Creek past Point Reyes Station for about 4 miles into the hills.

0.25   The channel bends right—north—soon leaving the trees.

0.9   A midstream islet allows a landing spot, as do several beaches along the left bank, if you're careful about the mud and trampling sensitive marsh plants. Caution: The channel begins to silt up from here on, so be sure you have enough tide left to continue.

2.0   The channel banks end and the bay opens up to nearly 1 mile wide, making it a good turn-around point for less-energetic paddlers. To continue look for the knoll of Millerton Point (compass bearing 310° MN) another 1.5 miles in the distance. Although you'll eventually angle right toward the base of the point, aim for the point for the next mile or so to stay in deeper water, following a line of wooden stakes. Caution: If you continue on, look back to memorize the correct channel so that you can find it on your return. If you have a GPS, mark a waypoint (N38 05.50 W122 50.00).

3.7   The first clump of trees to the right of Millerton Point is Alan Sieroty Beach (N38 06.44 W122 50.74), a good landing spot with an outhouse. The platform atop a pole supports an osprey nest.

Where to Eat and Where to Stay

Restaurants: Station House Cafe (stationhousecafe.com; 415-663-1515) in Point Reyes Station serves fresh seafood and local oysters, and don't miss local favorite Bovine Bakery (thebovinebakery.wordpress.com). **Lodging:** For countless options, from the Point Reyes Youth Hostel (norcalhostels.org/reyes; 415-663-8811) to the elegant Point Reyes Seashore Lodge (pointreyesseashore.com; 415-663-9000), contact the West Marin Chamber of Commerce (pointreyes.org; 415-663-9232). **Camping:** Samuel P. Taylor State Park (reserveamerica.com; 800-444-7275) and Olema Ranch Campground (olemaranch.com; 415-663-8106).

Route 17
Drakes and Limantour Esteros

The four fingers of Drakes Estero and the double thumb of Limantour Estero form a 20-mile network of narrow bays that presses into the marshy center of Point Reyes National Seashore like a giant, deformed handprint. The only road access is at Drakes Bay Oyster Farm at the tip of the middle finger, a 3.5-mile paddle across the palm to the sea. Beyond the put in, the estero feels quiet and remote. The only access to its shores is by boat or trail, and no motorized craft are allowed. Rolling grassy hills surround the waterways. Here curious harbor seals shadow your strokes, and the estuary's fertile mudflats attract a wide variety of birdlife. For advanced paddlers Drakes Estero provides access to miles of uninhabited ocean shoreline.

Trip highlights: Peaceful, remote, with good birding and harbor seal watching.

Trip rating:

Beginner: 1 to 14+ miles round-trip on shallow, protected water.

Intermediate–Advanced: 1 to 14+ miles round-trip with surfing and coastal touring possibilities for those with previous experience.

Trip duration: Part or full day.

Navigation aids: USGS: Point Reyes National Seashore and Vicinity (15 minute), Point Reyes National Seashore map from Bear Valley Visitor Center, and NOAA chart 18647 (charts.noaa.gov/OnLineViewer/18647.shtml).

Weather information: NWS zone forecast: "Coastal waters from Point Reyes to Pigeon Point" (forecast.weather.gov/MapClick.php?zoneid=PZZ545); buoys: Bodega Bay, Point Reyes, and San Francisco.

Tidal information: At least 3 feet recommended. Extensive mudflats begin to uncover below 2 feet, and the launch beach gets muddy below 3 feet. Strong currents at mouth.

Cautions: Drakes and Limantour Esteros closed to boating March 1 to June 30 during harbor seal pupping season. Mud, strong afternoon winds, and dangerous currents at the mouth during ebb tide.

Trip planning: Except at the mouth, tide height is more of a concern in this shallow estuary than tidal currents, and it is good to have at least 3 feet. Although it's possible to find channels around the mudflats during lower tides, a high, rising tide simplifies route finding and makes the launch beach less muddy. Strong afternoon winds tend to funnel down Schooner Bay toward the mouth so start your return trip early or save some energy and use the bluffs as wind breaks whenever possible. Some paddlers, unable to make progress against the wind, have had to abandon their boats and hike out via Drakes

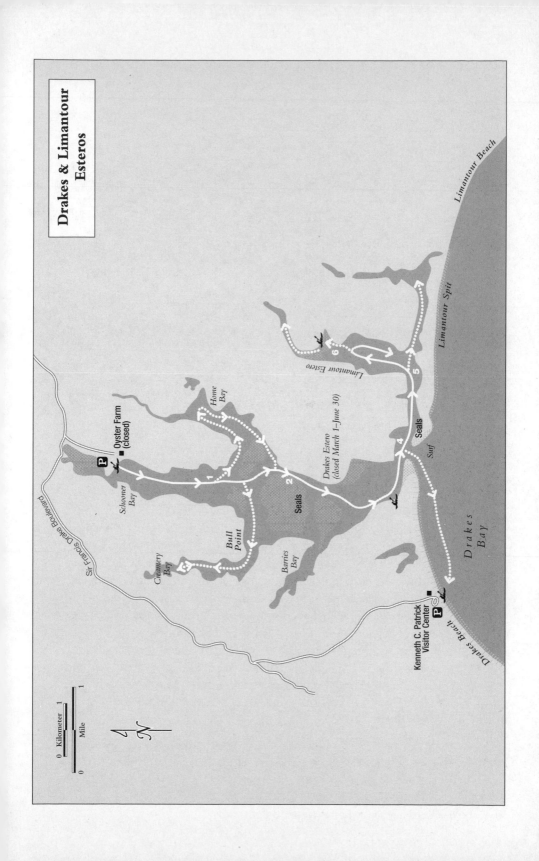

Drakes & Limantour Esteros

Drakes Estero
(closed March 1–June 30)

Limantour Estero
(closed March 1–June 30)

Sir Francis Drake Boulevard

Oyster Farm
(closed)

Schooner Bay

Home Bay

Creamery Bay

Bull Point

Barries Bay

Seals

Seals

Seals

Surf

Kenneth C. Patrick
Visitor Center

Drakes Beach

Drakes Bay

Limantour Spit

Limantour Beach

2
3
4
5
6

0   Kilometer   1
0   Mile   1

N

Going nowhere fast on Drakes Estero **SUSAN DEQUATTRO**

Beach, so check your weather radio for a day when wind is less than 15 knots. Links: National Park Service information for kayaking around Point Reyes National Seashore (nps.gov/pore/planyourvisit/kayak.htm).

Launch site: To reach the site of the now-closed oyster farm (formerly Johnson's Oyster Farm; 17171 Sir Francis Drake Blvd., Inverness) from Highway 101 in San Rafael, head west on Sir Francis Drake Boulevard and turn right where it joins Highway 1 North in Olema. Just south of Point Reyes Station, turn left off Highway 1 to stay on Sir Francis Drake where it heads west again at the sign for Tomales Bay State Park. Continue past Inverness 4 miles into the park, then turn left at the road to Drakes Estero. Just before you reach the buildings, park on the right near the water next to the outhouse. Facilities: Outhouse but no water; free parking. Aerial photo: Looking from the sea into the mouth of the estero (californiacoastline.org, image 200505408).

Miles and Directions

0.0   From the put-in by the old oyster farm (N38 04.95 W122 55.95), paddle along the steep left bank out of Schooner Bay, where you'll tend to find deeper water.

1.5 The estero widens at the mouth of Home Bay. Side trips: Explore the 1-mile length of Home Bay on your left or cross to the right shore and head 1.5 miles into narrow Creamery Bay. Caution: Be careful not to spook the harbor seals hauled out throughout the estero from this point on.

2.5 The estero narrows again, and the hillsides steepen around Barries Bay, the smallest "finger" off Drakes Estero. Side trip: Narrow Barries Bay extends 1 mile.

3.4 Land to the far right of the mouth of Drakes Estero (N38 02.12 W122 56.43) in a small cove at the end of the bluffs, avoiding the mouth. This makes a good lunch stop, with a picnic table and some wind protection; a short walk across the sandspit reveals good views of Drakes Bay and the Pacific. Caution: Be careful around the mouth for two reasons: to avoid disturbing the seals hauled out on the left at the end of Limantour Spit, and to avoid ebb currents, which can be dangerous—at least one inexperienced kayaker has been swept out into the surf and drowned here. Tide rips, rip currents, and heavy surf are not uncommon.

Side trip: The sandspit at the mouth of Drakes Estero is a good place to land and assess sea conditions. Experienced kayakers can paddle through the surf onto Drakes Bay and find good long-boat surfing breaks on the sand bars around the mouth, or continue to Drakes Beach (another 1.5 mile), or farther along the bluffs (see Route 18).

5.0 Continue toward Limantour Estero to the opening of its main bay where landings may be possible at higher tides on small beaches around the mouth or on the adjacent sandspit, but this area is shallow with extensive mudflats near shore. Side trip: Head straight along Limantour Spit another mile to the end.

6.0 Paddle to a small beach on the right (N38 02.90 W122 54.42) near the back of Limantour. Side trip: At high tide, continue another 0.2 mile to the very end of the bay, and follow the narrow tidal creek as it meanders another 0.5 mile into the pickleweed marsh. Caution: This channel dead-ends, so turn around before it gets too narrow to do so.

Where to Eat and Where to Stay

Restaurants: Drakes Beach Cafe (drakescafe.com; 415-669-1297) nearby (serving lunch, open seasonally) is the only restaurant for miles. **Lodging:** For countless options, from the Point Reyes Youth Hostel (norcalhostels.org/reyes; 415-663-8811) to the elegant Point Reyes Seashore Lodge (pointreyesseashore.com; 415-663-9000), contact the West Marin Chamber of Commerce (pointreyes.org, 415-663-9232). **Camping:** Samuel P. Taylor State Park (reserveamerica.com; 800-444-7275) and Olema Ranch Campground (olemaranch.com; 415-663-8106).

DRAKES CLOSED FOR SEAL-PUPPING SEASON

Drakes Estero (along with South Blue Gums Beach and the east side of Hog Island) is closed to boating from March 1 through June 30 to allow the area's harbor seals *(Phoca vitulina)* to bear their young free of human disturbance. Each spring some 7,000 seals—20 percent of the state's mainland breeding population—haul out along the seashore's beaches. Able to swim at birth, pups are just 2 feet long and weigh about 20 pounds. But their size doubles within a month on a diet of seal milk that is nearly 50 percent fat. When Drakes reopens, it's important to stay 100 yards or more from seal haul outs to avoid spooking the colony. Seals haul out on land to warm up because they are unable to maintain their body temperature if they remain in the water all the time. Not only will the animals get cold if frightened into the water, but also pups sometimes become separated from their mothers or even crushed by stampeding adults. Watch for movement among the resting animals, when you see their heads rise, you are too close—time to back paddle or move off to the side. Volunteers routinely monitor seals with telescopes, and kayakers can be cited for flushing seals off their resting beaches. If you find a pup on the beach, leave it alone; chances are it is not abandoned. Mothers often leave pups ashore while hunting, but they won't return if humans are around. The best thing to do is leave the area and report the location to park rangers, or call marine mammal rescue personnel (415-289-SEAL; marinemammalcenter.org) who can handle any truly deserted pups.

Route 18
Drakes Beach to Chimney Rock and the Point Reyes Headlands

Although Spanish explorer Don Sebastian Vizcaino named the massive headland here "Kings Point" because the day in 1603 that he first laid eyes on it was the Feast of the Three Kings, Point Reyes lives up to its regal title any day of the year. Literally one of the more outstanding points on the California coast, Point Reyes punches a rocky right fist into the Pacific—with its thumb sticking out and down. Below the point, the semisheltered crescent of Drakes Beach, which in this fist analogy stretches down the lower wrist to the thumb tip, is the most-protected oceanfront beach on the entire Point Reyes National Seashore, making it the best place in the park to gain coastal touring experience. Several miles of flat sandy beach fringes the base of the bluffs at low tide, providing both good landing access through (generally) small surf and fine scenery. At the far end of the beach, the chalky sandstone cliffs of Drakes Bay give way to the craggy granite knuckles of the Point Reyes Headlands, a 3-mile seawall of 400-foot cliffs that, for experienced paddlers, provides one of the most dynamic and dramatic roundings on the West Coast.

Trip highlights: Solitude, excellent scenery, and surfing.
Trip rating:
Beginner: 1- to 7-mile round-trip as far as Chimney Rock for advanced beginners accompanied by an experienced coastal paddler on a day with surf less than 1 foot at Drakes Beach and winds to 10 knots.
Intermediate: 1 to 7+ miles with good surf zone practice for those with previous coastal touring experience on days with surf to 3 feet and winds below 15 knots. It's not recommended that you go beyond Chimney Rock without advanced leadership.
Advanced: 7 to 17+ miles round-trip along Point Reyes Headlands with landing possible beyond the lighthouse if surf on exposed South Beach is below 4 to 6 feet. (Although it's possible to paddle the headlands in swells in excess of 10 feet, it's difficult to appreciate the scenery in seas above 6 feet.)
Trip duration: Part to full day.
Navigation aids: USGS: Point Reyes National Seashore and Vicinity (15 minute), Point Reyes National Seashore map from Bear Valley Visitor Center, and NOAA chart 18647 (charts.noaa.gov/OnLineViewer/18647.shtml).
Weather information: Zone forecast: "Coastal waters from Point Reyes to Pigeon Point" (forecast.weather.gov/MapClick.php?zoneid=PZZ545); buoys: Bodega Bay, Point Reyes, and San Francisco.

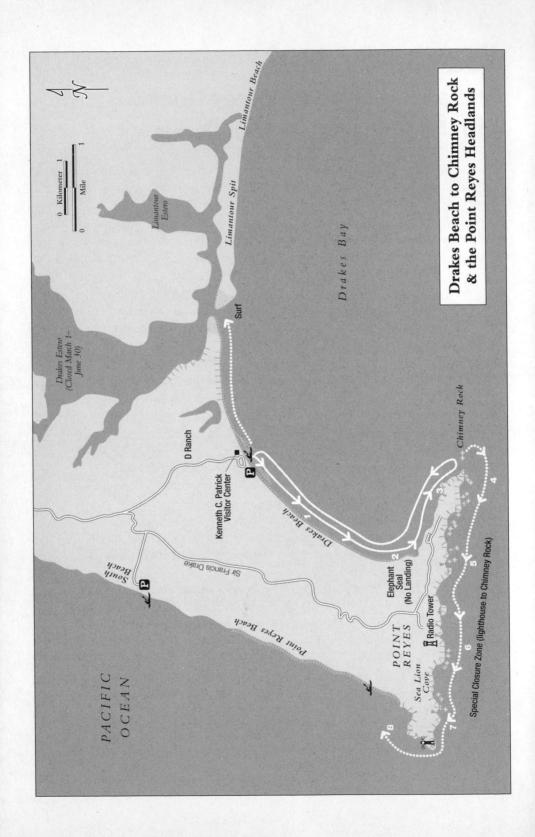

Drakes Beach to Chimney Rock & the Point Reyes Headlands

Tidal information: Lower tides leave better beach access along cliffs.

Cautions: Afternoon, offshore wind; surf; submerged rocks; and fog. Although the beach's southerly exposure gives it good protection from prevailing seas, wind whipping over the peninsula can create dangerous offshore conditions if you stray too far from shore. Several areas closed to kayaking: Drakes Estero from March 1 to June 30; year-round at Chimney Rock Boat Launch and the Elephant Seal Beach at the south end of Drakes Beach (maintain 100 yard distance from marine mammals or any beaches with seals on them). Note: All boaters are now required to stay at least 1,000 feet from shore along the seaward side of Point Reyes Headlands Special Closure zone between Chimney Rock and the Lighthouse, and 100 yards from the point around the lighthouse, to avoid disturbing elephant seals and other wildlife in the area.

Trip planning: Although you can usually land along the bluffs between Drakes Beach and Elephant Seal Beach except at high tide, more beach will be exposed along cliffs on days when tides are lower. These cliffs provide some protection, so stay close to shore to minimize the effects of offshore winds; this will be easier to do on a day with smaller surf. Links: National Park Service information for kayaking around Point Reyes National Seashore (nps.gov/pore/planyourvisit/kayak.htm).

Launch site: To reach Drakes Beach (1 Drakes Beach Rd., Inverness) from Highway 101 in San Rafael, head west on Sir Francis Drake and turn right where it joins Highway 1 North in Olema. Just south of Point Reyes Station, turn left off Highway 1 to stay on Sir Francis Drake where it heads west again at the sign for Tomales Bay State Park. Continue through Inverness and past Drakes Estero toward Point Reyes Lighthouse, turning left at the sign for Drakes Beach and the Kenneth C. Patrick Visitor Center. Facilities: Restaurant, restrooms, cold showers, and water available; no fee. Aerial photo: Drakes Beach (californiacoastline.org, image 200505397).

Miles and Directions

0.0 From Drakes Beach (N38 01.63 W122 57.68) paddle southwest along the cliffs and the long sandy beach. Caution: Stay close to shore to reduce your exposure to offshore winds. Side trips: Head east toward the mouth of Drakes Estero (with good kayak surfing over the sand bar at the mouth) and beyond. Caution: Exposure to wind and surf increases as you continue toward the estero (see Routes 17 and 19). Drakes and Limantour Esteros closed March 1 through June 30.

2.5 The gentle curve of beach angles hard left just after a beach often used by elephant seals. Caution: According to the Marine Mammal Protection Act, it is a federal offense to approach within 100 yards of any seals or other marine mammals.

Point Reyes Headlands CASS KALINSKI

3.5   Chimney Rock, at the southeast tip of Point Reyes, makes a good turn-around point. On calm days you may be able to round the point for a peek at the wave-pounded headlands. Caution: Extreme exposure beyond Chimney Rock. For experienced coastal paddlers, the next 3.5 miles of cliffs to the lighthouse is spectacular; however, it is now prohibited to paddle within 1,000 feet of shore along the headlands (see "Cautions" above).

7.5   Point Reyes Lighthouse; stay 100 yards offshore.

8.5+   South Beach, possible landing site. Caution: Landing on the northwest-facing beach beyond Point Reyes Lighthouse is not recommended unless scouted first from the South Beach parking lot and it's a very calm day: Point Reyes Beach is among the roughest, most-exposed beaches in the state.

Where to Eat and Where to Stay

Restaurants: Drakes Beach Cafe (drakescafe.com; 415-669-1297) at the put in (serving lunch, open seasonally) is the only restaurant for miles. **Lodging:** For countless options, from the Point Reyes Youth Hostel (norcalhostels.org/reyes; 415-663-8811) to the elegant Point Reyes Seashore Lodge (pointreyesseashore.com; 415-663-9000), contact the West Marin Chamber of Commerce (pointreyes.org; 415-663-9232). **Camping:** Samuel P. Taylor State Park (reserveamerica.com; 800-444-7275) and Olema Ranch Campground (olemaranch.com; 415-663-8106).

Punching out through the surf, the author takes one on the head. SANDY RINTOUL-SCHUMANN

Route 19

Point Reyes National Seashore Outer Coast Camping Tour—Drakes Beach to Coast Camp and Stinson Beach

One of the premier open-coast camping trips in the state, the lower half of the Point Reyes National Seashore is a southerly version of Mendocino's Lost Coast: a 20-mile stretch of roadless, uninhabited coastal wilderness, with rugged cliffs and remote beaches, providing ample challenge for experienced paddlers. It is possible to do just the upper section as an overnighter, 6 miles each way to Coast Camp and back. Or go for the full effect and paddle the entire 23 miles down to Stinson Beach in one to three days, camping along the way. Either way you'll pass some of the wildest coastal real estate in the country, as its "National Seashore" designation would suggest.

Trip highlights: Open-coast camping, rock gardens, solitude, and scenery.
Trip rating:
  Intermediate: 12-mile round-trip to Coast Camp and back for those with previous coastal touring experience in waves below 4 feet and winds to 15 knots. Because of the exposure, advanced trip leader is recommended.
  Advanced: 16-mile round-trip or 23 miles one-way to Stinson Beach; surf landings difficult in waves greater than 6 feet; rough seas in winds above 20 knots.
Trip duration: Full day or overnight(s).
Navigation aids: USGS: Point Reyes National Seashore and Vicinity (15 minute), Point Reyes National Seashore map from Bear Valley Visitor Center, and NOAA chart 18647 (charts.noaa.gov/OnLineViewer/18647.shtml).
Weather information: Zone forecast: "Coastal waters from Point Reyes to Pigeon Point" (forecast.weather.gov/MapClick.php?zoneid=PZZ545); buoys: Bodega Bay, Point Reyes, and San Francisco.
Tidal information: Lower tides on open coast leave more beaches exposed for landing.
Cautions: Standard open-coast hazards: fog, strong afternoon winds, boomers, rough seas, and surf landings on steep beaches. Extreme exposure: If camping overnight en route, worsening conditions could leave you stranded, forcing a long hike out without your boat. Avoid the Special Closure zones at Point Resistance and Double Point (see below). Drakes Estero closed to kayaking March 1 through June 30.

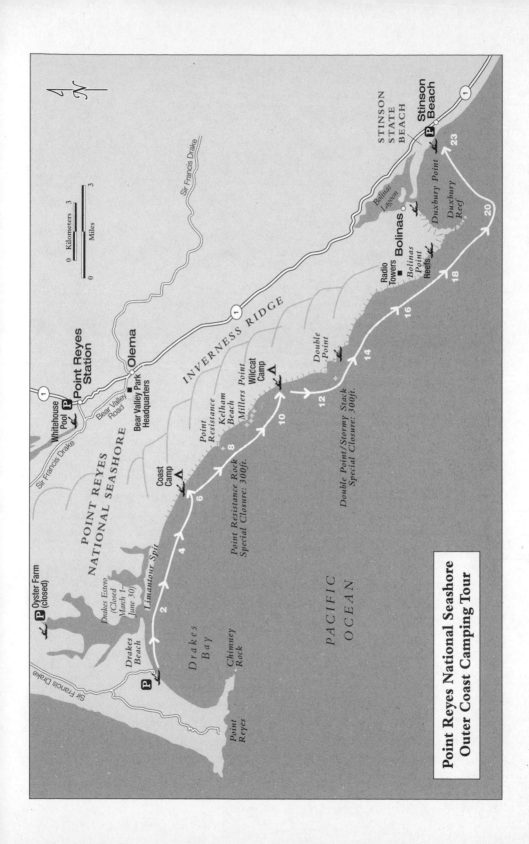

**Point Reyes National Seashore
Outer Coast Camping Tour**

Surf zone launch on the Point Reyes National Seashore SANDY RINTOUL-SCHUMANN

Trip planning: Paddle early; wind and seas tend to get worse in afternoon. Bring extra food and be prepared for weather layovers. Camping within the seashore, permitted only in established sites at Coast and Wildcat Camps, requires backcountry permit from park service (see "Camping"). You'll also need someone to drop you off, as overnight parking is not allowed at the put in. If going all the way to Stinson, you could park your shuttle vehicle on a side street near the public beach, then walk out onto the beach and identify some landmarks, so you'll be able to find the closest place to land at journey's end. Or convince whoever dropped you off in the beginning to pick you up afterwards. Links: National Park Service information for kayaking around Point Reyes National Seashore (nps.gov/pore/planyourvisit/kayak.htm).

Launch site: To reach Drakes Beach (1 Drakes Beach Rd., Inverness) from Highway 101 in San Rafael, head west on Sir Francis Drake and turn right where it joins Highway 1 North in Olema. Just south of Point Reyes Station, turn left off Highway 1 to stay on Sir Francis Drake where it heads west again at the sign for Tomales Bay State Park. Continue through Inverness and past Drakes Estero toward Point Reyes Lighthouse, turning left at the sign for Drakes Beach and the Kenneth C. Patrick Visitor Center. Facilities: Restaurant, restrooms, and water available; no fee. Aerial photo: Drakes Beach (californiacoastline.org, image 200505397).

Landing site: Stinson Beach Park (3514 Hwy. 1, Stinson Beach), part of Golden Gate National Recreation Area.

Miles and Directions

0.0   From Drakes Beach (N38 01.63 W122 57.68) head east along the cliffs.

1.4   The beach at the end of the bluffs (N38 01.89 W122 56.42) just before the mouth of Drakes Estero is a good place to reassess sea conditions before committing yourself to the much more exposed shorelines beyond. Caution: Tide rips, rip currents, and heavy surf are common off the mouth of Drakes.

6.0   Continue east to the beach below Coast Camp (N38 01.00 W122 51.39), a mile or so past where the bluffs begin again at the end of Limantour Spit. It's a long carry uphill to the campground. If you leave your boat down on the beach, be sure it's secure from marauding raccoons, which can be extremely pesky here, and well

The author surfing an unnamed break on a remote stretch of the Pt. Reyes National Seashore
SANDY RINTOUL-SCHUMANN

above the tide line. Caution: Carefully reassess sea conditions before continuing down the coast. It's only 5 miles of open water back to the mouth of Drakes Estero but an increasingly exposed, 16-mile commitment to Stinson Beach, and landing beaches on this stretch are all steep and dumpy.

8.0 Point Resistance Rock (N37 59.92 W122 49.75) is a Special Closure zone: no one is permitted within 300 feet to protect nesting seabirds.

11.0 Look for Wildcat Camp (N37 58.16 W122 47.48), your next campsite option, atop a flat bluff just past the steepest section of cliffs so far. Caution: The beach here is steep and exposed.

12.5 Double Point/Stormy Stack Special Closure zone (N37 56.82 W122 47.17) restricts entry within 300 feet of Stormy Stack to protect nesting seabirds, so you'll want to swing 100 yards out to seaward until you round the second point. Several small beaches in the lee of the southern point provide possible landing options.

18.0 Caution: The gently sloping sand beaches in the lee of Bolinas Point are less exposed than those to the north, but reefs can make for interesting landings, creating both protection and rocky hazards, depending on swell and tide height.

19.0 Beyond Duxbury Point, conditions should get calmer. Caution: Duxbury Reef, an amazing and potentially hazardous land form, stretches its rocky grasp nearly 1 mile out to sea. If the tide is high and the swell is low, you might paddle right over the reef next to shore without noticing it. But if the tide is down and the swell high, you'll need to detour well out to sea beyond the wave-pounded rocks early, before the prevailing winds blow you into danger.

23.0 Look for lifeguard towers and restrooms to find your landing spot on Stinson Beach.

Where to Eat and Where to Stay

Restaurants: Drakes Beach Cafe (drakescafe.com; 415-669-1297) at the put in (serving lunch, open seasonally) is the only restaurant for miles. **Lodging:** For countless options, from the Point Reyes Youth Hostel (norcalhostels.org/reyes; 415-663-8811) to the elegant Point Reyes Seashore Lodge (pointreyesseashore.com; 415-663-9000), contact the West Marin Chamber of Commerce (pointreyes.org; 415-663-9232). **Camping:** Samuel P. Taylor State Park (reserveamerica.com; 800-444-7275) and Olema Ranch Campground (olemaranch.com; 415-663-8106).

Route 20

Bolinas Lagoon and Duxbury Reef

A birder's dream, this shallow, salt marsh lagoon at the wild southern edge of Point Reyes National Seashore is simple to paddle at high tide, when much of its 2-mile length is accessible. At low tide, however, the extensive mudflats that hungry migratory birds find so enticing limit boating to narrow channels. There are rumblings afoot to ban paddling in the lagoon because in the past some unwitting boaters have scared seals off haul outs and frightened migratory waterfowl off the water (see below). Therefore maintaining a low profile (i.e., launching along Highway 1 to ease parking pressures in town) and a respectful attitude toward wildlife may be essential to continued access for kayakers. Beyond the lagoon the sandbar off its mouth is a popular place to practice kayak surfing in the often gentle waves, and the protection of Duxbury Reef, the largest shale reef in North America, makes it a good spot for introductory coastal touring on calm days.

Trip highlights: Excellent bird watching, seals, protection, access to surfing, and semiprotected coastal touring.

Trip rating:

Beginner: 1 to 4 miles of protected water at high tide.

Intermediate: 1 to 4 miles with surf practice at the mouth during a rising tide, and a 2-mile introductory coastal tour to Duxbury Reef in waves to 3 feet and wind to 15 knots.

Advanced: 4+ miles with good kayak surfing at the mouth in waves to 6 feet or more and access to coastal touring (see Route 19).

Trip duration: Part to full day.

Kayak rental: Stinson Beach Surf and Kayak (stinsonbeachsurfandkayak.com; 415-868-2739) rents sit-on-tops in Stinson Beach.

Navigation aids: USGS: Bolinas (7.5 minute) and NOAA chart 18647 (charts.noaa .gov/OnLineViewer/18647.shtml).

Weather information: Zone forecast: "Coastal waters from Point Reyes to Pigeon Point" (forecast.weather.gov/MapClick.php?zoneid=PZZ545); buoys: Bodega Bay, Point Reyes, and San Francisco.

Tidal information: Extensive mudflats exposed at tide heights below 3 feet; strong currents at mouth during ebb.

Cautions: Mud, wind, tidal currents, and surf at mouth; avoid disturbing sensitive seal haul outs and birding areas.

Trip planning: Paddle early to avoid wind and during rising tide to avoid getting stuck in the mud. The higher the tide, the more places you can paddle; launching from Highway 1 sites requires 3 to 4 feet of tide minimum. At lower

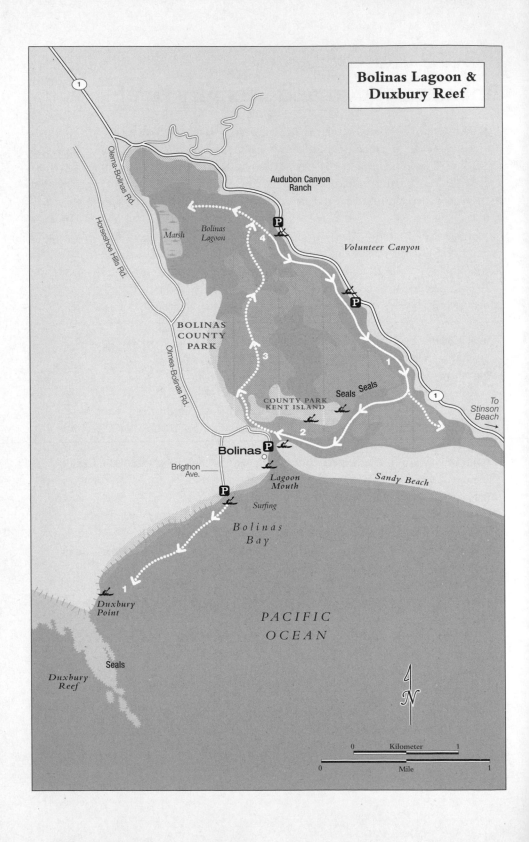

**Bolinas Lagoon &
Duxbury Reef**

1

Audubon Canyon
Ranch

P

Marsh

*Bolinas
Lagoon*

Volunteer Canyon

4

P

Olema-Bolinas Rd.

Horseshoe Hills Rd.

**BOLINAS
COUNTY
PARK**

3

1

Olema-Bolinas Rd.

COUNTY PARK
KENT ISLAND

Seals Seals

2

1

*To
Stinson
Beach*

Bolinas

P

Brigthon
Ave.

P

*Lagoon
Mouth*

Sandy Beach

Surfing

*Bolinas
Bay*

1

*Duxbury
Point*

*PACIFIC
OCEAN*

Seals

*Duxbury
Reef*

N

0   Kilometer   1

0   Mile   1

tides, use the alternate launch site at the mouth of the lagoon and follow the boat channel, which is navigable for a mile or more except during extreme low tides. Links: Marin County Parks (marincountyparks.org/Depts/PK/Divisions/ Open-Space/Bolinas).

Launch sites: There are several roadside launch sites off Highway 1 where it borders Bolinas Lagoon between the Bolinas turnoff and Stinson Beach. The best pullouts are at highway marker 15.67 (0.3 mile south of the entrance to Audubon Canyon Ranch) and 15.32 (0.1 mile south of Volunteer Canyon). Look for the small, green signs warning not to disturb the harbor seals.

Alternate launch sites: To reach the mouth of the lagoon, turn west off Highway 1 to the unsigned Olema-Bolinas Road (xenophobic locals tear down the signs), which follows the lagoon's north shore. Turn left at the T intersection to stay on Olema-Bolinas Road where Horseshoe Hills Road joins it from the north. Follow it through "downtown" Bolinas to a dead end at the lagoon mouth, or turn right onto Brighton Avenue for a surf launch with better parking. Aerial photo: Looking from the sea into the mouth of the lagoon (californiacoastline .org, image 200400139).

Miles and Directions

0.0 Head southwest from highway marker 15.67 (N37 55.55 W122 40.84), following the channel that parallels the road. Caution: Watch out for mud and don't disturb the seals hauled out on the mudflats. Side trip: At high tide you can wander north across the mudflats and marshes at the north end of the lagoon.

0.5 Alternate launch site at highway marker 15.32 (N37 55.43 W122 40.50).

1.25 Channel bends west away from highway and toward the lagoon mouth. Caution: There are many seals in this area. Side trip: At high tide you can continue along the highway and explore the mudflats in the lagoon's southeastern arm.

2.25 Landing options at either side of lagoon mouth or on Kent Island at high tide. Caution: Ocean-going currents in mouth during ebb tide; waves and surf. Helmets and surf zone experience required beyond the mouth. Side trip: At high tide you can explore the narrow boat channel that winds around Kent Island and into the salt marsh, retracing your route before the tide turns or completing the clockwise loop back to the launch site at extreme high tide. Caution: Don't get caught in the mud by a falling tide.

4.0 Return to launch site.

Other options: Ocean paddlers can shred the classic kayak surfing break at the mouth or explore another 1.5 mile to Duxbury Reef or round the reef and continue north up the much more exposed and rugged coastline beyond. Caution: Continuing up the coastline north of the reef recommended for experienced coastal paddlers only.

Taking advantage of a rising tide to explore a tidal channel in Bolinas Lagoon R. SCHUMANN

Where to Eat and Where to Stay

Restaurants: Few choices, but try Coast Cafe (bolinascafe.com; 415-868-2298) in Bolinas. There are a few more options in Stinson Beach: Parkside Snack Bar (415-868-1272) and Surfer's Grill (surfersgrill.com; 415-868-1777) for quick and casual, or Sand Dollar Restaurant (stinsonbeachrestaurant.com; 415-868-0434) for mid-priced seafood. **Lodging:** The Sandpiper (sandpiperstinsonbeach.com; 415-868-1632) has cabins with fireplaces within a short walk to the beach. (See Route 11 for other options.) **Camping:** There is camping and cabins at nearby Steep Ravine Environmental Camp, part of the Golden Gate National Recreation Area (415-331-1540; reservations: reserveamerica .com; 800-444-7275).

PADDLING RESPONSIBLY AROUND WILDLIFE

Launch sites along Highway 1 display signs reminding paddlers that Bolinas Lagoon is a sensitive resting and pupping habitat for harbor seals. When resting seals raise their heads to look at you, one sign explains, you are too close and should back off. Frightening seals off their haul outs not only reduces breeding success and increases the likelihood they will abandon the site, it is a federal offense carrying fines up to $10,000. Lagoon birdlife, too, is sensitive. Although shorebirds are fairly tolerant of kayakers, waterfowl are not. Over a dozen species of ducks frequent the lagoon between November and February. Used to being hunted, these skittish ducks are easily spooked by boats and flailing paddles. Not realizing Bolinas is a rare "safe harbor," they may fly off to other areas where hunting is permitted. The locals like their wildlife, so it's important for kayakers not to drive it away if we want to continue paddling this fine lagoon.

Quick Trip Tips: Other Launch Sites in Point Reyes Area

Stillwater Cove Regional Park (Intermediate to Advanced)

This aptly named Sonoma County Park is a popular launch site for abalone divers, with a campground and protected launch beach. The cove is very small, however, and quickly opens up to an exposed, rocky shoreline.

Fort Ross (Beginner–Intermediate to Advanced)

Fair protection in Fort Ross Cove on calm days to poke around among the rocks for a mile or so, with miles of rugged, rocky shoreline beyond.

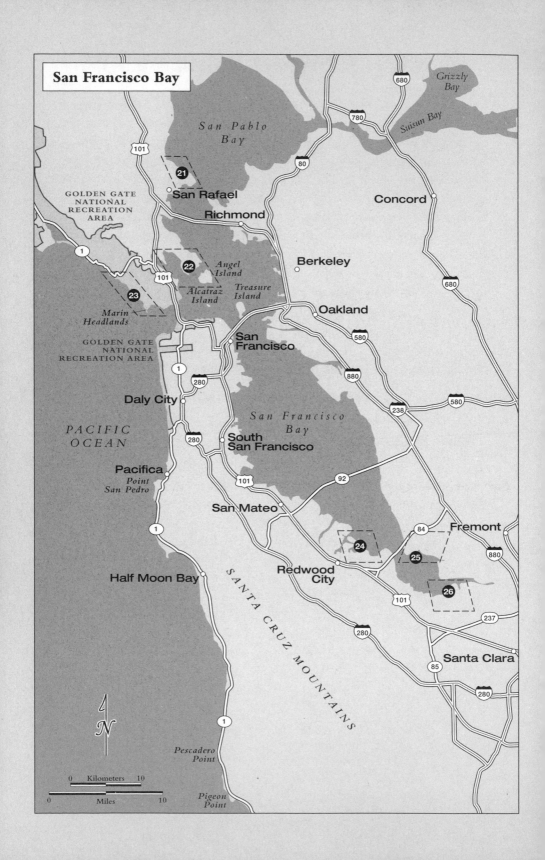

San Francisco Bay

Route 21
China Camp and Marin Islands Reserve

The convoluted shoreline of this 1,500-acre park stretches 3 miles along rocky bluffs backed by rolling hills of thickly forested oak woodland, offering panoramic views of San Pablo Bay and the East Bay hills. This series of points and small coves fringed with salt marsh creates great feeding grounds for the nearby heron and egret rookeries on Marin Islands Reserve, and narrow, winding channels give kayakers access to the marsh at high tide. Essentially undeveloped, the area retains much of the character (as well as several original structures) from the days when it was a Chinese fishing village. For a historical perspective, stop by the small museum near the launch beach.

Trip highlights: Flat-water paddling, bird watching, and scenery.

Trip rating:

Beginner: 1 to 5+ miles round-trip of calm water in winds to 10 knots.

Intermediate: 1 to 10 miles; those with open-water skills can paddle out to Marin Islands to explore the egret rookery in winds below 15 knots.

Trip duration: Part to full day.

Navigation aids: China Camp State Park map, available at visitor center, also describes the area's rich cultural and natural history; NOAA chart 18653 (charts.noaa.gov/OnLineViewer/18653.shtml).

Weather information: Zone forecast: "San Francisco, San Pablo, Suisun Bays and the West Delta" (forecast.weather.gov/MapClick.php?zoneid=PZZ530); buoys: Golden Gate.

Tidal information: Tides below 2 feet expose broad mudflats near shore.

Cautions: Mud, offshore winds, closed areas, fishing lines, and light boat traffic.

Trip planning: Paddle early before wind with at least 2 to 3 feet of tide; a rising tide is best.

Launch site: China Camp Historic Area (on North San Pedro Point Road). From points south: Heading north on Highway 101 take Central San Rafael exit and turn right onto 2nd Street (which merges into third, becomes Point San Pedro Road, and then becomes North San Pedro Point Road). Follow signs to China Camp State Park. From points north: Heading south on Highway 101, take North San Pedro Road exit and follow signs to China Camp State Park: head east on North San Pedro Point Road through the park to the beach at China Camp Historic Area. There is an $8 day-use fee with snack concession, museum, restrooms, and picnic area.

Alternate launch sites: Bullhead Flat, 0.5 mile north of the historic area, has restrooms and fee as well as an outdoor shower but fewer parking sites and

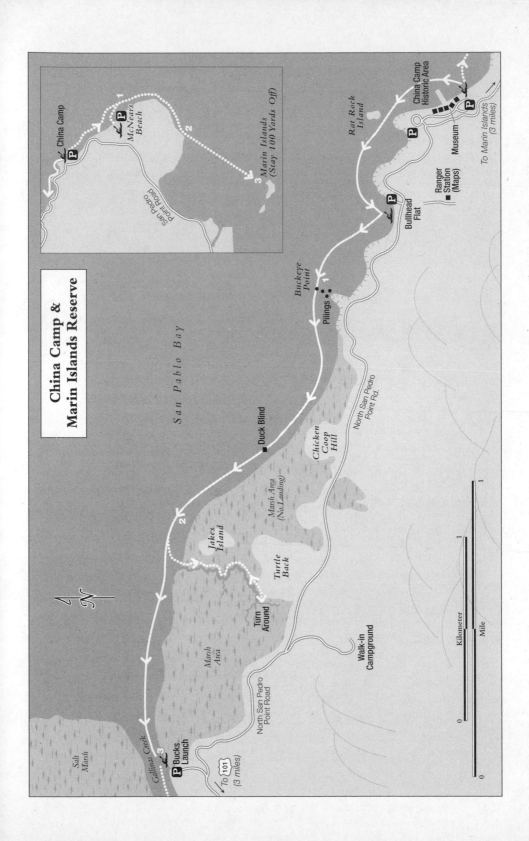

Looking for a route into the pickleweed marsh at China Camp R. SCHUMANN

less wind protection; or try McNears Beach County Park, a mile south, $8 parking fee, or Bucks Launch ($5).

Miles and Directions

0.0 From the beach at China Camp Historic Area (N38 00.00 W122 27.65), head northwest along the shore. Side trips: Experienced open-bay paddlers may paddle south around Point San Pedro to explore the egret rookery at Marin Islands bird refuge. Caution: This is an open-bay crossing of about 1.5 miles each way and subject to strong offshore winds; absolutely no landing permitted on these refuge islands nor approach within 100 yards.

0.25   Tiny Rat Rock Island—off the first point—is more picturesque than its name suggests. Caution: In spring this can be the nesting site of Canada geese; do not disturb.

0.7   Bullhead Flat (N38 00.21 W122 28.04), an optional launch site with restrooms.

1.0   Beyond the pilings off Buckeye Point, the salt marsh begins.

2.0   Except during extreme high tides, Jakes Island looks like a point of land surrounded by the salt marsh. Side trip: A narrow tidal creek just past Jakes (N38 00.85 W122 29.39) is navigable for 0.5 mile to the northwest edge of Turtle Back, where it forks and is wide enough to turn around. For adventurous paddlers, several other tidal creeks along the marsh offer the chance for exploration.

3.0   The mouth of Gallinas Creek and site of Bucks Launch (N38 00.95 W122 30.21), a good spot for a snack and rest. Side trip: Continue up Gallinas Creek for another 1.5 miles to Santa Margarita Island Preserve.

Where to Eat and Where to Stay

Restaurants: Snack bars at China Camp Historic Area (415-459-9877) and Bucks Launch (415-472-1502) and many restaurants in nearby San Rafael. **Lodging:** San Rafael Chamber of Commerce (srchamber.com; 415-454-4163). **Camping:** Walk-in sites at China Camp Back Ranch Meadows campground (reserveamerica.com; 800-444-7275).

Route 22
Richardson Bay to Angel Island

Richardson Bay offers aspiring intermediates a great introduction to open-bay paddling with all the rewards and challenges of the greater bay—scenery, tidal currents, exposure, boat traffic, fog, and wind—in a more protected setting. Less-experienced kayakers can stay near shore or confine their exploration to the back of the bay, while more-experienced paddlers can venture out toward "the Gate" (the Golden Gate Bridge, the waters, and the general vicinity beneath the bridge) or cross Raccoon Strait to Angel Island for a day trip or overnight camping. On the island, climb to the summit of Mount Livermore for excellent views of the bay and the Golden Gate Bridge or visit the museum at the old immigration station, the colonial garrisons, and the Ayala Cove coffee shop.

Trip highlights: Views of the Golden Gate Bridge, overnight camping, paddling in tidal currents, and bird watching.

Trip rating:

Beginner: 2 to 5 miles, depending on conditions; stay along shore in Richardson Bay or explore the salt marsh in the back of the bay.

Intermediate: 5 to 15 miles. For those with previous experience paddling in currents and strong open-water rescue skills, a crossing to Angel Island is possible on days when winds are below 15 knots and tidal currents are weak (or during slack tide). A trip leader with previous local experience is suggested. Yellow Bluff tide rips are an excellent training ground during ebb currents of 1 to 3 knots.

Advanced: 5 to 15 miles; same as intermediate trip but in stronger winds and currents; tide rips play in 3- to 6-knot currents at Yellow Bluff and Raccoon Strait during big ebbs.

Trip duration: Part day, full day, or overnight.

Kayak rentals: Sea Trek (seatrek.com; 415-332-8494) at Schoonmaker Bay has a wide selection of sea touring and sit-on-top kayaks for rent, 7 days a week year-round. Reservations suggested on weekends.

Navigation aids: NOAA chart 18649 (charts.noaa.gov/OnLineViewer/18649 .shtml) or 18653 (charts.noaa.gov/OnLineViewer/18653.shtml).

Weather information: NWS zone forecast: "San Francisco, San Pablo, Suisun Bays and the West Delta" (forecast.weather.gov/MapClick.php?zoneid=PZZ530); buoys: Golden Gate. Web cams: Looking south from Sausalito across the bay to San Francisco (rntl.net/sausalitocam.htm); Ayala Cove "Angel Cam" (angelisland.org/angelcamnew); overlooking the bay from high on the hill above Sausalito (webmarin.com).

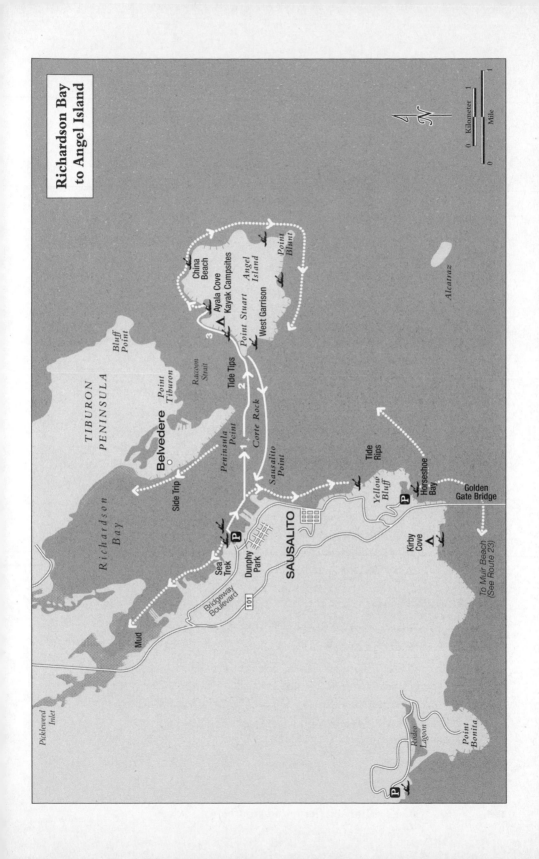

Richardson Bay
to Angel Island

Pickleweed Inlet

Richardson Bay

Mud

TIBURON PENINSULA

Belvedere

Bluff Point

Point Tiburon

Raccoon Strait

China Beach
Ayala Cove
Kayak Campsites
Point Stuart
West Garrison

Angel Island

Point Blunt

Alcatraz

Peninsula Point

Tide Tips

Side Trip

Sea Trek
Dunphy Park
Bridgeway Boulevard
101

SAUSALITO

Sausalito Point
Corte Rock

Tide Rips

Yellow Bluff

Horseshoe Bay
Golden Gate Bridge

Kirby Cove

Rodeo Lagoon

Point Bonita

To Muir Beach
(See Route 23)

N

0   Kilometer   1
0   Mile   1

Tidal information: Complex tidal flows make San Francisco Bay the place to learn about paddling in currents. Cross Raccoon Strait during slack tide to avoid tide rips (or at maximum if you like to play rough).

Cautions: Boat traffic, strong currents, and challenging tide rips—especially in Raccoon Strait and off Yellow Bluff during ebb tide—strong afternoon winds and heavy fog. Don't cross to Angel Island if you're not comfortable reading tide and current tables or navigating by compass in fog. If planning to circumnavigate Angel Island, expect afternoon winds to cause confused seas and surf along the island's southwest shore—helmets and surf zone experience recommended for landings.

Trip planning: Paddle early before wind and use tidal currents to your advantage: Explore the back-bay marsh on an incoming tide to avoid being stuck in the mud; ride the ebb currents to Yellow Bluff and return on the flood; or cross to Angel Island at slack after a morning ebb and return with the afternoon flood, avoiding peak ebb and the tide rips in Raccoon Strait. Autumn has less fog and wind. Winter and spring runoff creates stronger ebbs. Bring money for the park fee and also to ride the ferry ($14) back across Raccoon Strait to Tiburon if the wind comes up too much to paddle.

Launch site: To reach Dunphy Park (300 Napa St., Sausalito) take the Sausalito/Marin City exit off Highway 101 and head south on Bridgeway Boulevard into Sausalito. Turn left on Napa (the first street after the light at Easterby), then take a right into the parking lot at Dunphy Park. The farther into the lot you can park the better because the launch beach is on the far end of the park on the other side of the gazebo. Facilities: Porta-potties; no fee; overnight parking is allowed.

Alternate launch sites: Sea Trek (85 Libertyship Way, Sausalito; seatrek.com; 415-332-4465) at Schoonmaker Bay has a nicer beach but finding parking spaces can be difficult. From Horseshoe Bay Marina (see Route 23), experienced bay paddlers can make the longer crossing to Angel Island during the opposite tide scenario (morning flood with afternoon ebb).

Miles and Directions

0.0 From Dunphy Park (N37 51.69 W122 29.25) head northeast toward the boat channel, following the docks on your right.

0.25 When you reach the channel, you can bear right and follow it along the docks, or better yet, cross the channel and skirt its left edge to avoid boat traffic. Side trips: Turn left and follow the shore into the back of the bay at high tide to explore 3 miles or more into the protected marshes.

Rescue practice near Point Cavallo **KIM GRANDFIELD**

0.5   Anywhere along this stretch offers the shortest crossing to the cliffs on Belvedere Peninsula. The most conservative and scenic route is to cross toward Cone Rock (N37 51.83 W122 28.19), staying well inside Richardson Bay (as opposed to heading straight to Peninsula Point), checking your drift against the midbay buoys and the far shore. There are no good landing beaches along Belvedere's cliffs, so don't cross unless you are prepared to be in your boat for a while. Side trips: Instead of crossing to Belvedere, continue along the Sausalito shore for another 2.5 miles to Yellow Bluff or follow the shore for another mile to Horseshoe Cove for views of the Golden Gate. Caution: Strong currents and tide rips occur at Yellow Bluff, especially during ebb tide, and the change happens early and fast, usually within an hour of slack. (Those who come to play on the tide rips want to arrive an hour or more before maximum ebb at the Golden Gate.) Expect rougher conditions when approaching the Gate.

1.5   Follow the cliffs toward Peninsula Point, gawking at the amazing homes perched there.

1.75 In the protection of Peninsula Point is a good place to reassess conditions for crossing Raccoon Strait. Caution: Be aware of strong currents that sometimes sweep toward the point from several hundred yards inside Richardson Bay. At the point, tide rips, submerged rocks, and exposure to wind can create challenging conditions. Out in the strait some of the bay's more exciting or excruciating tide rips (depending on your abilities) form. If your skills are up to the conditions, cross to Point Stuart on Angel Island, using a ferry angle to compensate for currents.

2.25 From Point Stuart continue northeast along the island toward Ayala Cove. Side trips: Head to the right around Point Stuart for 0.25 mile to land at the West Garrison to stretch or to use the public restroom.

2.5 A small beach in the middle of the cove gives access to the trail to the kayak campsite.

3.5 Land in Ayala Cove on the right side in front of the lawn to hike, picnic, or investigate the coffee shop and museums. Also, this is where you are supposed to pay your $3 day-use fee. Side trips: Continue another 0.7 mile to a quieter beach at China Cove and tour the museum at the old immigration station. Circumnavigators can finish the 4-mile loop back to Point Stuart. Caution: Westerly winds funneling through the Gate onto Point Blunt are consistently recorded as among the strongest in the bay, often causing confused seas to batter the cliffs between Points Blunt and Stuart.

4.5 To return from Point Stuart (mile 7.5 for circumnavigators), head straight back toward Sausalito Point if it is windy in order to gain some wind protection from the shore.

Where to Eat and Where to Stay

Restaurants: Among Sausalito's multitude of choices, Sartaj India Cafe (43 Caledonia St.; 415-332-7103) near Dunphy Park is quick and casual; Arawan Thai, a few doors down (47 Caledonia St.; 415-332-0882), is slightly more upscale, and downtown has many fancier options. **Lodging:** Larkspur Hotel Mill Valley (larkspurhotels.com/larkspur-hotels/mill-valley; 800-258-3894), Fireside Motel (415-332-6906) or Fountain Motel (motelinmarin.com; 415-332-1732). **Camping:** Plan well in advance to reserve the kayak campsite on the northwest corner of Angel Island (reserveamerica.com; 800-444-7275). Several other "environmental sites" (i.e., "walk-in") are also available on the island, depending on how far you are willing to walk uphill with your gear.

Route 23
Golden Gate to Point Bonita and Muir Beach

From the seat of a kayak, the enormous scale of the scenery as you paddle out beneath the Golden Gate—the bridge towering nearly 700 feet overhead, the 600-foot cliffs of the Marin Headlands, and perhaps the skyscraper hull of a passing supertanker—can be mesmerizing. But you'll need to pay full attention to the water. Twice a day all of San Francisco Bay (as well as some 80 percent of the state's freshwater runoff from the Sacramento River, San Joaquin, and most Sierra rivers) funnels out through the barely mile-wide gap beneath the bridge; and twice each day the Pacific floods back in, creating the strongest, most challenging tidal currents in California. During peak flows, currents faster than you can paddle, sometimes in excess of 6 knots, can sweep you away with them. Understanding the complexities of the tides—how to hitch a ride on these powerful liquid conveyer belts and how to pick a time and a day to avoid them—are essential skills for the well-rounded kayaker. For those ready to bump their skills up a notch, the waters of the Gate are the master teacher. Beyond the Gate to Point Bonita, several semi- protected beaches make good lunch stops, and beyond Bonita, the cliffy open-coast vistas are rugged and spectacular, as is the rock garden paddling between Point Bonita and Muir Beach.

Trip highlights: Awesome views of the Golden Gate Bridge and Marin Headlands; state's premier spot for learning about tidal currents.

Trip rating:

Beginner: 1-mile, open-bay crossing as far as the Gate not recommended unless led by experienced paddler on a calm day during a weak flood tide.

Intermediate: 4-mile round-trip to Point Diablo (8 miles round-trip to Point Bonita). Going beyond the Gate not recommended without previous experience paddling in currents and strong open-water skills; ability to read local current guides a must; experience navigating in fog and a trip leader with previous local experience suggested.

Advanced: 10-mile round-trip to Rodeo Beach (or 8.5 miles one-way from Muir Beach) recommended in seas below 6 feet, winds below 20 knots.

Trip duration: Part to full day.

Navigation aids: NOAA chart 18649 (charts.noaa.gov/OnLineViewer/18649 .shtml).

Weather information: NWS zone forecast: "San Francisco, San Pablo, Suisun Bays and the West Delta" (forecast.weather.gov/MapClick.php?zoneid=PZZ530);

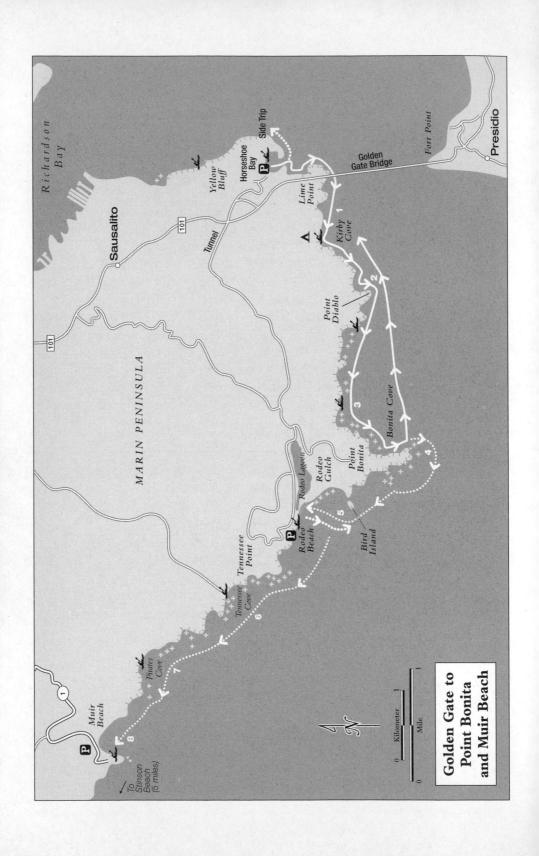

Golden Gate to Point Bonita and Muir Beach

buoys: Golden Gate. Web cam: Looking south from Sausalito across the bay to San Francisco (rntl.net/sausalitocam.htm). Overlooking the bay from high on the hill above Sausalito (webmarin.com).

Tidal information: The swiftest currents in the state flow through the Golden Gate. Plan your trip to go with them.

Cautions: Strong currents and tide rips. Small Craft Advisories for winds above 20 knots are standard most spring and summer afternoons. The bay is (in)famous for fog. Don't paddle here unless you are comfortable navigating by compass. Boat traffic of every description: The bay is one of the world's major commercial and recreational ports. Avoid crossing shipping lanes; freighters move deceptively fast and can't stop. Dumping waves on beaches outside the gate are common, so surf landings and helmets are often necessary. The open coast around Point Bonita to Rodeo Beach can be as dynamic as it gets, with large waves flushing into rocks and cliffs. Be careful not to flush nesting seabirds, especially around Bird Island.

Trip planning: Ride the ebb on your way out and use the flood on your way back. Unless you're looking for excitement, pick a day with currents less than 3 knots or so, and/or avoid the Gate during times of maximum current. Check your weather radio throughout the day; expect strong westerlies in the 20-knot range to funnel through the Gate. Hug the shore to minimize effects of wind, current, fog, and boat traffic. The best places for tide-rip play are Yellow Bluff on the ebb and North Tower on the flood.

Launch site: Beach in front of the Presidio Yacht Club (on Sommerville Road, Sausalito) in Horseshoe Bay Marina: From Highway 101, exit on Alexander Avenue (just north of Golden Gate bridge) and head downhill about 0.25 mile toward Sausalito. Take the first left at sign for Fort Baker. Take the first right (sort of a U-turn) just before the tunnel to Rodeo Beach, and head downhill toward the water. At the bottom of the hill, take a right at the stop sign and continue toward the water. Take the second left onto Sommerville Road (not signed) and follow the waterfront past the Coast Guard Station for 0.25 mile to where the road winds up and around the Yacht Club and back down to the gravel parking lot on the other side, where you'll see the short trail down to the beach. Facilities: Nearest toilets are the porta-potties against the hill on the far side of the marina (until the bar opens at the Yacht Club after 11 a.m. on weekends). Free parking. Aerial photo: Looking in through the Golden Gate at Horseshoe Bay Marina with Angel Island in the distance (californiacoastline .org, image 201007641).

Alternate launch sites: Rodeo Beach: Follow the directions above, but head through the tunnel and follow the signs 3.5 miles to the beach. Muir Beach is 6 miles north on Highway 1; turn left on Pacific Way and follow signs 0.5 mile to beach.

Checking out the underbelly of the Golden Gate Bridge R. SCHUMANN

Miles and Directions

0.0 From the beach (N37 50.01 W122 28.46) paddle out the jetties of Horseshoe Bay, head right around the fishing pier, and follow the cliffs toward the Gate. Caution: Paddle well beyond fishing lines when passing the pier. Side trip: Turn left and follow the shore to Yellow Bluff for more protection or to play in the tide rips during an ebb, or to access small beaches 0.5 mile beyond Yellow Bluff.

0.5 The lee of Lime Point beneath the unmistakable Golden Gate Bridge provides a great photo op and a good place to reassess conditions. Caution: On rough days conditions immediately worsen on rounding Lime Point: Wind, ocean swells, and current can create confused seas. Swing wide to avoid washing into the cliffs. Avoid this area during strong ebbs when currents faster than you can paddle against sweep seaward. All boats are required to stay 25 yards from the bridge towers.

1.5 Kirby Cove (N37 49.60 W122 29.41), the long beach with a staircase on its far end, makes a good place for a break. It is one of the few beaches in the area protected from prevailing swell and winds, and it has pit toilets hidden in the trees. Caution: Surf looks nonexistent, but it often dumps quick and hard on this beach. Far left side is more protected; helmets are recommended.

2.0 Point Diablo, the distinct point with the navigational horn, is where conditions generally get rougher still, so it's a good turnaround on many days. Caution: On calm days there are some decent rock gardens to play in along this stretch, but they are tight and technical and sneaker waves can catch you off guard. Watch for harbor seals hauled out so you don't spook them.

2.5 Several scenic pocket beaches dot Bonita Cove. Caution: Dumping surf on steep beaches can make for challenging landings in all but the smallest swell.

4.0 Point Bonita makes a good turn-around spot for all but advanced open-coast kayakers. Routinely battered by waves and strong winds, the steep cliffs beyond the point are as exposed as they are dramatic. Side trips: Depending on conditions, experts may find the rock gardens and arches from the point onward extremely challenging and beautiful—or extremely hazardous. Caution: Avoid nesting seabirds in this area, especially around Bird Island, which is currently under consideration as a Special Closure zone and would be off limits to all boating within 300 yards. Check for updates (dfg.ca.gov/mlpa).

5.0 A sandy but exposed beach at Rodeo Beach (N37 49.82 W122 32.26) offers the only landing spot on this stretch of cliffs for several miles, but when surf is above 6 feet, it's recommended for experts only.

Other options: Advanced coastal paddlers can launch from Rodeo Beach or Muir Beach for round-trips, or run a shuttle and enter the Gate. This section of coast is extremely scenic and extremely exposed, with towering cliffs and few beaches besides Tennessee and Pirates Cove and the launch sites listed here north to south: Stinson Beach (10 miles to Point Bonita), Muir Beach (4.5 miles), and Rodeo Beach (1 mile).

Where to Eat and Where to Stay

Restaurants: Presidio Yacht Club (presidioyachtclub.org; 415-332-2319) serves a limited menu of burgers (and is only open to the public Thurs through Sun), but has a great view of the Golden Gate; downtown Sausalito has many fancier options. **Lodging:** Larkspur Hotel Mill Valley (larkspurhotels.com/larkspur-hotels/mill-valley; 800-258-3894), Fireside Motel (415-332-6906), or Fountain Motel (motelinmarin.com; 415-332-1732). **Camping:** Sites available at Kirby Cove, through Golden Gate National Recreation Area (recreation.gov; 877-444-6777 for reservations; 415-331-1540 for information). But these sites (only 4) usually book the day reservations become available, 90 days in advance.

Route 24
Bair Island Reserve
and Corkscrew Slough

Bair Island Ecological Reserve, a 1,600-acre tidal marsh tucked away at the edges of urban sprawl, is a wilderness for the myopic: surrounded by city, traversed by power lines, but chockablock with shorebirds. And once you slip into its maze of narrow, winding channels, it's not hard to lose oneself in the solitude. This area is especially convenient for South Bay residents looking for a local alternative to the long drive to Elkhorn Slough or Tomales Bay. New flow restrictors and levee breaches designed to restore original wetland areas are opening up new paddling areas, but creating much faster flows in many areas.

Trip highlights: Good birding, solitude, and tidal currents play.
Trip rating:
   Beginner: 1 to 7 miles or more of protected exploration for paddlers with a basic understanding of tides and boat traffic and a good sense of direction.
   Intermediate: Longer flat-water trips with some currents and access to open bay and strong currents around new levee breaches.
Trip duration: Part to full day.
Navigation aids: USGS Redwood Point (7.5 minute) and NOAA chart 18651 (charts.noaa.gov/OnLineViewer/18651.shtml).
Weather information: NWS zone forecast: "San Francisco, San Pablo, Suisun Bays and the West Delta" (forecast.weather.gov/MapClick.php?zoneid=PZZ530).
Tidal information: Although much paddling is still possible at low tide, you'll need 2 to 3 feet of tide height to get through Corkscrew Slough and to explore smaller side channels. Expect moderate to "strong" currents in constricted channels, especially around the new flow restrictors and breaches during big tide changes.
Cautions: Winds, boat traffic in harbor, currents, and mud. New flow restrictors and levee breaches now create much stronger flows and may become impassible except around slack. For updates see http://biac.wildapricot.org/Default.aspx?pageId=1493592.
Trip planning: Choose a high, rising tide and give yourself plenty of time.
Launch site: To reach the Redwood City Marina Boat Ramp (601 Chesapeake Dr., Redwood City), exit Highway 101 at Seaport Boulevard/Highway 84 West/Woodside Road and follow signs to the Port of Redwood City. Turn left on Chesapeake Drive to where it ends at the boat ramp, 0.5 mile on your right. There is a $5 launch/parking fee.

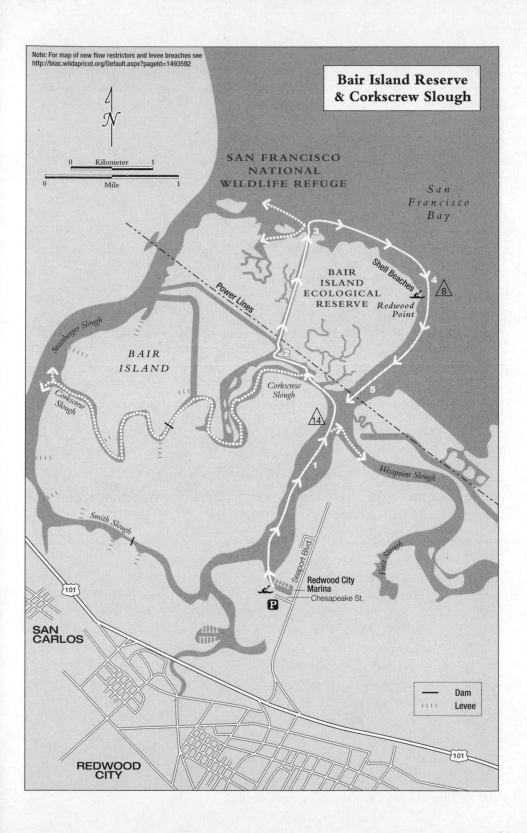

Cruising the channels of Corkscrew Slough R. SCHUMANN

Miles and Directions

0.0   Launch from dock or boat ramp (N37 30.15 W122 12.88) and follow the right shore northeast toward the bay.

1.5   Turn left into Corkscrew Slough (N37 31.40 W122 12.37) at the red #14 channel marker just before you would pass under the power lines. Side trip: You can also paddle several miles into Westpoint Slough on the right side of the channel if you're looking to try someplace new.

1.75   First channel on the right is a dead end (but it is noted here to distinguish it from the next channel).

2.0 The second channel on your right (N37 31.60 W122 12.70), the narrow, "secret passage" through the heart of the Bair Island Ecological Reserve, is the scenic route to San Francisco Bay. It's smaller than the first channel you just passed, with small, mud mounds that partially block the entrance. Turn right into the channel and follow the right-hand bank for 0.25 mile to where a straight channel branches off to the right and cuts under the power lines (N38 31.78 W122 12.82), bearing 5° MN. Side trip: You can also continue through the deeper Corkscrew Slough if you want more mileage: The counterclockwise loop through Corkscrew and Steinberger Sloughs to Smith Slough and back to the marina is another 7 miles; the clockwise trip around Bair Island adds another 10. Caution: Flow restrictors and levee breaches ahead.

2.25 Follow this channel for 0.75 mile. From here it's a straight shot along the levee to the bay. Caution: You'll want a good 2 to 3 feet of tide to attempt this shortcut. Side trip: Some smaller channels on your left are navigable if you're in the mood to explore dead ends.

3.0 Views of San Francisco Bay and the East Bay hills open up at the edge of Bair Island, as does exposure to the wind. On windy days you may want to retrace your path; otherwise continue clockwise around the island. Side trip: A maze of channels angles back into Bair Island on your left (bearing 220° MN) for those who enjoy meandering (and have a good sense of direction). For a workout turn left and take the long way home down Steinberger Slough and return via either the more scenic Corkscrew (about 8 miles back to the put in) or the shorter Smith Slough (6 miles). Caution: Flow restrictors and levee breaches ahead.

3.6 Although white shell beaches along this stretch make for a good landmark and apparently offer mud-free landings, it is prohibited to land on Bair Island.

4.4 Turn right at channel marker #8 at Redwood Point, which is the last shell beach and the most accessible at lower tides.

5.2 Cross under power lines at the mouth of Corkscrew Slough, looking for egret nests on the towers, to complete your loop around Bair Island.

6.8 Return to the marina.

Where to Eat and Where to Stay

Restaurants: There are no restaurants in the immediate area. Follow Seaport Boulevard under Highway 101 into Redwood City for a selection of fast-food chains. **Lodging and camping:** Not exactly a "destination" location, the light industrial area offers no lodging or camping nearby.

Route 25
Newark Slough Wildlife Refuge

The Newark Slough's narrow channel meanders through the salt marsh of Don Edwards San Francisco Bay National Wildlife Refuge, the nation's largest urban wildlife refuge at 20,000 acres. Particularly convenient for both East and South Bay residents, this launch site lies within a mile of refuge headquarters and its extensive visitor center, with its fine exhibits interpreting the fascinating ecology and biology of the marshlands and the hundreds of wildlife species residing there.

Trip highlights: Good birding, peaceful marsh.

Trip rating:

Beginner: 1 to 10+ miles of narrow protected waterway, easy paddling in winds to 10 knots.

Intermediate–Advanced: 14+ miles with access to open bay.

Trip duration: Part day.

Navigation aids: USGS: Newark (7.5 minute) and NOAA chart 18651 (charts.noaa .gov/OnLineViewer/18651.shtml).

Weather information: NWS zone forecast: "San Francisco, San Pablo, Suisun Bays and the West Delta" (forecast.weather.gov/MapClick.php?zoneid=PZZ530).

Tidal information: Tidal currents and mud can cause problems during low and falling tides. You'll want at least 2 feet of tide or more at the put in if you want to avoid a muddy launch, but it is possible to slide into the water with less.

Cautions: Mud, currents, and afternoon winds.

Trip planning: Launch an hour or two before high tide (don't forget to make the correction). Very muddy at low tides. With no good landing sites in the marsh, paddle out only half as far as you want to go without getting out of your kayak to rest, then turn around and head back. Paddle early before the wind and make time to see the refuge's visitor center exhibits in the afternoon.

Launch site: To reach Jarvis Landing boat launch (Thornton Avenue and Marshlands Road, Newark), from Highway 84 east, take Thornton Avenue south (the Paseo Padre exit if you're heading west on 84) and turn right on Marshlands Road. The boat ramp is in the parking lot at this corner. Facilities/ fees: None.

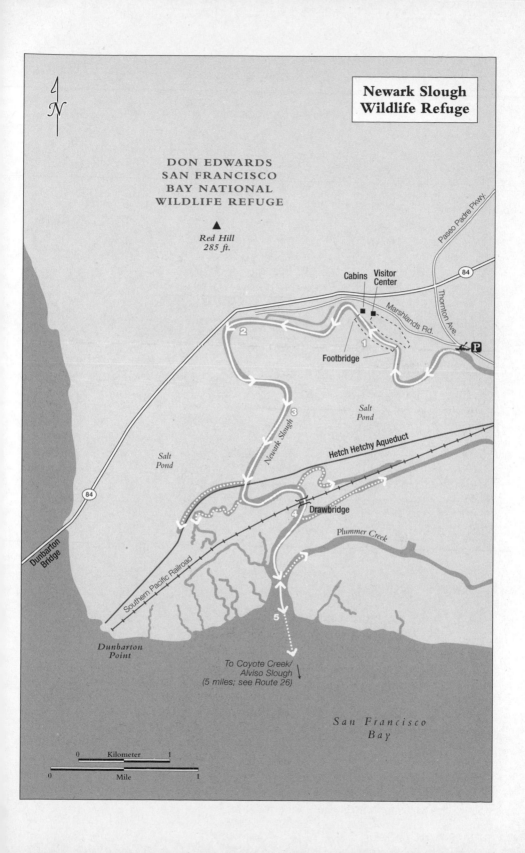

Newark Slough
Wildlife Refuge

DON EDWARDS
SAN FRANCISCO
BAY NATIONAL
WILDLIFE REFUGE

Red Hill
285 ft.

Cabins Visitor
Center

Marshlands Rd.

Paseo Padre Pkwy.

Thornton Ave.

84

Footbridge

Salt
Pond

Newark Slough

Salt
Pond

Hetch Hetchy Aqueduct

84

Drawbridge

Plummer Creek

Southern Pacific Railroad

Dunbarton
Bridge

Dunbarton
Point

To Coyote Creek/
Alviso Slough
(5 miles; see Route 26)

San Francisco
Bay

0   Kilometer   1

0   Mile   1

Narrow channels of Newark Slough R. SCHUMANN

Miles and Directions

0.0 Head right from Jarvis Landing (N37 31.72 W122 03.81), meandering along the bends in the channel. Side trip: Shallow marshlands on right can be explored at high tide.

0.8 Pass under a footbridge as you follow a straightaway that parallels the main hiking trail from the visitor center.

1.2 After a second footbridge, pass the historic cabins on the right just before the channel bends hard left.

2.0   Slough nears Dunbarton Bridge before curving left and heading back into the marsh. Caution: If continuing beyond here, expect the wind to be in your face on the return.

3.5   At Hetch Hetchy Aqueduct (N37 30.93 W122 05.35) a side channel branches off to the right. Side trip: It is the first of several channels over the next 0.5 mile (2 on the right and 2 on the left) where adventurous paddlers could meander off to explore the pickleweed marsh. All of these are dead ends, eventually narrowing to naught. Turn around before their width is less than your kayak is long, unless you want to practice your backing up skills, and avoid these channels if the tide is falling.

4.0   Railroad tracks and drawbridge are among the more obvious landmarks in this marsh maze.

4.7   Plummer Creek (N37 30.35 W122 05.09) angles off behind you to the left and into the salt ponds.

5.0   Mouth of Newark Slough with views of the open bay is probably a good place to turn around unless you have open-water paddling experience. Caution: Currents and choppy seas are common on the bay. Side trip: Ambitious paddlers with good navigational skills could make the 5-mile open-water crossing to the mouth of Coyote Creek and paddle another 4 miles up Alviso Slough to the launch ramp (see Route 26) for a 14-mile downwind trip to the other end of the Don Edwards Refuge.

Where to Eat and Where to Stay

Restaurants and lodging: Not exactly a "destination" spot; various chain restaurants and lodging are available in Newark and the surrounding East Bay sprawl. **Camping:** None nearby.

Route 26
Alviso Slough

While this might not be the sort of place you'd be willing to drive hours out of your way to paddle, for South Bay locals Alviso Slough's new launch facility is just way too convenient to pass up. Along with its proximity, it offers both a boat ramp and a low dock for easy launch access (so no more mud launches), a regularly dredged channel out to San Francisco Bay that's navigable at any tide height, tons of birdlife to see along the way, and even wash racks (bring your own hose) and plenty of free parking. It's great for a quick fitness paddle after work or a Sunday morning dawdle.

Trip highlights: Good birding, peaceful marsh, excellent proximity to South Bay residents.

Trip rating:

Beginner: 1 to 8 miles round-trip of narrow protected waterway, with easy paddling in winds to 10 or 15 knots.

Intermediate–Advanced: 10+ miles round-trip with access to open bay.

Trip duration: Part day.

Navigation aids: USGS: Milpitas and Mountain View (7.5 minute) and NOAA chart 18651 (charts.noaa.gov/OnLineViewer/18651.shtml).

Weather information: NWS zone forecast: "San Francisco, San Pablo, Suisun Bays and the West Delta" (forecast.weather.gov/MapClick.php?zoneid=PZZ530).

Tidal information: Although the area gets very shallow at low tide, the main channel is dredged and open at all tide heights.

Cautions: Mud shoals if you leave the slough, currents, afternoon winds, harbor seals, and boat traffic.

Trip planning: Currents can be strong on big tide changes. Leave an hour or two before low tide to ride the ebb current out to the bay and then return to the launch with the beginning of the flood. Launch early before the wind (which typically comes in from the bay) begins to blow, to have it at your back on the return. If paddling into the wind on an outgoing tide, expect a wet ride as it creates a 6-inch chop that splashes you in the face. No landing sites in the slough; paddle out only half as far as you want to go without getting out of your kayak to rest, then turn around.

Launch site: To reach Alviso Marina Boat Dock (Hope Street and Mills Street, San Jose) take Highway 237 from either 880 or 101 and exit on Great America Parkway. Eastbound travelers: turn left on Yerba Buena and left again on

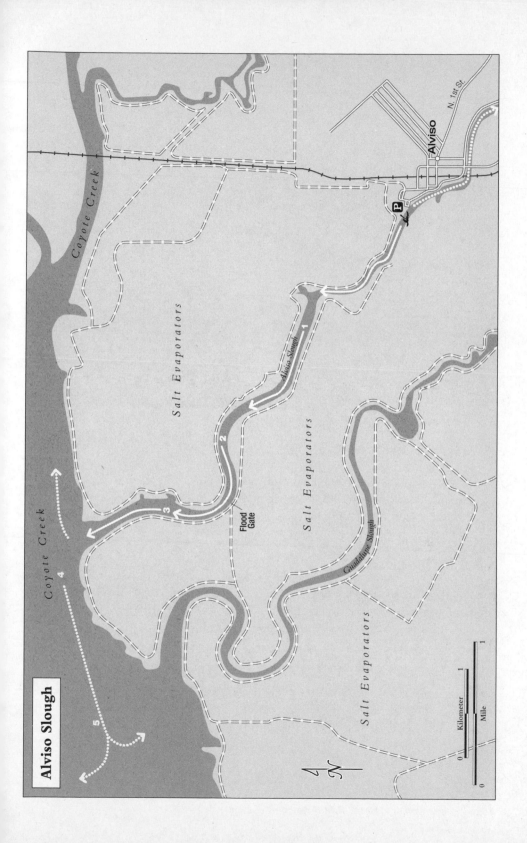

Alviso Slough

New boat launch at Alviso Slough, with low dock on right for easy launching R. SCHUMANN

Lafayette/Gold Street. Westbound: turn right on Gold Street Connector and left onto Gold. Follow Gold to the end and turn left on Elizabeth Street, then right onto Hope Street and follow it into the parking lot. Facilities: Restrooms and water; no fees.

Miles and Directions

0.0 From the launch ramp (N37 25.77 W121 58.91), head toward the bay, meandering along the bends in the channel. Side trip: At high tide (9 feet or so) you can paddle the other direction up the Guadalupe River for a couple miles.

1.0 The slough bends left to the west and away from the hiking trail that's been following the left bank and passes an abandoned boat on the right bank.

2.6 Flood control gate (N37 26.81 W122 01.10) on left, where the slough curves sharply back to the right and north. Caution: Breaks in the levee along the left bank, although navigable, are closed to boaters.

3.8   At Coyote Creek (N37 27.75 W122 01.47) the channel widens considerably as it passes beneath power lines. If it is beginning to get windy, this makes a good turn-around point. Caution: At lower tides, the water can be shallow in this area, so try to stick to mid-channel if you are going to continue. Side trips: Head west on Coyote Creek for another 1.25 mile to the #20 navigational marker at the mouth of Guadalupe Slough if the tide hasn't turned too strongly yet against you. You can head several miles up Guadalupe Slough if you have time and energy or out onto the open bay. From the mouth of Alviso Slough, you could also head east up Coyote Creek for a couple miles, but if the tide starts to flood, you'll be fighting it on your way back.

Where to Eat and Where to Stay

Restaurants: Maria Elena's (408-946-5336) just up the street is a popular mom-and-pop place serving authentic Mexican food. **Lodging:** Not exactly a "destination" location, there are chain hotels available in the surrounding South Bay sprawl. **Camping:** Nearest camping in the Santa Cruz area: New Brighton or Henry Cowell State Parks (reserveamerica.com; 800-444-7275).

Quick Trip Tips: Other Launch Sites in San Francisco Bay Area

Coyote Point Recreation Area (Beginner to Advanced)

A few miles south of San Francisco airport, Coyote Point offers excellent launch access to the mid-bay from a very protected marina in the lee of the point or from a more-exposed beach to the north. Typically calm in the mornings, this is a popular windsurfing spot most afternoons.

Oakland Estuary (Beginner to Advanced)

Launch site near Jack London Square offers several miles of protected waterways with access to the open bay for more experienced paddlers. Kayak rentals from California Canoe and Kayak (calkayak.com).

Brooks Island (Beginner to Advanced)

Several well-protected launch sites around Richmond Marina with access to the open bay. The island is only 0.5 mile offshore, but is downwind of the launch and no landings are allowed without arranging a tour with East Bay Parks first. Call their reservations department at 888-327-2757, option 2, or visit EBParksOnline.org for the current schedule of tours.

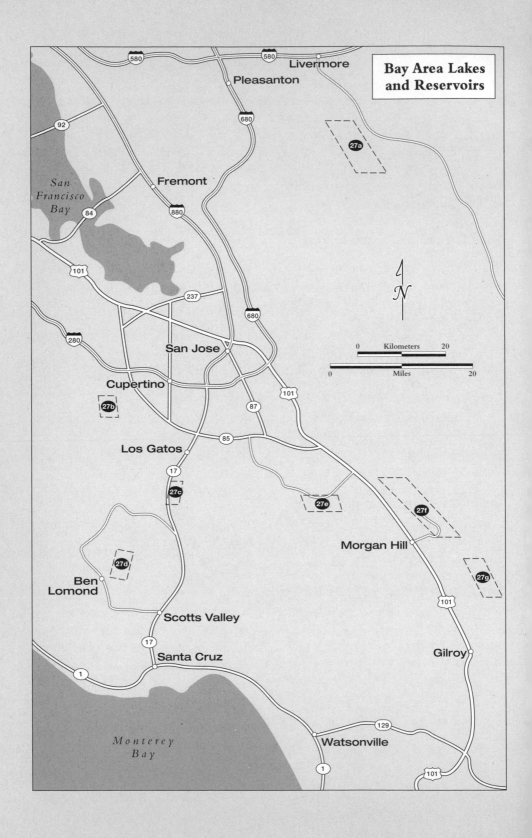

Special Section: Bay Area Lakes and Reservoirs

Route 27
Bay Area Lakes

Set in the quintessential "golden rolling hills of California," these seven Bay Area lakes and reservoirs are an especially good option for paddlers who live near them on days when the sea is rough, or you just want to enjoy some warm, fresh water closer to home. All are known for good fishing. Those that allow powerboats have quieter "environmental areas," low-speed zones where you can paddle away from boat noise and wakes if you choose, and all of them are much quieter midweek or off-season. Although the lakes close to boating a half-hour before sunset, experienced paddlers with their own boats can join the popular, naturalist-led Full Moon Paddles run by Santa Clara County Parks (408-846-5622) on several of the lakes.

Cautions: Afternoon winds (typically out of the northwest), fishing lines, boat traffic on those lakes that permit powerboats, mandatory zebra/quagga mussel inspections. Most do not allow swimming.

Trip planning: Check the hours and days of operation via the websites or phone numbers below as some lakes are not open year-round. All are open 8 a.m. to sunset, seven days a week from April 16 through October 14. Some remain open all year, while others either close completely for boating during the off-season or for a couple days during the week. Plan your routes to return with the wind or paddle early to avoid it. Leave time for mandatory mussel inspections (see Don't Move a Mussel below).

27A Lake Del Valle

Five miles long, Lake Del Valle allows swimming, which is good since it is farther inland, so generally a bit hotter than the other lakes. Although powerboats are also allowed, what makes Del Valle good for kayaking is their strictly enforced 10 mph speed limit and total ban on Jet Skis, keeping wakes and noise to a minimum. Bald eagle and osprey are not uncommon sights. The lake also has campsites, and kayak rentals are available lakeside through Sunrise Mountain Sports (kayakdelvalle.com; 925-447-8330) seven days a week during summer and other times by arrangement.

Trip rating:
  Beginner: 10-mile round-trip in winds to 10 knots.
Navigation aids: Park map, info, and current hours of operation (ebparks.org/Page115.aspx#reach).
Launch site: Boat ramp, or even better from the beach nearby, next to the swim area (7000 Del Valle Rd., Livermore) open year-round. Facilities: Toilets,

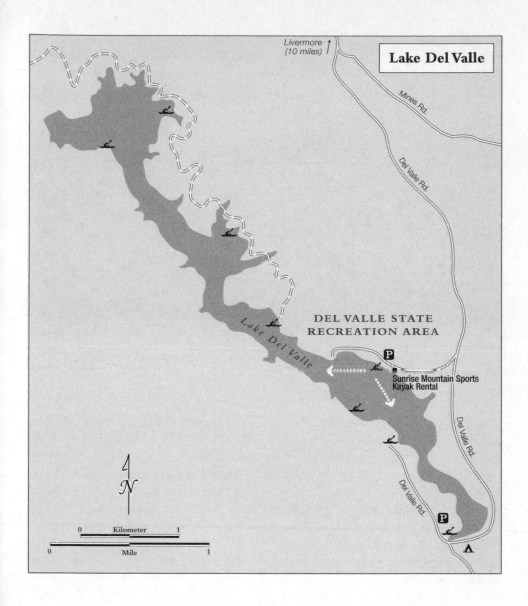

water, snack bar, campground; $6 entrance fee, $4 launch fee, $4 mussel inspection (the fee is good for 30 days, but you'll still have to get your boat inspected every time you use the lake).

Where to Eat and Where to Stay

Restaurants: Snack bar near the boat ramp. **Lodging:** None at the lake. **Camping:** Lakeside sites are available when water levels are high; at lower levels they are dry-creek-side sites, but still close to the lake (reserveamerica.com; or call directly, 888-327-2757).

Overview of Lake Del Valle KIM GRANDFIELD

27B Stevens Creek Reservoir

Small but sweet, this is a favorite destination for Bay Area paddlers. Although little more than a mile long and less than half as wide, it's among the most scenic of the local lakes, tucked away in a steep, forested fold of the Santa Cruz Mountains that snakes its way up Stevens Creek into the redwoods. It's also very peaceful, being one of the few non-powerboating lakes in the area, and one of two offering kayak rentals (outbackadventures .com; 510-440-8888; weekends during summer or midweek by arrangement). Paddling here is easy as the canyon is mostly protected from afternoon winds, with several sites where you can pull out for a rest or picnic.

Trip rating:
  Beginner: 2.5-mile round-trip loop.
Navigation aids: Park map, info, and current days and hours of operation (sccgov
  .org/sites/parks/Maps%20Here/Pages/default.aspx).
Launch site: Boat ramp (11401 Stevens Canyon Rd., Cupertino) is open
  seasonally, April 15 to October 14. Facilities: Porta-potties; $6 entrance fee; $7
  mussel inspection.

Where to Eat and Where to Stay
No food, lodging, or camping available at the lake.

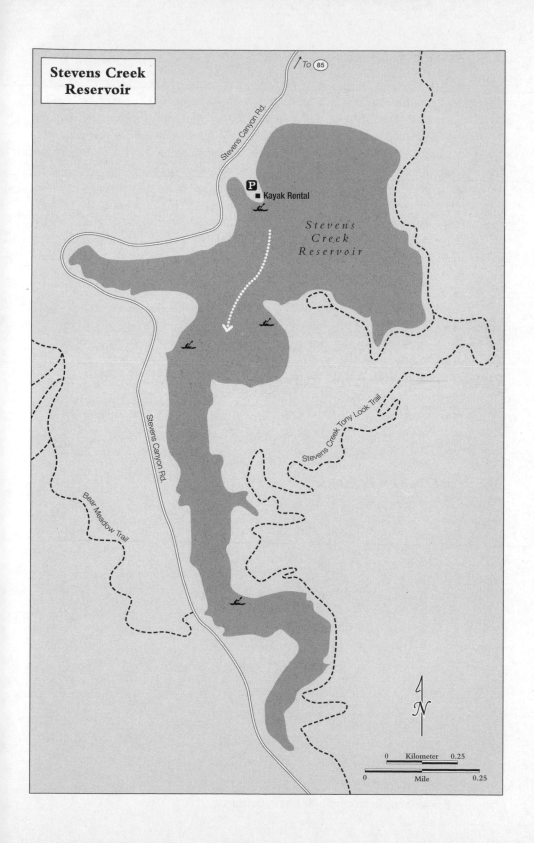

Stevens Creek Reservoir

To (85)

Stevens Canyon Rd.

P
■ Kayak Rental

Stevens Creek Reservoir

Stevens Creek Tony Look Trail

Stevens Canyon Rd.

Bear Meadow Trail

N

| 0 | Kilometer | 0.25 |

0   Mile   0.25

27C Lexington Reservoir

Cradled in the foothills of the Santa Cruz Mountains overlooking Santa Clara Valley, Lexington Reservoir displays an interesting tapestry of habitats. The lake's steep shores sport a fascinating blend of "ecotones"—areas of overlapping habitat, rich in diversity and sharing the flora and fauna of each other. The coastal-scrub chaparral, which dominates the drier, south-facing slopes, blends into areas of oak woodland and mixed-evergreen and riparian forests laced with strands of redwood groves in shady canyons and on north-facing slopes. No swimming or gas motors are allowed at this popular fishing lake, so it's a peaceful place to paddle. The most interesting paddling is found in the narrows where Los Gatos Creek drains into the lake on the southern end, with greater access earlier in the season when water levels are higher. Unfortunately the put in is at the lake's northern end, meaning that the 2.5-mile return to the launch site will be into the wind most afternoons. Paddle early to avoid wind or pick a day when the weather forecast is for winds below 15 knots.

Trip rating:
> *Beginner:* 5-mile round-trip, becomes intermediate in northwest winds between 10 and 20 knots.

Navigation aids: Park map, info, and current hours of operation (sccgov.org/sites/parks/Maps%20Here/Pages/default.aspx).

Launch sites: Boat ramp (17770 Alma Bridge Rd., Los Gatos,) is open seasonally, April 15 to October 14. Facilities: Porta-potties; $6 entrance fee, $5 launch fee, $7 mussel inspection.

Where to Eat and Where to Stay

No food, lodging, or camping available at the lake.

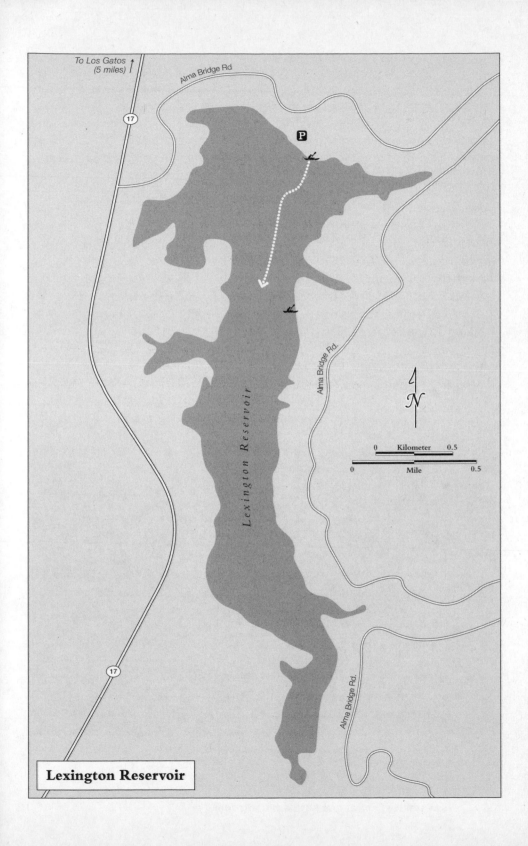

To Los Gatos ↑
(5 miles)

Alma Bridge Rd

17

P

Alma Bridge Rd.

N

0   Kilometer   0.5

0   Mile   0.5

Lexington Reservoir

Alma Bridge Rd.

17

Alma Bridge Rd.

Lexington Reservoir

27D Loch Lomond

Nestled among the redwoods in the Santa Cruz Mountains, 2 miles long and typically less than a couple hundred yards wide, Loch Lomond feels more like paddling on a North Coast river than a lake. Although it is arguably the most scenic of all the lakes, and serene, since no gas motors are allowed, it is now the most challenging to access. Because of mussel restrictions, only those willing to pay $200 to store a kayak there for the entire season are allowed to paddle the loch.

Trip rating:
   Beginner: 4-mile round-trip.
Navigation aids: Park map, info, and current hours of operation (cityofsantacruz
   .com/index.aspx?page=426).
Launch site: Boat ramp (100 Loch Lomond Way, Felton) open seasonally 7 days
   a week, March 1 to Labor Day, then weekends only through October 14.
   Facilities: Toilets, water, small store; $6 entrance/launch fee (or $60 season
   pass); $25 season mussel inspection.

Where to Eat and Where to Stay

No food, lodging, or camping available at the lake.

Paddling early to beat the wind, a paddler glides across Lake Del Valle. **K. GRANDFIELD**

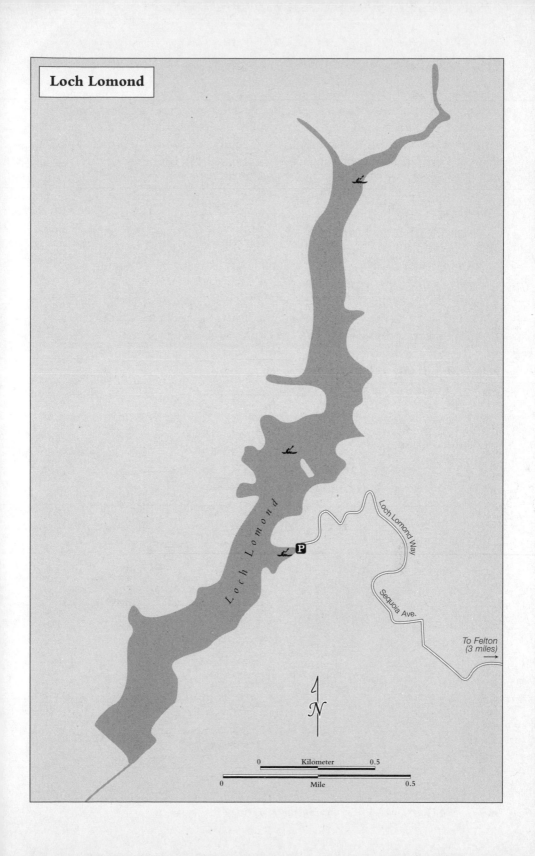

Loch Lomond

Loch Lomond

Loch Lomond Way

Sequoia Ave.

To Felton
(3 miles)

N

Kilometer
0   0.5

Mile
0   0.5

27E Calero Lake

Like most of the other lakes in the area Calero gets busy with powerboats on summer weekends, but it is less than a mile paddle across the lake from the launch ramp to the "no wake zone" in Cherry Cove. Most power craft shun this narrow, picturesque finger of water where oak-clad hillsides rise steeply on either side as you paddle up Cherry Canyon. Here birdlife is common, and the park has placed bat boxes, so check out the Full Moon Paddles run by Santa Clara County Parks (408-846-5622).

Trip rating:
> *Beginner:* 10-mile round-trip in winds to 10 knots; intermediate in winds from 10 to 20 knots.

Navigation aids: Park map, info, and current hours of operation (sccgov.org/sites/parks/Maps%20Here/Pages/default.aspx).

Launch site: Boat ramp (23205 McKean Rd., San Jose) open seasonally, April 15 to October 14, and closed on Mon through Tues the rest of the year. Facilities: Porta-potties; $6 entrance fee, $6 launch fee, $7 mussel inspection.

Where to Eat and Where to Stay

No food, lodging, or camping available at the lake.

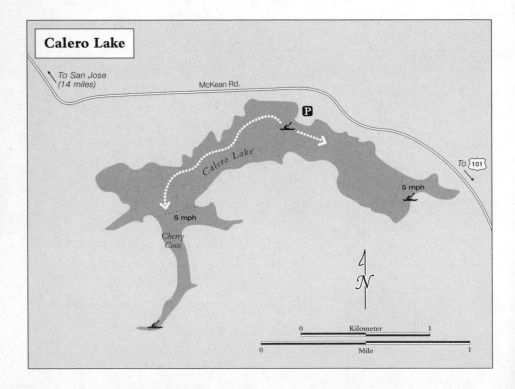

27F Anderson Lake

At 7 miles long, Anderson is the largest of the local lakes. Only 2 miles below its upstream neighbor on Coyote Creek, Anderson is a 2X version of Coyote Lake. It's also narrow, straight, framed by rolling, oak-clad hills, and busy with powerboats on summer weekends, but quiet the rest of the time with "environmental areas" on either end. The southern end where Coyote Creek enters the lake is especially good at higher, early-season water levels, when you can paddle a mile or more past the bridge on E. Dunne Avenue, but plan your return to the launch ramp before the wind kicks up. One bonus here is the chance to see the Tule elk herd that frequents the northeast shore, members of which are often heard bugling during the fall rut.

Trip rating:

Beginner: 14-mile round-trip; becomes intermediate in winds between 10 and 20 knots (and boat wakes 1 to 3 feet).

Navigation aids: Park map, info, and current hours of operation (sccgov.org/sites/parks/Maps%20Here/Pages/default.aspx).

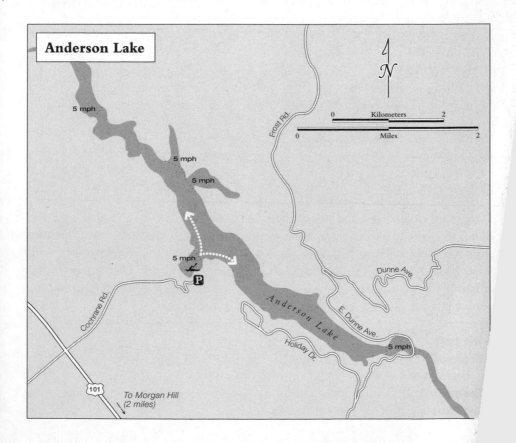

DON'T MOVE A MUSSEL!

First found in the Great Lakes in the late 1980s, quagga and zebra mussels have since spread west to bodies of water in Southern California. Not only do these tiny, Eurasian invasives clog water pipes, causing expensive damage to drinking-water systems and hydroelectric plants, they throw fresh-water habitats out of balance. By filtering out phytoplankton at the base of aquatic food webs with deadly efficiency, these rapidly reproducing pests quickly grow in clusters to inch-long adults and set off a cascade of problems that leads to heavier aquatic plant growth, lowered oxygen levels, and fish die-offs. The result is that infested waterways get closed to boating altogether. To help stop the spread, you should thoroughly dry your kayak (especially inside hatches) and equipment whenever you've paddled fresh water, since microscopic juveniles can survive up to five days out of water in hot weather and up to thirty days in cool, wet conditions. Feel your boat and gear for gritty spots that feel like sandpaper, which may be young mussels. To pass mussel inspections at lakes, all your gear needs to be totally dry and clean. If anything is damp or gritty, your boat could be quarantined and you could be fined for transporting mussels, even if unknowingly. For more information see the Fish and Game website (dfg.ca.gov/invasives/quaggamussel).

Launch site: Boat ramp (19245 Malaguerra Ave., Morgan Hill) open seasonally, April 15 to October 14, and closed on Wed and Thurs the rest of the year. Facilities: Toilets, water; $6 entrance fee, $6 launch fee, $7 mussel inspection.

Where to Eat and Where to Stay

No food, lodging, or camping available at the lake

G Coyote Lake

ee miles long, narrow and straight, Coyote Lake is surrounded by oak-covered hills. ough busy with powerboats on summer weekends, there are 5 mph "environmental on either end, and it is one of only two lakes with a campground. When water are high, the Coyote Creek area on the south end is nicest, its cattail marsh full life. On windy days, however, the north end might be a better choice, with the st wind at your back on your return to the launch site.

ng:

6-mile round-trip; intermediate in winds from 10 to 20 knots (and akes 1 to 3 feet).

aids: Park map, info, and current hours of operation (sccgov.org/sites/ ps%20Here/Pages/default.aspx).

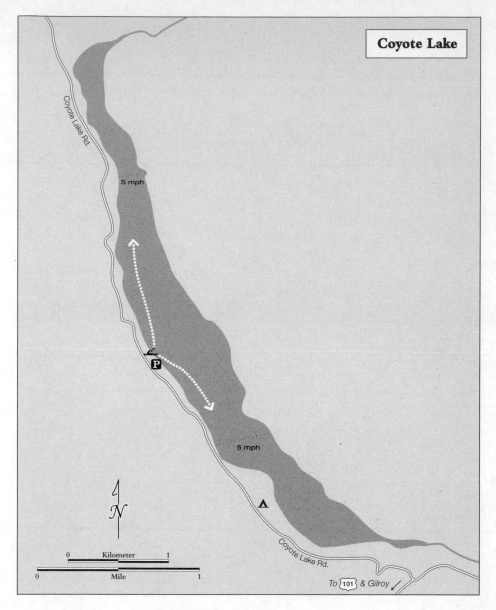

Launch site: Boat ramp (10840 Coyote Lake Rd., Gilroy) open seasonally, April 15 to October 14. Facilities: Toilets, water; $6 entrance fee, $6 launch fee, $7 mussel inspection.

Where to Eat and Where to Stay

No food or lodging available at the lake.

Camping: Campsites on the south end of the lake can be reserved (gooutsideandplay .org; 408-355-2201).

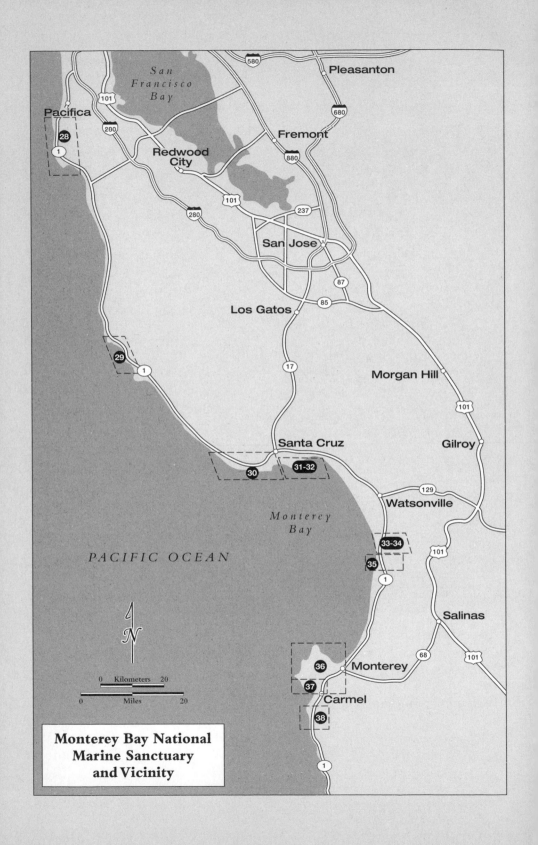

Monterey Bay National Marine Sanctuary and Vicinity

Monterey Bay National Marine Sanctuary and Vicinity

Route 28
Pillar Point Harbor and Devil's Slide

Set against a backdrop of coastal mountains and the Pillar Point headlands, this picturesque harbor makes an excellent destination for beginners and experts alike. Within the protection of the breakwater is a 3-mile loop tour with several sandy beaches good for fine tuning basic skills and practicing rescues. Beyond the harbor intermediates can access a semisheltered beach for surf zone practice, while advanced paddlers are within 1 mile of some of the better surfing and rock garden paddling on one of the more-challenging coastlines in California. This is the Tsunami Rangers' backyard, and several segments from their videos were filmed nearby. Outside the harbor is also the realm of Mavericks surf break, in winter one of the biggest waves in the Pacific. The harbor is also the end point for one of the area's classic advanced coastal day trips: the 10-mile, one-way stretch below the towering cliffs of the infamous Devil's Slide.

Trip highlights: Good flat-water touring and excellent access to surfing and open coast.

Trip rating:

Beginner: 1- to 3-mile flat-water loop around harbor in winds 10 to 15 knots.

Intermediate: 3-mile round-trip for surf zone practice in waves to 3 feet, winds below 15 knots.

Advanced: 2 to 10+ miles of exposed coast, rock gardens, and surfing.

Trip duration: Part to full day.

Kayak rentals: California Canoe and Kayak (calkayak.com; 510-893-7833) and Half Moon Bay Kayak Co. (hmbkayak.com; 650-773-6101) both offer a wide range of single and double touring kayaks and sit-on-tops.

Navigation aids: USGS Montara Mountain and Half Moon Bay (7.5 minute) and NOAA chart 18682 (charts.noaa.gov/OnLineViewer/18682.shtml).

Weather information: NWS zone forecast: "Coastal Waters from Point Reyes to Pigeon Point" (forecast.weather.gov/MapClick.php?zoneid=PZZ545); buoys: Half Moon Bay.

Tidal information: Little effect in the harbor except more beach for landing at lower tide. On the coast, more beaches and offshore rocks exposed at lower tide, and generally better surfing conditions.

Cautions: Boat traffic in harbor; wind blowing out toward harbor mouth can make return difficult. Standard coastal hazards beyond the harbor: sneaker waves, submerged rocks, and fog. Be aware that paddling too close to the rocks off Pillar Point has cost one paddler his life.

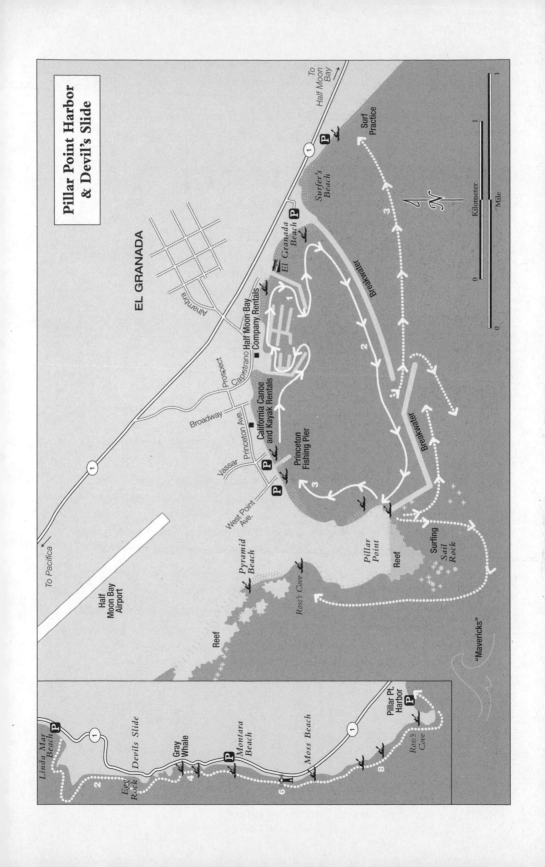

Pillar Point Harbor & Devil's Slide

EL GRANADA

To Half Moon Bay

Surf Practice

Surfer's Beach

El Granada Beach

Breakwater

Capistrano Half Moon Bay Company Rentals

California Canoe and Kayak Rentals

Alhambra

Prospect

Broadway

Vassar

Princeton Ave.

West Point Ave.

Princeton Fishing Pier

Breakwater

Surfing

Sail Rock

Reef

Pillar Point

Reef

Pyramid Beach

Ross's Cove

Half Moon Bay Airport

To Pacifica

"Mavericks"

N

Kilometer

Mile

Linda Mar Beach

Devils Slide

Egg Rock

Gray Whale

Montara Beach

Moss Beach

Pillar Pt. Harbor

Ross's Cove

Trip planning: Calmest paddling usually in the mornings although it can be very foggy. If heading south toward Surfer's Beach to surf, save some energy for the return against the wind.

Launch site: The beach in front of the yacht club (214 Princeton Ave., Half Moon Bay) is one of several launch options. From Highway 1 in El Granada (4 miles north of Half Moon Bay) turn west on Capistrano Road into Pillar Point Harbor. Either take the first left toward Johnson Pier (to launch off the beach at HMB Kayak Co., or the boat ramp another 0.2 mile farther) or continue for 0.5 mile to turn left at Prospect Way, left again on Broadway, and right onto Princeton Avenue; follow Princeton for two blocks and turn left on Vassar Avenue into the dirt lot beside the yacht club (or one block farther at the end of West Point Avenue). Facilities: None, but may be able to use bathrooms and water at California Canoe and Kayak shop. Parking free.

Alternate launch sites: On Highway 1 near Surfer's Beach.

Miles and Directions

0.0 Head left from the beach (N37 30.16 W122 29.45), contouring along the shore toward the marina jetty. Side trips: Head out the harbor toward Surfer's Beach or portage the sandspit at Pillar Point (see below).

0.5 At entrance to inner harbor/marina, follow jetty around to left for a 0.5-mile loop behind the boat docks, underneath the gangplanks, and out the other side. Caution: Watch for traffic, ceding right of way to larger vessels in the narrow channels.

1.5 Beyond the boat launch at the far side of the harbor is El Granada Beach, a good rest stop with restrooms. Caution: There is boat traffic in front of launch ramp. If the wind has come up, this is a good place to turn around and retrace your route, using the inner harbor jetties as windbreaks; if you continue along the jetty to the main harbor entrance, returning to the beach against winds above 10 or 15 knots can be difficult.

2.25 Harbor mouth. Caution: Boat traffic; wind exposure.

2.75 The shallow, sandy beach against the cliffs at Pillar Point has the best protection from northwest winds in the harbor, making it a good place to practice skills and a prime lunch spot. Cross the sandspit at the end of the jetty for views of the reef in front of Mavericks and the wild, open sea beyond. Side trips: Experienced paddlers can portage the sandspit for access to the open coast (see "Other options" below).

3.25 Return to launch beach.

The author carving some early morning glass on Pillar Point Harbor **SANDY RINTOUL-SCHUMANN**

Other options: Intermediates can paddle out harbor mouth 1.5 miles for surf zone practice just south of Surfer's Beach where the bluffs start. (Parking/launching available here for those who just want to surf.) Caution: Stay well away from swimmers and surfers at Surfer's Beach, but don't go too far south: The beach gets steeper and rougher farther down. For beginners and intermediates we don't recommend practicing here in waves above 3 feet or at high tide. Scout the waves from shore first; don't just paddle out of the harbor and assume you can land safely. A second calm day option for intermediates with previous coastal paddling experience or with an advanced paddler leading is to portage the sandspit at Pillar Point for a 1-mile tour along the outside of the breakwater and back in the harbor mouth. Caution: Stay close to the jetty, especially where it bends sharply to the left, to avoid the shallow reefy area beyond. Experienced surfers will find nice rights at Microwave/Mushroom Rock, a reef break just east of Sail Rock (the square, shed-sized rock near the end of the reef), or head up the coast 3 miles toward Fitzgerald Marine Reserve for excellent rock-garden paddling. Landings are possible (but not always easy) at Ross's Cove and Pyramid Beach.

Bill Vonnegut waiting for a wave below Devil's Slide CASS KALINSKI

Devil's Slide: A more ambitious option is the 10-mile run down from Pacifica State Beach past Devil's Slide. Caution: Advanced skills are required for this trip. Landings along this dramatic, cliffy coast are few, often difficult, and exposed (especially at Gray Whale Cove, which is "clothing optional," and subject to an entrance fee whether you enter by land or sea). North of Gray Whale is pure cliffs to Pacifica, but a small beach just south may be an option, as is Montara Beach (but it's often crowded with board surfers, and the beach break can be vicious). Farther south are cliffs again for several miles, except for a couple small, north-facing coves around Moss Beach, along with a couple possibilities in the last mile before Ross's Cove, just north of Pillar Point. The area around Egg Rock is now a Special Closure zone, so stay 300 feet to seaward and don't pass between the rock and shore.

Where to Eat and Where to Stay

Restaurants: Several seafood choices in the harbor, but Barbara's Fish Trap (650-728-7049) has a take-out window, convenient for sandy kayakers; Half Moon Bay Brewing Co. (hmbbrewingco.com; 650-728-2739) serves great microbrews and upscale pub fare; Cafe Classique (cafeclassique.com; 650-726-9775), a local hangout straight across Highway 1, serves gourmet sandwiches, bakery treats, and coffee drinks. **Lodging:** Point Montara Lighthouse Hostel (norcalhostels.org/montara; 650-728-7177) has inexpensive lodgings in a converted lighthouse. For fancier digs try Pillar Point Inn (650-728-7377) on the waterfront in the harbor. **Camping:** Beachfront camping is available at Half Moon Bay State Beach (reserveamerica.com; 800-444-7275).

Route 29
Pigeon Point to Franklin Point Rock Gardens

At first glance there is little to set this 5-mile stretch apart from the other 60 miles of wild open coast between Santa Cruz and San Francisco. Cliffy and scenic, it makes a fine coastal tour, but that's nothing unique here. That two of the area's prominent points were named after ships wrecked on them—the *Carrier Pigeon* and the *Sir John Franklin*—gives a clue. Since the first Spanish mariners, this jagged piece of coast has had a reputation for destruction. But on calm days, the same offshore rocks and low reefs that played such havoc with early navigators form a playground for skilled rough-water paddlers. In the last mile below Franklin Point, a patchy barrier reef paralleling the coast forms a maze of chutes, surge channels, and pourovers, much of it fairly protected and accessible. Other parts require the same precise maneuvering and judgment of kayaking as whitewater rivers do—producing the same level of thrills mixed with the same level of danger. And then, of course, there are the sharks (see Paddling the Red Triangle). Rugged and remote, this rock garden play spot is not everyone's cup of sea, but accomplished paddlers with an adrenaline habit will find it addicting.

Trip highlights: Excellent rock garden play spot, seabirds, solitude, and scenery.
Trip rating:
> *Intermediate:* 1 to 6 miles one-way or round-trip, recommended only for those with previous open-coast experience and only in the company of an experienced paddler, during mid- to lower tides when swells are below 3 to 4 feet and winds below 15 knots.
> *Advanced:* 6 miles one-way of open coast with excellent rock garden play in swells to 6 feet; not recommended above 8 feet when waves wash over protective outer reefs.

Trip duration: Part to full day.
Navigation aids: USGS Pigeon Point and Franklin Point (7.5 minute).
Weather information: NWS zone forecast: "Coastal Waters from Point Reyes to Pigeon Point" (forecast.weather.gov/MapClick.php?zoneid=PZZ545) and "Pigeon Point to Point Piños" (forecast.weather.gov/MapClick.php?zoneid =PZZ560); buoys: Half Moon Bay.
Tidal information: In general the lower the tide, the more protection the reef gives around Franklin Point, although some of the shallower channels may become inaccessible.

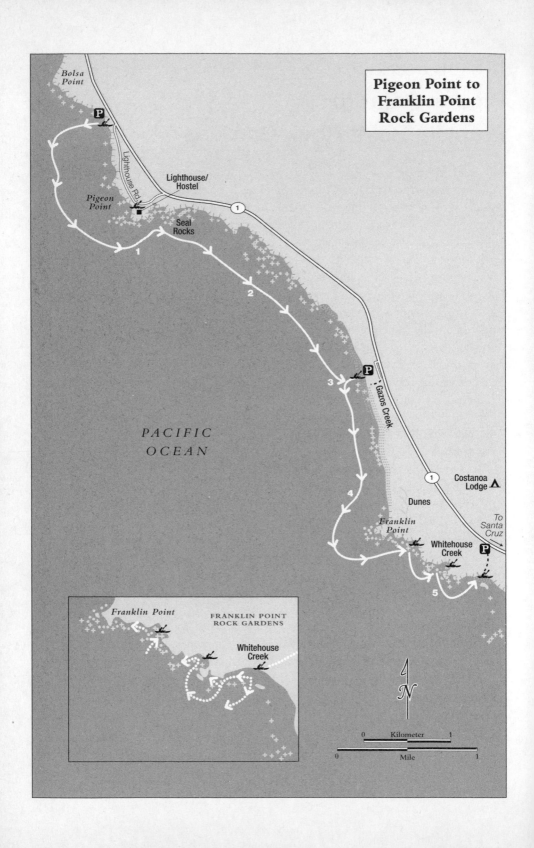

**Pigeon Point to
Franklin Point
Rock Gardens**

Bolsa
Point

P

Lighthouse Rd

Lighthouse/
Hostel

1

Pigeon
Point

Seal
Rocks

1

2

3

P

Gazos Creek

PACIFIC
OCEAN

4

1

Costanoa
Lodge △

Dunes

Franklin
Point

Whitehouse
Creek

P

To
Santa
Cruz

5

Franklin Point

FRANKLIN POINT
ROCK GARDENS

Whitehouse
Creek

N

Kilometer
0   1
Mile
0   1

Cautions: Fog so thick you can't see shore from beyond the surf zone, strong wind, waves, and submerged rocks. You must pick your day, especially if planning to play in rock gardens. A solid combat roll is highly recommended here for two reasons: first, in tighter rock gardens, other forms of capsize recovery may be impossible; second, the area is barely 2 miles from the elephant seal rookery at Año Nuevo where many great white sharks have been identified and tagged, so it's not the best place to be out of your boat. As for elephant seals, while uncommon, I was once confronted at Whitehouse by a 14-foot, one-ton, territorial male, forcing me to land elsewhere.

Trip planning: For a first visit, smaller swell and lower tide offer more protection for exploration behind the reefs. For a thrill the best conditions are a 4- to 6-foot swell with a longish swell period (12 to 14 seconds or so) and a 3- to 4-foot tide height, allowing waves to wash over and through slots in the reefs. This forms the best runs through surge channels and pourovers (if not sure what these terms mean, go with someone who does). Scout Whitehouse Creek by foot first to check landing conditions, to help recognize the beach from seaward, and to pick a line through the rocks. Run a shuttle for a north-south trip and save energy for the 0.25-mile carry, or launch and land at the south end. For rock garden park-and-play, we often launch from Whitehouse and spend the entire day playing in the lee of Franklin Point.

Tony Johnson prepares for splashdown, Franklin Point. CASS KALINSKII

Launch site: The sandy beach in the lee of Bolsa Point (Pigeon Point Road, Pescadero), is just off Highway 1, 0.75 mile north of Pigeon Point Lighthouse below the dirt pullout where the lighthouse road rejoins the highway. Facilities/fees: None.

Alternate launch sites: Gazos Creek State Beach, 2 miles south of the lighthouse, is okay on calm days, but it's exposed to surf and has rocks in the surf zone, so it can be a challenging place to launch. Facilities: Porta-potties; no fee. Whitehouse Creek is a small, unsigned dirt pullout at a state park trailhead 1.5 mile south of Gazos. Look for a small cluster of roadside mailboxes and state park trailhead signs directly across the highway from Whitehouse Canyon Road (unsigned dirt road). Facilities/fees: None. Aerial photo:

PADDLING THE RED TRIANGLE: WHITE SHARK FACT AND FICTION

Nothing puts the *wild* in wilderness, it's been said, like the presence of some large and fangy alpha predator. Alaska has its grizzlies, the Serengeti its lions, and our coast its great white sharks. But what are the actual risks to kayakers? True, the area between the elephant seal rookeries at Año Nuevo, the Farallon Islands, and Point Reyes is known as the Red Triangle, an area of ocean that's reputed to have had more shark attacks on humans than any other on earth. However it's not necessarily a shark breeding ground, as locals often proclaim. Truth is, shark scientists don't know where whites go to breed. Anyway it's not breeding that presents a problem but rather feeding, so an understanding of sharks' hunting behavior is probably your best defense. Elephant seals are the sharks' favorite prey, so they like to hunt around seal colonies. Sharks generally attack from below with one lightning-like strike, then back off and wait for the seal to bleed to death. This hit-and-run technique protects them from injury, as shark researchers, who photo ID the animals, have noted teeth marks on some sharks where seals have bitten back with their bear-sized canines. The movie *Jaws* aside, white sharks are not "eating machines" (one seal may last a shark days or even weeks), nor are they "man-eaters." Of the millions of people who take to our waters each year, very few end up on the menu. On average fewer than two or three divers or surfers annually get attacked along the entire

Franklin Point looking south into the rock gardens (californiacoastline.org, image 200907259).

Miles and Directions

0.0 From the beach at Bolsa Point (N37 11.55 W122 23.90), head south along the bluffs toward the lighthouse. Caution: Numerous offshore boomers along this stretch. The safest route is well out beyond them.

1.0 Just south of Pigeon Point Lighthouse, seas should get calmer. Caution: Confused seas, submerged rocks, and reefs extend well out to sea off the point. In the lee of the point, stay well right of the sea stacks and the seals hauled out on them.

California coast, and they usually survive to tell the tale when the shark, perhaps expecting tasty blubber instead of neoprene, doesn't return to finish the meal. Mistaken identity is the likely culprit; shark eyes (lacking cones for color vision) probably distinguish little more than seal-shaped silhouettes, so forget anything you may have heard about their attraction to "yum-yum yellow." So far, knock on wood, no full-length touring kayaks have been hit (although one was seriously "mouthed" for several very long seconds recently by a 15-footer near Santa Barbara); perhaps from below they appear to be skinny but full-grown bull elephant seals—no easy meal. In recent years, however, attacks on paddlers fishing from sit-on-tops are becoming an annual event; although no one has been injured (short of fouling their pants), several have been blasted violently off their boats. Generally these have been short, plump kayaks (in the 8- to 12-foot range with distinctly seal-shaped silhouettes) whose unwitting owners were floating immobile off by themselves for long periods near seal colonies, perhaps trailing fish blood into the water. Apparently this is a good way to lure sharks, who may target solo seals sleeping at the surface (so be mindful of what you might be using as bait). Statistically, your chances of getting struck by lightning are more than a hundred times better than becoming shark bait; however, you do increase your odds by climbing around on the lightning rod in a thunderstorm. To lower your risks, stay away from seal colonies, keep it moving, and paddle with partners, especially those in shorter boats (sometimes referred to as "chum boats"), and by far the most dangerous part of your paddling day will be the drive home in traffic.

3.0   Gazos Creek (N37 09.89 W122 21.77) gives access to a 1-mile-long stretch of sandy beach punctuated by dumping surf and the occasional submerged rock.

4.0   Sandy beach gives way to the jagged black rock of Franklin Point. Caution: Stay well outside the point and watch for boomers. As protection increases and conditions grow calmer in the lee, the best rock gardens begin.

4.5   A narrow, rocky channel leads into a calm cove with protected rock gardens and a sandy, private beach (N37 08.89 W122 21.31) for a rest break.

5.0   Another more protected cove (N37 08.79 W122 21.10) for landing on your own private beach.

5.5   Take out at mouth of Whitehouse Creek (N37 08.74 W122 20.80) on small, sandy beach behind a bus-sized rock in the surf zone; some great kayak surfing is available off the reefs to the south, but the entire area is scattered with submerged rocks, so be extra careful landing or surfing.

Where to Eat and Where to Stay

Restaurants: Cascade Bar and Grill (costanoa.com/cascade-bar-and-grill.html) across the highway is much fancier than its name might imply. Twenty miles south, local favorite Whale City Bakery Bar and Grill (831-423-9803) features coffee drinks and bakery treats. **Lodging:** Costanoa Lodge offers a variety of upscale-rustic lodging (costanoa.com; 877-262-7848). Pigeon Point Lighthouse Hostel (norcalhostels.org/pigeon; 650-879-0633) is more basic but features what *Budget Travel* magazine called "the most spectacular hot tub on earth." **Camping:** Camp among the redwoods at Butano State Park (reserveamerica .com; 800-444-7275), or at the Costanoa KOA (koa.com/campgrounds/santa-cruz-north; 650-879-7302). (Also see Route 30.)

Route 30

Santa Cruz Harbor to Three-Mile Beach and Davenport Down

Point Santa Cruz, better known locally as Lighthouse Point, forms the northern boundary of Monterey Bay and creates a wide arc of semisheltered water for kayakers. Aspiring intermediates will find some protection from prevailing wind and seas most days, making this area an excellent choice for first trips onto open water. Sea lions, seals, and otters frequent these waters, along with many of the area's best board surfers, who are drawn to the world-famous waves that curl around the point. For experienced paddlers, exposure increases rapidly as you paddle northward toward Natural Bridges State Beach. Beyond it lie some of the sanctuary's wilder shores, including the challenging and remote 11-mile roadless stretch from Davenport down to Natural Bridges.

Trip highlights: Relatively protected ocean paddling, marine mammals, and seabirds, including nearby access to remote and challenging coastal touring.

Trip rating:

Beginner: 1- to 4-mile round-trip, either staying inside harbor (1.5 miles), or, on calm days, adventurous beginners with open-water rescue skills (and ideally an intermediate in the lead) may find suitable conditions as far as Lighthouse Point or the kelp beds off Black Point (to the east), both about 4 miles round-trip.

Intermediate: 3 to 6 miles round-trip to Lighthouse Point with a surf landing on Cowell Beach, which is generally protected enough in swells to 4 feet and winds to 15 knots; or if these conditions hold beyond the point, you might continue to the beach at Mitchell Cove.

Advanced: 5 to 16 miles round-trip (or 15 miles one-way from Davenport Landing to the harbor) of remote, exposed cliffs to Natural Bridges and beyond to Four-Mile Beach, with rock gardens, surf breaks, and even a cave or two.

Trip duration: Part to full day.

Kayak rentals: Venture Quest (kayaksantacruz.com; 831-425-8445) on the Santa Cruz Wharf and Kayak Connection (kayakconnection.com; 831-479-1121) in the harbor both rent sit-on-tops and sit-inside kayaks.

Navigation aids: USGS Santa Cruz (7.5 minute) and NOAA chart 18685 (charts .noaa.gov/OnLineViewer/18685.shtml).

Weather information: NWS zone forecast: "Monterey Bay" (forecast.weather.gov/ MapClick.php?zoneid=PZZ535); buoys: Monterey Bay. Web cams: Looking

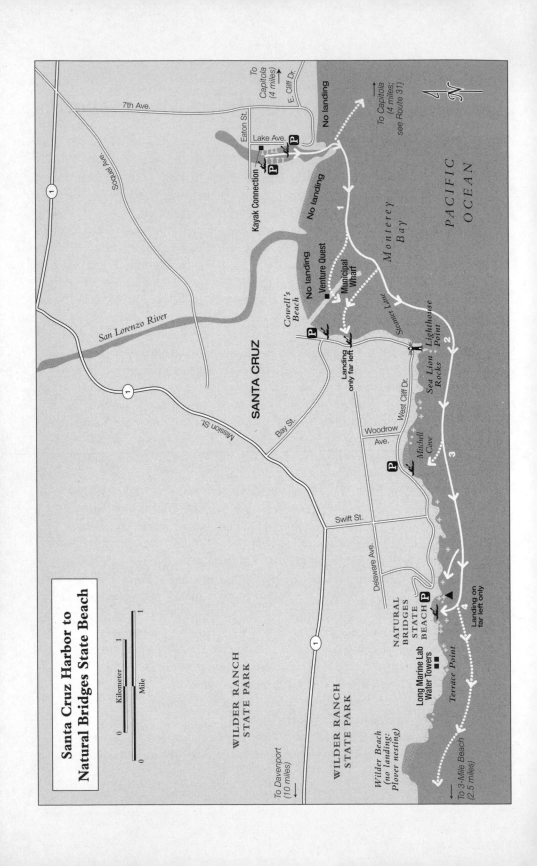

Santa Cruz Harbor to
Natural Bridges State Beach

out the Santa Cruz Harbor entrance (santacruzharbor.org/harborCams/harborEntrance.html) and at Lighthouse Point (santacruzharbor.org/harborCams/lightHousePoint.html).

Tidal information: Little effect beyond some light currents inside the harbor during large tidal changes; some low-tide beaches beyond Natural Bridges may not be above water during extreme highs.

Cautions: Tricky harbor entrance: Narrow mouth with "blind spot" behind jetty makes approaching boat traffic difficult to see; waves break in mouth during certain conditions. There are occasional offshore winds, fog, and sneaker waves. Landing is prohibited except on the west end of Cowell Beach, Mitchell Cove, and the north end of Natural Bridges (although beach lifeguards sometimes prohibit this when the beach is crowded).

Trip planning: Scout harbor mouth from shore before launching to assess sea conditions. Less wind generally makes mornings safer, assuming it's not too foggy to see. Links: Santa Cruz Harbor info for launch ramps, restaurants, web cams, weather, etc. (santacruzharbor.org).

Launch site: The small-boat launch dock (at the end of Mariner Park Way, Santa Cruz) near the Murray Street Bridge is a popular spot to launch kayaks (and other small craft). Facilities: Restrooms and water near the bridge; the harbor now charges $10/vehicle to launch/park. Aerial photo: Beaches at mouth of harbor launch site (californiacoastline.org, image 201009184).

Alternate launch sites: Santa Cruz Harbor boat ramp (2218 E. Cliff Dr., Santa Cruz) gives you the option to launch from the ramp or off dock. Facilities: Restrooms and water. Parking/launch fee, $10 per vehicle. Natural Bridges State Beach (West Cliff Drive and Swanton Boulevard, Santa Cruz) is a surf launch that lifeguards may not allow if the beach is busy. Facilities: Restrooms, water, cold showers; $10 day use. Davenport Landing (252 Davenport Landing Rd., Davenport), 1.5 miles north of Davenport off Highway 1. Facilities: Vault toilets. Fees: None.

Miles and Directions

0.0   From the launch dock (N36 58.04 W122 00.21), follow the boat channel toward the harbor mouth. Caution: Boat traffic—stay well to the right and out of the way.

0.5   At the harbor mouth, swing wide around the west jetty and head right along the beach. Caution: Watch for fast-moving boat traffic and waves breaking in the harbor mouth, and stay well clear of waves breaking on the jetty. After leaving the harbor, paddle outside the buoys marking the swimming area; no landings permitted until you are beyond the swim buoys on Cowell's Beach on the north side of the wharf. Side trip: Head left from the harbor 0.5 mile to look for otters in the kelp beds off Black Point, or round Pleasure Point to Capitola (see Route 31).

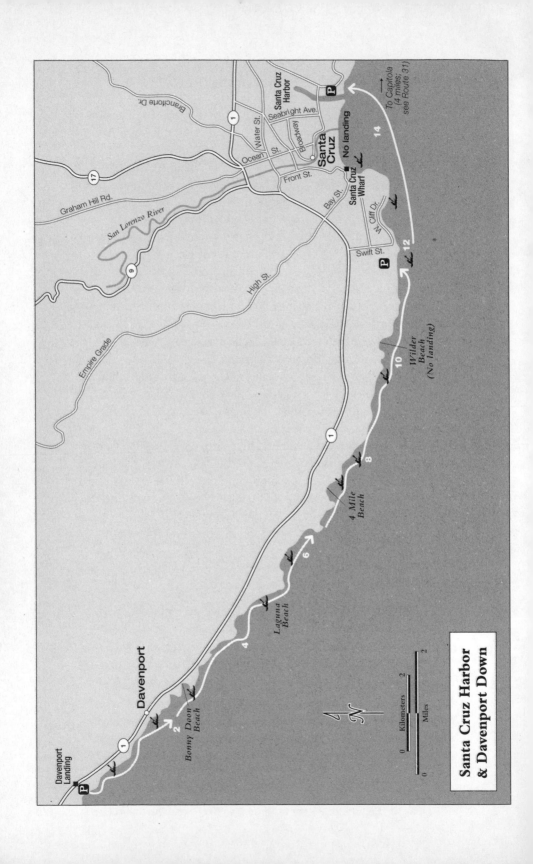

Santa Cruz Harbor & Davenport Down

Harbor Mouth on a calm morning, Santa Cruz **R. SCHUMANN**

1.4   Skirt the end of the Municipal Wharf, looking for sea lions on the pilings, but keep your distance from them and fishing lines. Caution: Boats prohibited within 50 yards of wharf (except at the signed kayak-crossing area at the Venture Quest rental dock toward the shoreward end). Side trip: Assuming the surf is small, and you have a helmet and some surf zone training, landing is allowed on the far left of Cowells Beach west of the swim area buoys.

1.5   Look for otters and sea lions along the kelp beds or watch the surfers at world-renowned Steamer Lane. Caution: Keep your distance from the cliffs: Territorial board surfers have been known to hurl insults, and sneaker waves have washed several kayaks into the cliffs. Side trip: Paddle out to the sea lion rocks off Lighthouse Point.

3.0   There is a fairly protected landing at Mitchell Cove (N36 57.16 W122 02.45). Side trip: Advanced paddlers with bomber rolls might try the rock gardens east of the cove, but be careful not to flush any seabirds or seals.

SOOTY SHEARWATERS

I'm a half-mile offshore about to practice open-water rescues with my surf zone class when we first see the birds. Skimming low across the water, first hundreds—then thousands upon thousands—of dark gray birds looking like chubby seagulls engulf us like a swarm of giant bees. Within moments the flock is so thick it blocks our view of others in our group. "Sooty shearwaters," calls out Steve, a friend who teaches birding classes, "among the most numerous birds on Earth." Shearwaters are a pelagic (open-ocean) species that spends most of its life at sea, except for a few months of our winter when they breed on land in the Southern Hemisphere. After that the birds head to sea, chasing summer and schools of fish across the North Pacific in flocks numbering into the tens or even hundreds of thousands. Deep water near shore, rich in prey, draws them into Monterey Bay, where they can sometimes be seen from the beach. Or from the seat of a kayak.

4.0   Natural Bridges (N36 56.98 W122 03.56), the last beach in town, makes a good landing spot for those with strong surf zone skills, and a good alternate launch site for advanced trips up the rugged north coast. Caution: On busy weekends the lifeguards may not permit launching or landing.

5.2   Sandy and inviting, Wilder Beach is nonetheless closed to landings to protect nesting habitat for endangered snowy plovers. Landings on small pocket beaches along this stretch are sometimes possible but challenging. Caution: Only experienced coastal paddlers recommended north along the exposed and roadless cliffs beyond Natural Bridges. Landings are few and remote, and strong winds with rough seas are common.

7.5   The best landings can be found at Three-Mile Beach (N36 57.68 W122 06.78) or a mile farther on Four-Mile Beach, but both are fairly popular surf breaks, so expect surf landings.

Other options: Davenport Down, the extremely exposed 11-mile roadless stretch from Davenport Landing to Natural Bridges, makes an excellent one-way trip for advanced coastal kayakers. Speaking of exposure, en route camping is no longer possible at Red White and Blue Beach "Clothing Optional" campground, which has closed to the public, so this is best done as a day trip. From Davenport Landing, the first stretch of beaches 0.5 mile south around the point should give you a good idea of how difficult any landings will be that day on most of the beaches on the rest of the route. If you can land here, then landing should be possible on Davenport Beach (1.5 miles south), Bonny Doon Beach (2.5 miles south), and Laguna Beach (4.7 miles south), and possibly a handful of secluded pocket beaches in between. If these are too rough, your next possibility of a more-protected landing might be a pocket beach in the lee of Sand Hill Bluff at mile 5.5 (N36 58.66 W122 08.84), or at Four-Mile Beach (mile 7.5). After that, Natural Bridges is at mile 11.5, assuming the conditions (and lifeguards) will allow landing that day; it is as exposed as the beaches farther north. Otherwise continue to the harbor at mile 15.

Where to Eat and Where to Stay

Restaurants: Many options, including the Crow's Nest (crowsnest-santacruz.com; 831-476-4560), a lively bar and seafood restaurant with a killer ocean view, and local favorites Betty Burgers (bettyburgers.com; 831-475-5901), featuring a wide choice of burgers and hand-dipped shakes, and Seabright Brewery (seabrightbrewery.com; 831-426-2739), serving award-winning microbrews and upscale pub fare. **Lodging:** Santa Cruz is a beach town with countless hotels. Contact the chamber of commerce (santacruzchamber.org; 831-475-3713). **Camping:** RV travelers can use the RV parking lot in the upper harbor by calling the office at (831) 475-3279. New Brighton State Beach has attractive tent sites on the bluffs, and Seacliff Beach State Park offers beachfront camping for RVs (reserveamerica.com; 800-444-7275).

Tour group exploring the kelp beds off Lighthouse Point R. SCHUMANN

Route 31
Santa Cruz Harbor to the Cement Ship

This 12-mile round-trip is a good challenge for budding coastal paddlers looking to stretch themselves, with a little of everything thrown in. It has a tricky harbor entrance, a rounding of a major point including a 3-mile stretch with no landing sites, numerous shallow reefs that break well offshore, and a decent possibility that you'll be paddling into headwinds (or fog banks) on the return to the harbor. In good weather, the route is straightforward. It's complicated, however, by the distance and amount of exposure, which leave plenty of room for conditions to change for the worse. If the fog rolls in, for example, or the northwest afternoon winds come up early, return to the harbor can get suddenly difficult. But what make these risks reasonable are the good bailout options around Capitola if things turn nasty. The rewards are great, as well, with common sightings of otters, seals, sea lions, and seabirds, and a historically interesting turn-around point at the Cement Ship.

Trip highlights: Challenge with a good safety net, and lots of marine wildlife.
Trip rating:
Beginner: 1- to 4-mile round-trip either staying inside harbor or on calm days adventurous beginners with open-water rescue skills (and ideally an intermediate in the lead) may find suitable conditions as far as Black Point, or over toward the Santa Cruz Wharf (see Route 30). On very calm days, and with an experienced paddler leading, the one-way trip to Capitola might be possible.
Intermediate: 12-mile round-trip semi-exposed coastal tour is generally protected enough in swells to 4 to 6 feet and winds to 15 knots if fog is not too thick to see shore. It is wise to have surf-landing skills equal to the size of the day's waves in case you need to come ashore.
Advanced: 12-mile round-trip semi-exposed coastal tour begins to get challenging if it is too foggy to see shore, or in winds above 15 knots and swells to 8 feet or so, when surf breaks around Capitola will be going off!
Trip duration: Part to full day.
Kayak rentals: Venture Quest (kayaksantacruz.com; 831-425-8445) on the Santa Cruz Wharf and Kayak Connection (kayakconnection.com; 831-479-1121) in the harbor both rent sit-on-tops and sit-inside kayaks.
Navigation aids: USGS Santa Cruz (7.5 minute) and NOAA chart 18685 (charts .noaa.gov/OnLineViewer/18685.shtml).

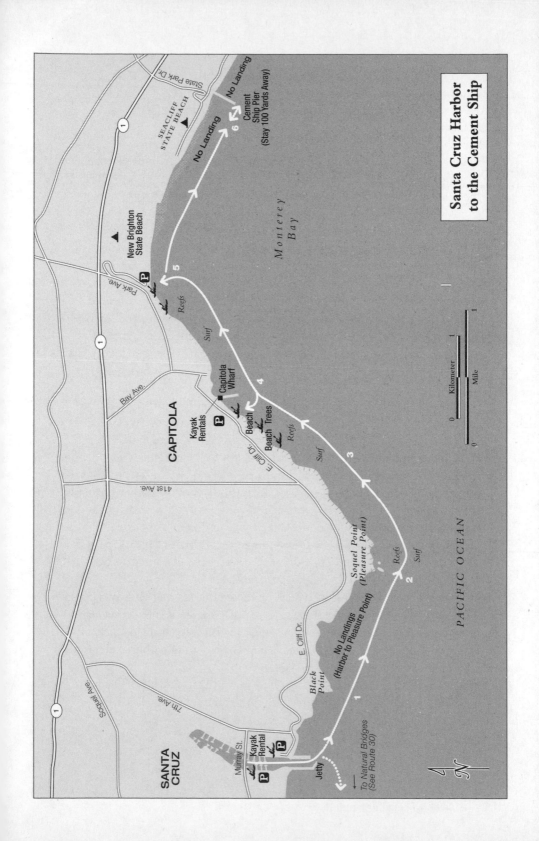

Santa Cruz Harbor to the Cement Ship

Monterey Bay

PACIFIC OCEAN

SANTA CRUZ

CAPITOLA

Kayak Rentals

Capitola Wharf

Beach

Beach Trees

New Brighton State Beach

SEACLIFF STATE BEACH

State Park Dr.

Cement Ship Pier
(Stay 100 Yards Away)

No Landing

No Landing

No Landings
(Harbor to Pleasure Point)

Soquel Point
(Pleasure Point)

Black Point

Jetty

Kayak Rental

To Natural Bridges
(See Route 30)

Reefs

Surf

Reefs

Surf

Surf

Reefs

Surf

Murray St.

7th Ave.

Soquel Ave.

41st Ave.

E. Cliff Dr.

E. Cliff Dr.

Bay Ave.

Park Ave.

Kilometer

Mile

1

2

3

4

5

6

Weather information: NWS zone forecast: "Monterey Bay" (forecast.weather.gov/MapClick.php?zoneid=PZZ535); buoys: Monterey Bay. Web cams: Looking out the Santa Cruz Harbor entrance (santacruzharbor.org/harborCams/harborEntrance.html) and at Capitola Beach (capitolabeach.net).

Tidal information: Little effect beyond some light currents inside the harbor during large tidal changes. Some low-tide beaches beyond between Pleasure Point and New Brighton may not be above water during extreme highs, and landings are generally more difficult on steep beaches along this stretch at high tide; at lower tides during larger swells, sneaker waves break far from shore inside the kelp beds.

Cautions: Tricky harbor entrance: Narrow mouth with "blind spot" behind jetty makes approaching boat traffic difficult to see; waves break in mouth during certain conditions. There are occasional offshore winds, fog, and sneaker waves that can break well offshore around Pleasure Point. Landing is prohibited from the harbor to Pleasure Point and is highly discouraged until you are past the surf break at Privates Cove due to the lack of beaches and numerous surf spots with sometimes territorial surfers. This stretch is generally too crowded with boardies for kayakers to be welcome (see Surfing Etiquette, page 194).

Trip planning: Scout harbor mouth from shore before launching to assess sea conditions. Less wind generally makes mornings safer, assuming it's not too foggy to see. Try to return before the afternoon wind picks up (typically between noon and 2 p.m.) or save energy to paddle the last 2 miles from Pleasure Point to the harbor against a 10- to 15-knot headwind. On days with questionable conditions for the return, run a one-way trip to New Brighton, or leave a vehicle in Capitola, just in case the return trip to the harbor gets nasty. If the wind has come up early, you can also run the trip in reverse, so you can return with the wind, although the launch sites at Capitola or New Brighton are not as simple as the harbor. Links: Santa Cruz Harbor (santacruzharbor.org) has info for launch ramp, restaurants, web cams, weather, etc.; New Brighton State Beach (parks.ca.gov/?page_id=542).

Launch sites: The small-boat launch dock (at the end of Mariner Park Way, Santa Cruz) near the Murray Street Bridge is a popular spot to launch kayaks (and other small craft). Facilities: Restrooms near the bridge. Parking/launch fee now costs $10/vehicle. Aerial photo: Beaches at mouth of harbor launch site (californiacoastline.org, image 201009184).

Alternate launch sites: Santa Cruz Harbor boat ramp (2218 E. Cliff Dr., Santa Cruz) gives you the option to launch from the ramp or off dock. Facilities: Restrooms and water. Parking/launch fee, $10 per vehicle.

The SS Palo Alto, *aka Cement Ship, off Seacliff State Beach* **R. SCHUMANN**

Miles and Directions

0.0　From the launch dock (N36 58.04 W122 00.21), follow the boat channel toward the harbor mouth. Caution: Boat traffic—stay well to the right and out of the way; however, it will probably be easier to cross to the left side of the boat channel after passing the last docks (a couple hundred yards before the entrance) where boat traffic is still moving slowly.

0.5　At the harbor mouth, swing wide left around the east jetty and head along the beach. Caution: Watch for fast-moving boat traffic and waves breaking in the harbor mouth, and stay well clear of waves breaking on the jetty. After leaving the harbor, paddle outside the buoys marking the swimming area; no landings permitted until you are beyond Pleasure Point.

1.0　Black Point at the end of the sand beach is a good turn-back point for the timid. Waves rebounding off the point can create choppy seas similar to what you should expect if you continue.

2.25   Soquel Point, better known locally as Pleasure Point, is the beginning of several miles of offshore reefs and surf breaks. Caution: Stay well to seaward of any surfers (and out of shouting range if you don't want to get shouted at). On days with big swell, waves can break several hundred yards from shore. Side trip: Experienced kayak surfers with reliable rolls might find a peak with no surfers, but often this area will be crowded if the waves are going off and kayak surfing here will not win you any friends.

3.75   The beach after the point at Trees surf spot (N36 58.04 W121 57.47) is the best one to land at in the area, although you might have a few options before that if there are no waves and no surfers. But Trees Beach is difficult to get to from land except during very low tides, so unlike other beaches, you are likely to have it all to yourself (which could be handy in case you were stopping to pee).

4.0   Capitola Wharf is an alternate launch site with restrooms. Landing is allowed either on the beach on the left side of the wharf or on the seasonal dinghy dock on the right side of the pier from May through October. (On summer weekends the Wharf House restaurant on the wharf serves alfresco lunches with live jazz on their sun deck.) Otherwise, paddle beyond casting range of any fishers on the wharf.

5.0   New Brighton Beach (N36 58.71 W121 56.33) allows landing (easiest on the far left side), but stay well clear of swimmers and waders and watch out for dumping shore break. This is another alternate launch site.

6.5   Cement Ship; no boats allowed within 100 yards, and no landing permitted along Seacliff Beach. Landing is allowed in front of the houses between New Brighton and Seacliff beaches.

Where to Eat and Where to Stay

Restaurants: Many options, including the Crow's Nest (crowsnest-santacruz.com; 831-476-4560), a lively bar and seafood restaurant with a killer ocean view, and local favorites Betty Burgers (bettyburgers.com; 831-475-5901), featuring a wide choice of burgers and hand-dipped shakes, and Seabright Brewery (seabrightbrewery.com; 831-426-2739), serving award-winning microbrews and upscale pub fare. **Lodging:** Santa Cruz is a beach town with countless hotels. Contact the chamber of commerce (santacruzchamber.org; 831-475-3713). **Camping:** RV travelers can use the RV parking lot in the upper harbor by calling the office at (831) 475-3279. New Brighton State Beach has attractive tent sites on the bluffs, and Seacliff Beach State Park offers beachfront camping for RVs (reserveamerica.com; 800-444-7275).

CEMENT SHIP

Built during World War I when steel was in short supply, the SS *Palo Alto*, better known as the "Cement Ship," never saw action. By the time the ship was finished, so was the war. Investors brought the ship to Seacliff in 1930, flooded the bilges so it would rest on the bottom, extended a pier out to meet the ship, and turned it into a high-class amusement center, complete with a ballroom, heated swimming pool, dining hall, and arcade. Operating successfully as *The Ship* for two summers, she faced a devastating blow in the winter of 1932 when storms cracked her hull, which would have required expensive repairs in a Depression-era economy. Stripped of anything valuable and left to the elements, the once grand ship lapsed into a simple fishing pier. Four years later the *Palo Alto* was sold to the state for one dollar, eventually to become part of the Seacliff Beach State Park. The pier remains a popular fishing spot, while the Cement Ship slowly deteriorates with the waves, fenced off to provide for the safety of the curious public, and serves as a haven for harbor seals and seabirds, especially the once-threatened brown pelicans.

Route 32

In the Lee of Pleasure Point: New Brighton to Capitola and Beyond

The most protected stretch of "open coast" on Monterey Bay, the lee of Soquel Point, better known locally as Pleasure Point, is a perfect place to gain ocean paddling experience, and it makes an excellent first coastal tour for those comfortable launching and landing through small surf or on days with no surf on the beach. In the kelp beds beyond the cliffs, sea otters and harbor seals are commonly seen, and occasionally bottlenose dolphin. Combined with a landing on the Capitola Wharf for brunch and live music on the sun deck, paddling here in the lee of Pleasure makes for a fine outing on a summer weekend. For experienced kayak surfers, the longboat surfing off several reef breaks is some of the best anywhere.

Trip highlights: Semiprotected coastal paddling, wildlife, scenery, and surfing.

Trip rating:

Beginner: 1 to 5 miles round-trip on calm days with small or no surf at the launch beach and less than 10 knots of wind.

Intermediate: 5+ miles round-trip to Pleasure Point requires open-water paddling skills and basic surf zone skills to negotiate the beaches. Not recommended if surf at New Brighton is above 2 to 3 feet, when dumping shorebreak can be difficult to dangerous.

Advanced: 10 miles round-trip to Santa Cruz harbor. Surfing at reef breaks along cliffs for those with bomber rolls, with clean shoulders in waves from 3 to 8 feet or more.

Trip duration: Part to full day.

Kayak rentals: Capitola Boat and Bait (capitolaboatandbait.com; 831-462-2208) rents sit-on-tops off the Capitola Wharf seasonally in the summer and fall.

Navigation aids: USGS Soquel (7.5 minute) and NOAA chart 18685 (charts.noaa .gov/OnLineViewer/18685.shtml).

Weather information: NWS zone forecast: "Monterey Bay" (forecast.weather.gov/ MapClick.php?zoneid=PZZ535); buoys: Monterey Bay. Web cam: Overlooking Capitola Beach (capitolabeach.net).

Tidal information: Tide heights less than 3 or 4 feet offer greater access to small beaches along cliffs.

Cautions: A dropping tide can create surf at the landing beach that wasn't there when you launched. No landings allowed on Capitola Beach on the east side of wharf. Be extremely careful of surf and rocks if attempting to land on

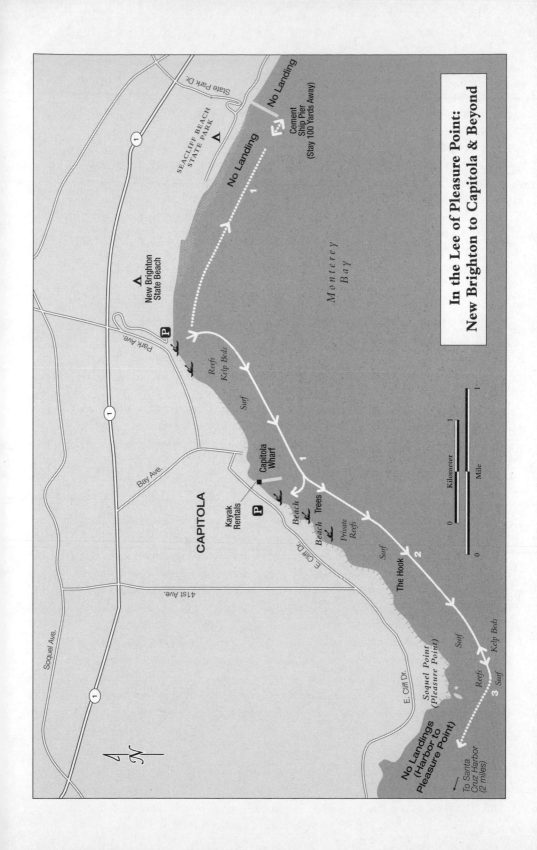

In the Lee of Pleasure Point:
New Brighton to Capitola & Beyond

No Landing

No Landing

Cement
Ship Pier
(Stay 100 Yards Away)

State Park Dr.

SEACLIFF BEACH
STATE PARK

1

New Brighton
State Beach

Monterey
Bay

Park Ave.

Reefs
Kelp Beds

Surf

Bay Ave.

Capitola
Wharf

1

CAPITOLA

Kayak
Rentals

Beach

Trees

Beach

Private
Reefs

E. Cliff Dr.

Surf

2

41st Ave.

The Hook

Soquel Ave.

Soquel Point
(Pleasure Point)

E. Cliff Dr.

Surf

Kelp Beds

Reefs

Surf

3 Surf

No Landings
(Harbor to
Pleasure Point)

To Santa
Cruz Harbor
(2 miles)

N

Kilometer

Mile

1

0

1

0

beaches at the base of cliffs. Localized afternoon winds sometimes blow from the east (up to 15 knots) against the usual northwest trend, causing choppy seas and making return to launch site a slog. Although generally quite calm and surfless, this whole area becomes a surfers' paradise when a big swell is running: Watch out for dumping waves on the beach, submerged rocks (boomers), and sneaker waves on shallow reefs far from shore, especially on falling tide, and especially, board surfers (see Surfing Etiquette on page 194).

Trip planning: Paddle early to beat wind, and, on busy summer weekends, to beat the beach crowds and find parking. A low tide will offer more landing beach options along the cliffs, and will also make boomers more numerous but easier to locate. Stay beyond the kelp to avoid sneaker waves on the reefs when a swell is running.

Launch site: New Brighton State Beach (on McGregor Drive at Park Avenue, Aptos) has a large parking lot on bluffs above the beach and is an excellent launch site despite the longish carry down the stairs or access road to beach. From Highway 1 on the south side of Santa Cruz, take the Park Avenue/New Brighton exit and follow signs toward beach. Take a left at first stop sign at Kennedy Street, then the first right into the park. Facilities: Restrooms up the trail to campsite, none in parking lot; day use fee $10. Aerial photo: New Brighton Beach launch site (californiacoastline.org, image 200810813).

Alternate launch site: Beach on west side of Capitola Wharf, but its parking is limited, especially on weekends. Offload your boat at the base of the wharf and find parking on the bluffs. Facilities: Porta-potty; parking meters, $1 per hour.

Miles and Directions

0.0 Launch from far right (west) side of New Brighton Beach (N36 58.71 W121 56.33), where the surf tends to be smaller, but stay well away from swimmers and rocks at the base of cliffs. Head west along sandstone cliffs, with the safest route being well out along the kelp beds where otters are common. Several low-tide beaches dot the cliffs from here to Pleasure Point. Caution: Stay well offshore; if there's a swell running, many shallow reefs cause intermittent waves to break up to several hundred yards from shore, making this a popular board-surfing area and a tricky place to land a kayak. Access to beaches can be deceptively difficult in all but the smallest swells. Side trips: Head east 1.5 miles to check out the Cement Ship (see Route 31), but don't approach within 100 yards or land on Seacliff Beach. Paddlers with strong surfing skills and reliable rolls may find good surf on reef breaks away from board surfers (see Surfing Etiquette on page 194).

Small waves lapping at the semi-protected launch site at New Brighton Beach **R. SCHUMANN**

1.0 You can land on the small beach on the far (west) side of Capitola Wharf (N36 58.25 W121 57.25), or use the seasonal dinghy dock on the pier from May through October. On summer weekends the Wharf House restaurant on the wharf serves alfresco lunches with live jazz on their sun deck. Caution: Landing on the west side beach can be dangerous in surf because waves tend to sweep into the pilings. Landings are prohibited on the main part of Capitola Beach east of the pier except during the off-season, when, if no swimmers are present, this rule is not enforced.

1.25 The first small, cliff-side beach (N36 58.04 W121 57.47), west of the pier at Trees surf spot, is generally easy to land on in small surf, and rarely has other people because they can only walk there at very low tides. The reef break off the point is a good entry-level surfing spot in waves to 3 feet provided there are no board surfers in the area and it isn't washing you directly into the cliffs, as it does in certain conditions. Otherwise there is generally a calm area in the reform zone between the reef break and shore where you can do a rescue if you swim. Beyond this point the reef extends out farther, so watch out for sneaker waves and surfers.

SURFING ETIQUETTE: SURVIVING SANTA CRUZ'S SOMETIMES SURLY SURF SCENE

When groups of surfers are out on the reefs, even if it looks totally calm, stay well clear of them—they're there for a reason. When big sets roll through, that calm sea can suddenly turn into walls of whitewater. If you are an experienced kayak surfer, stay on the *shoulder* (surfing *leftovers*) and out of the *line up,* and don't be a *kook* and *drop in* when anyone's paddling out *below* you. (If you are not sure what all the surf lingo in the last sentence meant, it might mean you shouldn't be in a kayak anywhere near board surfers.) Out-of-control kayakers in the surf are a major hazard. Please don't be one; you make it hard for the rest of us trying to get along in a tenuous relationship. While most boardies are laid-back and reasonable (and won't mind you hanging around if you show you can stay in control and out of the way, and don't steal all the waves), a few can be extremely territorial and intolerant of your presence (in some cases rightly so), and have been known to hurl insults and even fists. So if the vibe is "agro," brah, mo' better you go some udda' place, eh? If you want to be sure you are out of the surf zone, stay on the seaward side of the kelp forest.

1.5 The beach at Privates surf break (N36 57.89 W121 57.63) can be a bit steep and dumpy, but is not a bad place to land in small surf. Caution: The right side is an intermittent nude beach, if that sort of thing offends you.

2.0 This first obvious minor point is a popular surf spot, the Hook, at the end of 41st Avenue. Pleasure Point is the next point in the distance. Caution: Unless seas are calm and there are no surfers (or you are an experienced surfer), stay out beyond the kelp beds and avoid beach landings between here and Pleasure Point. This is an unofficial "no kayakers" zone when board surfers are numerous.

2.75 Pleasure Point makes a good turn-around spot because seas are typically much rougher on the windward side, and landing is prohibited between the point and Santa Cruz Harbor. Side trip: Experienced paddlers can continue another 2.0 miles to Santa Cruz Harbor for a lunch break and return with the wind, or run a shuttle for a one-way downwind trip to Capitola (see Route 31).

Where to Eat and Where to Stay

Restaurants: Wharf House Restaurant (wharfhouse.com; 831-476-3534) at the end of the Capitola Wharf serves fresh seafood and outstanding ocean views for an après paddle dinner or a mid-paddle lunch stop (to-go available for underdressed kayakers who can land on the dinghy dock); on summer weekends they feature live music and casual dining on their sun deck. Geisha Sushi (831-464-3328), just beyond the end of the esplanade, reopened (and deserves an award) as one of the few restaurants in the country featuring only "sustainable sushi"; so now you can eat sushi and actually feel good about it! The ever-popular local favorite, Pizza My Heart (pizzamyheart.com; 831-475-5714) sells by the slice from their walk-in counter for a quick, hearty snack for hungry kayakers. **Lodging:** Beach House Rentals (beach-houserentals.com; 800-330-2979) rents cottages and beach houses; of many hotels nearby, the closest is Capitola Venetian Inn (capitolavenetian.com; 831-476-6471) an all-suite, Mediterranean-style hotel right on the beach. **Camping:** New Brighton State Beach has attractive tent sites on the bluffs, and Seacliff Beach State Park offers beachfront camping for RVs (reserveamerica.com; 800-444-7275).

Route 33

Elkhorn Slough National Estuarine Research Reserve: Moss Landing to Kirby Park

Winding some 7 miles from the sea into rolling coastal hills, Elkhorn Slough is California's second-largest marine wetland after San Francisco Bay and one of only twenty-eight National Estuarine Research Reserves in the country. In addition to being one of the best places to view sea lions, seals, and sea otters from a kayak—numerous sightings are essentially guaranteed—the slough is renowned as one of the premier birding sites in the country. Its fertile mudflats and salt marshes support an incredible diversity of marine life, helping make it an essential feeding ground for birds traveling the Pacific Flyway (the major route for migratory birds along the West Coast). Because it provides a crucial link for these birds on their annual migrations between the Arctic and South America, the slough has been recognized as an Important Bird Area of International Significance. Until recently, in fact, Elkhorn Slough held the North American record for the most species of birds sighted in one place on one day, 116. In all, some 340 species reside in the area or migrate through during the year. The Moss Landing launch site, adjacent to the slough's opening to the sea, is more dynamic than the inland launch site at Kirby Park (see Route 34) having increased tidal flow and more boat traffic.

Trip highlights: World-class birding and excellent marine mammal viewing, kayak rentals.

Trip rating:

Beginner: 1 to 5 miles round-trip during tidal exchanges of less than 3 to 4 feet; experience reading tides recommended.

Intermediate: 5 to 9+ miles round-trip to Kirby Park with moderate tidal currents during large tide changes; surfing and coastal touring access on days with little wind and swells below 4 feet, but an advanced trip leader is recommended as the ocean can become rough quickly here.

Advanced: 9+ miles with access to surfing and open-coast side trips.

Trip duration: Part to full day.

Kayak rentals: This popular paddling spot has two rental shops: Monterey Bay Kayaks (montereybaykayaks.com; 800-649-5357), which also runs a shuttle service to Kirby Park, and Kayak Connection (kayakconnection.com; 831-724-5692).

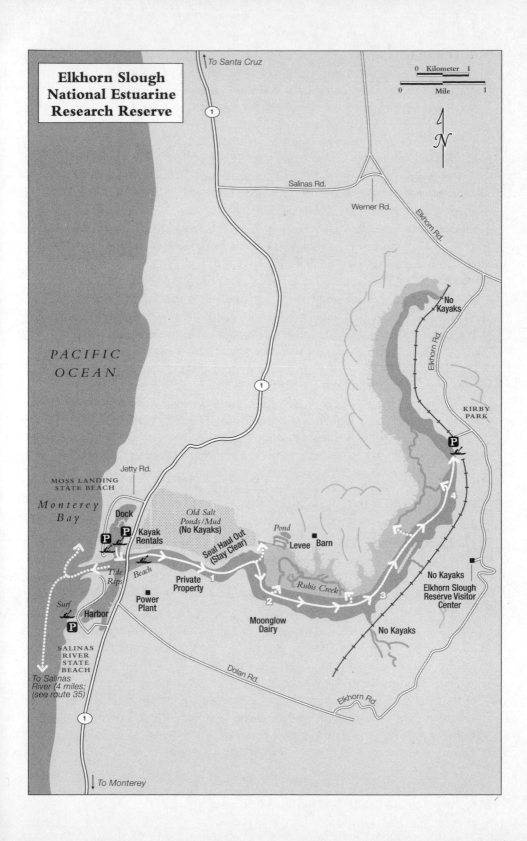

**Elkhorn Slough
National Estuarine
Research Reserve**

To Santa Cruz

1

0   Kilometer   1

0   Mile   1

N

Salinas Rd.

Werner Rd.

Elkhorn Rd.

No
Kayaks

1

KIRBY
PARK

Elkhorn Rd.

P

PACIFIC
OCEAN

Jetty Rd.

MOSS LANDING
STATE BEACH

*Monterey
Bay*

Dock

Old Salt
Ponds/Mud
(No Kayaks)

Pond

Levee   Barn

4

P
Kayak
Rentals

Seal Haul Out
(Stay Clear)

P   P

*Tide
Rips*

Beach

Private
Property

1

Rubis Creek

3

No Kayaks

Elkhorn Slough
Reserve Visitor
Center

2

Surf

Harbor

Power
Plant

Moonglow
Dairy

No Kayaks

P

SALINAS
RIVER
STATE
BEACH

*To Salinas
River (4 miles;
(see route 35)*

1

Dolan Rd.

Elkhorn Rd.

To Monterey

Navigation aids: Together with a local tide table, the *Elkhorn Slough Paddling Guide* is invaluable; this free map and informational flyer showing channels, mudflats, and closed areas is available online (for map only: elkhornslough.org/kayaking/kayak-map.htm) and at kayak shops near the launch site (for map with safety and natural history information), see "Kayak rentals" above, or from the Elkhorn Slough Foundation (elkhornslough.org; 831-728-5939); USGS Moss Landing (7.5 minute) and NOAA chart 18685 (charts.noaa.gov/OnLineViewer/18685.shtml) for coastal side trips.

Weather information: NWS zone forecast: "Monterey Bay" (forecast.weather.gov/MapClick.php?zoneid=PZZ535); buoys: Monterey Bay.

Tidal information: Mudflats make paddling outside the main channel difficult to impossible when tide heights drop below 2 feet; strong currents develop during tide changes over 3 or 4 feet.

Cautions: Tidal currents especially hazardous at the mouth of the slough during strong ebbs. Paddle and land only in designated areas so as not to disturb sensitive habitat; stay far enough away from marine mammals and birds not to change their behavior (minimum of 50 feet). Watch for boat traffic and fishing lines in the harbor area and the ubiquitous afternoon winds.

Trip planning: Use the currents. Days with a morning flood and afternoon ebb are best for heading into the slough from the mouth, but save some energy to fight the afternoon wind on your return. Note: Keeping close to the banks lessens the effects of contrary winds or currents. If exploring side channels, do so on a rising tide; beware of countless dead ends; try to follow the widest, deepest branch; and turn around before the branch gets narrower than the length of your boat, or you could have a lot of backing up to do. Also, avoid hitting the banks, which will cover your boat in sticky mud and cause erosion to sensitive habitat. If you want to ride the flood one way, all the way to Kirby Park, Monterey Bay Kayaks offers a shuttle service for $15 per person (see "Kayak rentals" above). Links: Elkhorn Slough Foundation (elkhornslough.org) for general natural history information; Moss Landing State Beach (parks.ca.gov/?page_id=574).

Launch sites: Moss Landing Boat Ramp (2390 Hwy. 1, Moss Landing) is on Highway 1, about 0.5 mile north of the bridge over the slough; turn toward the ocean at the sign for Moss Landing Boat Ramp, and launch from the dock or from the adjacent beach, which can be quite muddy at low tide. Stay to the left side of the beach to stay out of the way of the kayak shop's tours and rentals. Facilities: Restrooms and water. Pay parking/launching fees at the self-pay station on the side of the restroom. Aerial photo: Looking up slough from the launch site (californiacoastline.org, image 3200805448).

Alternate launch sites: Moss Landing State Beach across the water from the boat ramp is free, but the launch beach is a hundred-yard carry from the parking

Patty Andrews taking the channel less paddled, Elkhorn Slough R. SCHUMANN

lot. Park at the far end of the dirt lot at the end of the road and launch from the beach by the big black oil pipe (once used to fuel the power plant, which now runs on natural gas). Facilities: Porta-potties; no fee. Kirby Park, near the east end of the slough (on Kirby Road at Elkhorn Road in Elkhorn; see Route 34) is the launch site for a one-way trip. Salinas River State Beach is a popular kayak surfing spot; launch from the beach-access lot off Sandholdt Road where it crosses the lower harbor.

Miles and Directions

0.0 From the boat ramp (N36 48.77 W121 47.21), head toward the Highway 1 Bridge, avoiding the boat channel (marked by red and green buoys), and typically passing a group of one to two dozen sea otters resting or playing in the shallows in the small cove on your right. This group or "raft" of otters is a "bachelor group" of males, either too young or too old to hold their own feeding/breeding territories in the offshore kelp beds. Head east (left) into the slough, passing a dock covered with hundreds of barking California sea lions. Caution: Maintain a distance of at least 50 feet from both the otters and sea lions to avoid disturbing them. Also watch for boat traffic, fishing lines, and especially for strong currents under the bridge that can sweep you into pilings or even out to sea (if it's ebbing you might want to reconsider your trip plan). Side trips: Advanced paddlers will generally find challenging (sometimes hazardous) conditions out on Monterey Bay (see "Other options").

0.5   The sandy beach on right is private property above high tide, so according to state law any land below the tide line is technically held in the public trust, meaning that people are allowed to access it as long as they stay on the wet sand below the mean high tide line. Otherwise you are trespassing. Even if you stay below the line the owners may ask you to leave. All other places farther up the slough, except for the launch at Kirby Park, are part of the reserve and off-limits to landing to protect fragile habitat. Caution: All of the side channels along the north side until after Seal Bend are protected areas, so please don't paddle there. In the early summer, look for western gull (*Larus occidentalis*) nests and their cute, furry-looking chicks, lined up along the bank every 20 feet or so. These are the only gulls that nest in the slough. Keep your distance, however, as it is not uncommon for protective parents to dive-bomb paddlers who get too close. If they start cawing at you, back off. Their next step is to attack.

1.25   Seal Bend (N36 48.80 W121 46.22), the harbor seal haul out on the left bank (north) at the beginning of the big U bend, is the main birthing area in the slough and sensitive to disturbance, especially March through June, so keep at least 50 to 100 yards away. If seals raise their heads to look at you, you're getting too close. Look for another raft of otters, sometimes a dozen or more, in the small bay on the left beyond the seal haul out. This is a "nursery group" of mostly mothers and pups. Side trip: You can follow a channel into the pickleweed marsh in the back of the otter bay at high tide for another 0.5 mile or more. The channel mouth (N36 49.03 W121 45.90) can be difficult to spot from a distance and you'll need at least 2 to 3 feet of tide to avoid getting stuck in the muck. This makes a good turn-around spot for a short trip.

2.0   After rounding the big bend, the slough straightens out and passes Moonglow Dairy on the right (south) side just opposite the narrower of two openings to Rubis Creek (N36 48.85 W121 45.65). Side trip: Explore the twisting channels of Rubis here, or continue to the larger opening which is 0.5 mile farther on the left (north), where the oak-covered ridge comes closest to the slough.

2.7   A short way up the larger, eastern entrance to Rubis Creek (N36 49.00 W121 45.97) used to be a landing area, but is now closed, as Slough managers want to keep kayakers and kayaks from trampling the fragile mudflat. Note that the channel across the slough from Rubis on the south side is closed to kayaking beyond the railway bridge. Side trip: Explore 0.5 mile or so into the marsh at Rubis, or if the tide and your adventurous spirit are both running high, do a loop through the maze of twisting channels of Rubis Creek. To do this, follow Rubis's main channel until you get to the "deceptive left," a 90-degree bend (N36 49.04 W121 45.50) leading to a dead end. Take the smaller right channel straight ahead through a series of narrow S turns (where you'll be sure you are lost) until the channel widens again, bends to the left, and rejoins the slough across from the dairy.

3.5 Of the several tidal creek openings you can explore on your left, this one (N36 49.63 W121 44.72) near the north end of the midstream island offers the possibility of a through trip somewhere among its maze of multiple dead ends.

4.0 This large opening on the left is the exit to the previous maze as well as the entrance to another through-trip labyrinth that exits to the north of Kirby Park.

4.4 Kirby Park (N36 50.40 W121 44.60) launch ramp and dock, the only permitted landing site in the slough, has porta-potties, but no drinking water.

Other options: Advanced paddlers with strong surf zone skills can head north up the coast along the broad expanse of dunes for good views of Monterey Bay and surfing or head south about a mile to surf the point off Salinas River State Beach. Experienced paddlers sometimes run a shuttle for a 15- to 20-mile downwinder from Santa Cruz, Capitola, or New Brighton or from the Slough down to Monterey. Another option is to run a shuttle and paddle 5 miles south to the mouth of the Salinas River, portage across the sandbar to the lagoon (around N36 45.08 W121 48.27) about 0.25 to 0.5 mile north of the barge wreck, which makes an excellent landmark, then paddle 2 miles upriver to the Highway 1 bridge (see Route 35). Caution: Scout first. The mouth of Moss Landing Harbor can get quite rough, especially during an ebb when strong currents sweep seaward and waves can break inside the mouth along the south jetty. Submerged pilings extend off the north jetty. Before committing yourself to the downwind journey to the Salinas River, try a touch-and-go landing on the beach off the point at Salinas River State Beach, about a mile to the south; unless this is easy, don't expect to be able to handle the typically bigger surf you are likely to find at the mouth of the Salinas.

Where to Eat and Where to Stay

Restaurants: Sea Harvest Fish Market and Restaurant (831-633-8300) across the parking lot from the launch ramp serves fresh-caught seafood on their deck overlooking the slough, or clam chowder to go, if you're in a hurry. Whole Enchilada (wenchilada.com; 831-633-3038) serves California-style sit-down Mexican food, and Phil's Fish Market (philsfishmarket.com; 831-633-2152) across the bridge in the south harbor is a popular local spot to buy fresh fish to go, or stay and eat a good meal at a good price. **Lodging:** None nearby; try Santa Cruz or Monterey. **Camping:** Sunset Beach State Park, 5 miles north, has nice sites on bluffs above the bay (reserveamerica.com; 800-444-7275).

MARINE MAMMALS:
SEA LION, SEAL, OR OTTER?

One of the skills expected of kayakers in this area, it seems, is the ability to distinguish between sea lions, seals, and otters. California sea lions *(Zalophus californianus)* are what most people picture as the typical "circus seal," sitting upright with a ball balanced on its slender snout. Their familiar doglike bark sets them apart from their less vocal cousins. Sea lions become much larger, with fully grown adult bulls in the 8-foot, 600-pound range, and tend to be brownish-blond in color. A particularly distinguishing characteristic is that their rear flippers rotate forward, allowing them to sit upright and "walk." Kayakers typically see them barking on rocks, swimming fast and "porpoising" up and out of the water, or floating on the surface with one flipper in the air thermoregulating and looking unnervingly like a shark's fin. Harbor seals *(Phoca vitulina)* are chubbier, looking like 4- to 6-foot sausages in a variety of colors from black to light gray to speckled. They can't turn their rear flippers to walk, so they flop along on their bellies. Typically seen basking prone on rocks or beaches, the shy but curious creatures also like to float with just their heads showing as they sneak up behind your kayak. Sea otters *(Enhydra lutris)* rarely take to land and can be distinguished from harbor seals because they tend to float on their backs, often smacking shellfish open against a rock on their chests, with a telltale gull floating nearby, looking to steal scraps.

Route 34
Upper Elkhorn Slough—Kirby Park Area

More sheltered and less busy than the slough's ocean end (see Route 33), the waters around Kirby Park, 4 miles inland, are a good option for calm-water kayakers or on days with strong currents at the mouth. Although you're less likely to see seals and otters this far up the slough, the birding is still excellent. Extensive mudflats and pickleweed marshes make prime shorebird habitat, and the surrounding oak forests and grasslands are the preferred haunts of raptors, owls, and numerous other woodland species. Such varied microhabitats help boost the slough's overall bird count to over 300 species and gain it recognition as one of the nation's top birding hot spots. As the state's second-largest marine wetland, it's also protected as a National Estuarine Research Reserve. At higher tides, many mazelike channels provide miles of opportunity for marshland exploration.

Trip highlights: World-class birding and protected waterways.
Trip rating:
> *Beginner:* 1 to 4 miles round-trip to the end of the slough, with many side trips into the marsh possible, when winds are 10 knots or less. Experience reading tides recommended.

Trip duration: Part to full day.
Kayak rentals: Monterey Bay Kayaks (montereybaykayaks.com; 800-649-5357), which also runs a shuttle service to Kirby Park, and Kayak Connection (kayakconnection.com; 831-724-5692).
Navigation aids: Together with a local tide table, the *Elkhorn Slough Paddling Guide* is invaluable. This free map and informational flyer showing channels, mudflats, and closed areas is available online (for map only: elkhornslough .org/kayaking/kayak-map.htm) and at kayak shops in Moss Landing (for map with safety and natural history information), or from the Elkhorn Slough Foundation (elkhornslough.org; 831-728-5939); USGS Moss Landing (7.5 minute).
Weather information: NWS zone forecast: "Monterey Bay" (forecast.weather.gov/ MapClick.php?zoneid=PZZ535); buoys: Monterey Bay.
Tidal information: Mudflats make paddling outside the main channel difficult to impossible when tide heights drop below 2 feet, and 3 to 4 feet or more will be best for exploring the maze of tidal creeks in the area.
Cautions: Check the tides: Falling water can strand you in the mud. Paddle and land only in designated areas so as not to disturb the sensitive habitat, and stay far enough from marine mammals and birds (minimum of 50 feet) not to change their behavior. Expect strong afternoon winds.

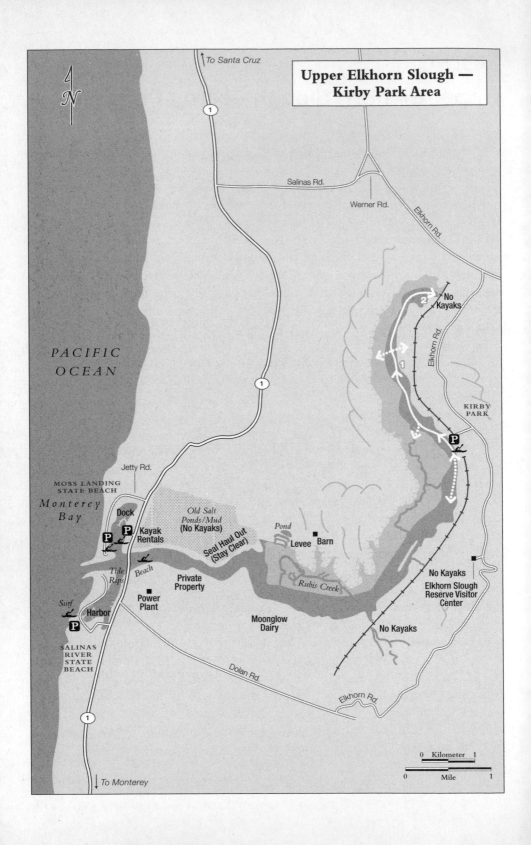

**Upper Elkhorn Slough —
Kirby Park Area**

N

To Santa Cruz

1

Salinas Rd.

Werner Rd.

Elkhorn Rd.

2 No
Kayaks

1

Elkhorn Rd.

KIRBY
PARK

PACIFIC
OCEAN

1

P

Jetty Rd.

MOSS LANDING
STATE BEACH

*Monterey
Bay*

Dock

P
P

Kayak
Rentals

*Old Salt
Ponds/Mud
(No Kayaks)*

Seal Haul Out
(Stay Clear)

Pond

Levee ■ Barn

No Kayaks

Elkhorn Slough
Reserve Visitor
Center

*Tide
Rips*

Beach

Private
Property

Rubis Creek

Surf

Harbor

P

■ Power
Plant

Moonglow
Dairy

No Kayaks

SALINAS
RIVER
STATE
BEACH

Dolan Rd.

Elkhorn Rd

1

To Monterey

0   Kilometer   1

0   Mile   1

Tim and Patty Andrews play follow-the-leader at the mouth of Rubis Creek. R. SCHUMANN

Trip planning: Paddle early morning or late afternoon to avoid wind. High, rising tides leave more room to explore with less chance of getting stuck in mud. In channels, beware of countless dead ends; try to follow the widest, deepest branch; and turn around before it gets narrower than the length of your boat, or you could have a lot of backing up to do. Also, avoid hitting the banks, which will cover your boat in sticky mud and cause erosion to sensitive habitat. If you want to ride the ebb tide one-way to Moss Landing, Monterey Bay Kayaks (800-649-5357) offers a shuttle service.

Launch site: Kirby Park (on Kirby Road at Elkhorn Road in Elkhorn) can be reached from Highway 1 just south of the Moss Landing Bridge: take Dolan Road east to Elkhorn Road, turn left, and follow it 5 miles to Kirby Park. If you are coming south from Santa Cruz on Highway 1, take Salinas Road east (about 5 miles north of Moss Landing), turn right on Werner Road, right again onto Elkhorn Road, and follow the signs to Kirby Park. Facilities: Porta-potties but no water. Free parking.

Miles and Directions

0.0   From the dock (N36 50.40 W121 44.60) head up slough to the right, crossing over to the more interesting left-hand bank. Side trip: Head left toward Rubis Creek or Moss Landing (see Route 33).

0.4   Entrance to the main maze of tidal creeks (N36 50.44 W121 45.07). Side trips: Meander your way along the main artery of this side channel for about a mile, searching for through channels back to the main channel among the many dead ends; or take the first fork to the left to work your way down to an exit about 0.5 mile south of Kirby.

0.75   The exit from the previous channel.

1.3   Channel entrances on either side of the slough are both good for exploration.

2.0   Railroad trestle marking the end of the slough.

Other options: Take advantage of the shuttle service, and the paddle to Moss Landing makes a great one-way "slough to sea" trip. With a nice morning ebb, kayaks will practically drift the 5 miles before lunch. More ambitious paddlers can catch the flood tide back to Kirby after lunch for a 10-mile round-trip. Caution: Beware of strong currents funneling under the Highway 1 bridge.

Where to Eat and Where to Stay

Restaurants: In Moss Landing try Sea Harvest Fish Market and Restaurant (831-633-8300), Whole Enchilada (wenchilada.com; 831-633-3038), or Phil's Fish Market (philsfishmarket.com; 831-633-2152). **Lodging:** None nearby; try Santa Cruz or Monterey. **Camping:** Sunset Beach State Park, 5 miles north, has nice sites on bluffs above the bay (reserveamerica.com; 800-444-7275).

Route 35

Salinas River National Wildlife Refuge

The secluded marshland at the mouth of the Salinas River is a well-known hot spot among local birders. Although there are fewer species here than at Elkhorn Slough, the birds tend to concentrate in large flocks by the river mouth and are easier to spot. Peaceful and remote, this short span of river passes through a nearly freshwater environment lined with willows and reeds, then gives way to flat grassy fields and coastal scrub, before opening up to a broad, brackish lagoon surrounded by dunes at the Pacific shore. Although the Salinas lacks facilities, this lack of amenities is made up for by the fact that you will likely be the only paddler on the water, making it especially attractive for adventurous misanthropes seeking to dodge the rental shops and tours at the more popular Elkhorn Slough.

Trip highlights: Great birding, solitude, views of Monterey Bay, and surfing options for advanced paddlers.

Trip rating:

Beginner: Protected 4-mile round-trip to river mouth.

Intermediate: 4+ miles with good surf zone practice and coastal touring possibilities on Monterey Bay in waves below 3 feet and winds to 15 knots.

Advanced: 4+ miles with good surfing off sandbar in waves to 6 feet.

Trip duration: Part to full day.

Navigation aids: USGS Monterey (7.5 minute).

Weather information: NWS zone forecast: "Monterey Bay" (forecast.weather.gov/MapClick.php?zoneid=PZZ535); buoys: Monterey Bay.

Tidal information: Freshwater inflow keeps the main channel navigable at any tide height, but there is more water in which to explore shallow areas during higher tides. Currents are generally weak except during the occasional flood year when the river breaches the sandbar separating it from the ocean (see "Cautions").

Cautions: Just reaching the launch site can be an adventure and is not recommended for low-clearance vehicles. Expect strong afternoon winds blowing upriver. Overgrown banks make landing difficult except at the mouth, and landing is prohibited entirely on the left bank (south) so you don't disturb any birds at the refuge. Ironically you are allowed to disturb birds by shooting them: duck hunting is permitted from mid-October to mid-January, so be aware of blinds and hunters, although this is not a popular hunting area. (Note: Serious birders won't add decoys to their life lists.) Avoid the river in flood. If the current is strong at the put in, only those with experience in currents should consider paddling. In years when the river is open to the sea,

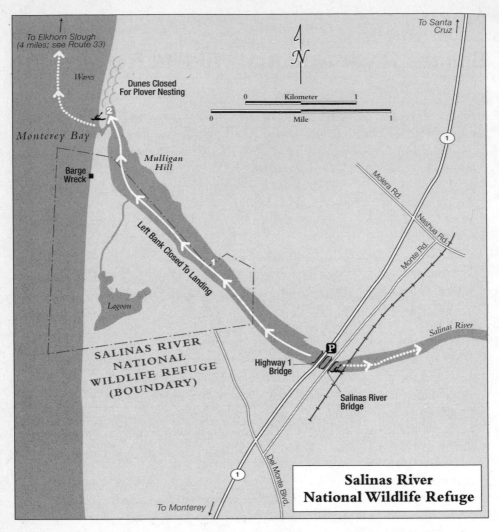

Salinas River National Wildlife Refuge

expect a slight current, especially during ebb tide, and avoid the channel at the mouth to keep from getting swept into the surf.

Trip planning: Head downriver early to avoid afternoon winds (which will be at your back on the return). Depending on water level, it's interesting to explore the narrow channels between islands, but sandbars and shallows can slow progress, and the deepest water is generally found from midchannel to the left (south) bank. Tidal ranges will be greater if the river is open to the sea. Calm conditions and scads of migratory birds make fall the best time of year for paddling and birding; summer is also good, but there are fewer species. Winter and spring are great for birding, but higher water levels can cause problems.

Launch site: The beach is hidden under the Highway 1 bridge on the river's north bank (268 Monte Rd., Castroville, is the approximate address). From Highway 1, about 1 mile south of Castroville, take the Nashua Road exit, cross over Highway 1, and head east. Turn right onto Monte Road just before the railroad tracks. Follow Monte for 0.7 mile to where the road takes a slight jog to the right, and you see a pullout on the right, just before a Narrow Bridge sign. If you have a low-clearance car and kayak wheels, you could park here and carry the final 0.2 mile to the river. Adventurous drivers with a little more clearance (I made it in my standard Toyota pickup fairly easily) can brave the bumpy, narrow dirt road to reach a wide turnout and easy, sandy beach launch beneath the Highway 1 bridge. This sometimes trashy put in belies a much more pristine paddling experience downstream, so don't be put off. Facilities/fees: None. Aerial photo: Shipwrecked barge near the mouth of the Salinas River (californiacoastline.org, image 200805521).

Nearing the mouth of the Salinas River R. SCHUMANN

Miles and Directions

0.0   Head west under the Salinas River Bridge (N36 43.92 W121 46.93) and downriver. Side trip: Head 1 mile or so upriver and look for birds in the willows and reeds. Although you can paddle a hundred miles upriver, the scenery gets no better as you continue into flat cropland.

1.0   Look for birdlife hidden in the bushes and reeds along both banks and on midriver islets, but please refrain from landing or walking on these fragile islets.

1.7   The small rise of Mulligan Hill on the right bank is a landmark near the river mouth.

2.0   At the river mouth (N36 45.04 W121 48.20) look for a spot along the right (north) side to land. Choose one where you won't flush the flocks of birds that tend to congregate there. Hike over the berm 100 yards or so for great views of the Monterey Bay and ocean birds—cormorants, surf scoters, and sandpipers—plying the waves, shore, and air or resting on the wreck of the barge 0.25 mile to the south. Dolphins and seals are sometimes seen here as well. Caution: Stay well to the right and out of the channel in the mouth if it is open to the sea unless you have strong surf zone skills. Avoid walking in the signed area in the dunes where endangered snowy plovers nest. Side trip: Those with helmets and surf zone skills can go for a coastal paddle north along the dunes or try surfing the sandbar at the river mouth, which can be fun in calm conditions but full of rip currents when the surf is up.

Where to Eat and Where to Stay

Restaurants: In Moss Landing try Sea Harvest Fish Market and Restaurant (831-633-8300), Whole Enchilada (wenchilada.com; 831-633-3038), or Phil's Fish Market (philsfishmarket.com; 831-633-2152). **Lodging:** None nearby; try Santa Cruz or Monterey. **Camping:** Sunset Beach State Park, 5 miles north, has nice sites on bluffs above the bay (reserveamerica.com; 800-444-7275).

Route 36

Monterey's Cannery Row and Around the Peninsula to Carmel

Nestled in the lee of Point Piños, Monterey's waterfront is one of the few coastal areas protected enough to give beginners access to an ocean paddling environment. Here lush forests of giant kelp harbor a world-renowned diversity of sea life, with near-guaranteed sightings of seals, sea lions, and sea otters. And each winter it's not uncommon for paddlers to spot migrating gray whales. On a few lucky occasions kayakers have even seen pods of orca and humpback whales near shore. In addition to wildlife viewing, this area is excellent for skills development. Sea conditions change gradually from the lake-like calm inside Monterey Harbor to the full exposure of the open Pacific as you paddle beyond Point Piños. These changes allow paddlers to progress by degrees, enticing them to return repeatedly to improve their skills, stamina, and comfort level. Experienced coastal paddlers ready to take on the "full Monte-rey"—a 14-mile rounding of the entire Monterey Peninsula—can run a shuttle to Carmel and enjoy views of the famous 17-Mile Drive from the ocean side (apparently the sea route cuts off 3 miles).

Trip highlights: World-famous scenery, excellent marine mammal viewing, ocean birding, whale watching in season, and skill building.

Trip rating:

Beginner: 2 to 5 miles, depending on conditions. Generally a good turn-around spot is the end of Cannery Row about 2 miles each way. On calm days beginners may go all the way to Lovers Cove, especially if accompanied by an experienced paddler. Even on rough days there is usually enough shelter that if you can get through the small surf at the launch beach, you can paddle for nearly 2 miles—out to the harbor mouth and inside the protection of the harbor breakwater. Helmets and a beginning surf zone class are recommended on days when surf is more than 1 foot.

Intermediate: A 5-mile round-trip to Lovers Point is accessible most days, and an 8-mile round-trip to Point Piños is possible when seas are less than 6 feet and winds below 15 knots. For surf zone practice, paddle east from the launch area down Del Monte Beach. Waves will grow gradually larger the farther you go.

Advanced: 8 miles round-trip to Point Piños and back, or 14 miles one-way to Carmel. While quite "doable" in rougher conditions, the Full Monte rounding of the peninsula will probably not have many opportunities for landing (or exploring among the rocks) in swells much above 6 feet and winds over 15 to 20 knots.

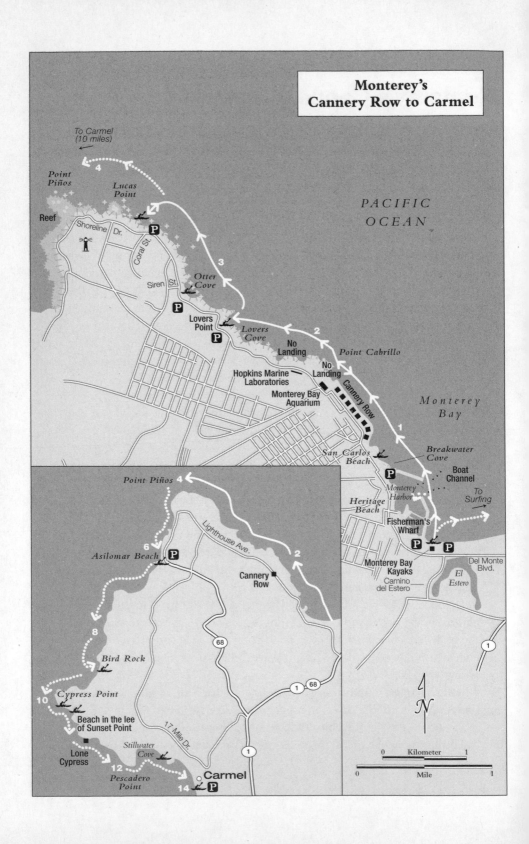

**Monterey's
Cannery Row to Carmel**

To Carmel
(10 miles)

Point Piños

Lucas Point

Reef

Shoreline Dr.

Coral St.

Siren St.

Otter Cove

Lovers Point

Lovers Cove

No Landing

Hopkins Marine Laboratories

Monterey Bay Aquarium

No Landing

Cannery Row

Point Cabrillo

PACIFIC OCEAN

Monterey Bay

San Carlos Beach

Breakwater Cove

Boat Channel

Monterey Harbor

To Surfing

Heritage Beach

Fisherman's Wharf

Monterey Bay Kayaks

Camino del Estero

El Estero

Del Monte Blvd.

Point Piños

Lighthouse Ave.

Asilomar Beach

Cannery Row

68

1 68

Bird Rock

Cypress Point

Beach in the lee of Sunset Point

Lone Cypress

Stillwater Cove

17 Mile Dr.

1

Pescadero Point

Carmel

N

0 Kilometer 1

0 Mile 1

Trip duration: Part to full day.

Kayak rentals: This popular destination has two rental shops. Monterey Bay Kayaks (montereybaykayaks.com; 800-649-5357) rents a variety of closed-cockpit sea kayaks and sit-on-tops, and Adventures by the Sea (adventuresbythesea.com; 831-372-1807) rents only sit-on-tops.

Navigation aids: USGS Monterey (7.5 minute) and NOAA chart 18685 (charts .noaa.gov/OnLineViewer/18685.shtml).

Weather information: NWS zone forecast: "Monterey Bay" (forecast.weather.gov/ MapClick.php?zoneid=PZZ535) and "Pigeon Point to Point Piños" (forecast .weather.gov/MapClick.php?zoneid=PZZ560); buoys: Monterey Bay and Monterey Waverider. Web cams: Looking out to sea from the Aquarium on Cannery Row (montereybayaquarium.org/efc/efc_lotb/webcam.aspx). View toward Cannery Row from Del Monte Beach (home.comcast.net/~georgek92).

Tidal information: During extreme highs some small landing beaches may be covered.

Cautions: Occasional small surf at launch beach, boat traffic around harbor, offshore winds, and submerged rocks near shore; habituated seals in the harbor have occasionally been reported trying to climb onto kayaks. Extreme exposure beyond Point Piños.

Trip planning: Winds generally calmer in mornings and evenings. Summer weekends can get crowded, especially from 10 a.m. to 4 p.m. Extreme low tides make for interesting kayak tide pooling along the harbor wall. If planning to round the peninsula, scout surf conditions off Point Piños, Asilomar, and Carmel Beach when you run the shuttle, and note some landmarks at Carmel so you can land near your car. Get to Carmel early if you want to find parking by the beach on summer weekends.

Launch site: Monterey State Beach (693 Del Monte Ave., Monterey) is just east of the harbor. From Highway 1 just north of Monterey, take the Pacific Grove/ Del Monte Avenue exit, follow Del Monte south through the stoplight at Camino del Estero, then turn right into the small parking lot for Monterey Bay Beach or take a right at the next light on Figueroa Street for more parking at Monterey Bay Kayaks (MBK) or more public parking for Monterey Harbor/ Fisherman's Wharf. MBK generously encourages kayakers to use their facilities, including launch beach, hot outdoor shower, and gear-rinsing tubs. Facilities: Restrooms and water. MBK's parking lot is a city lot that charges $1.50 per hour or $10 per day, the same as in the public lots next door. Aerial photo: Monterey State Beach next to the wharf in front of Monterey Bay Kayaks (californiacoastline.org, image 1799).

Landing site: Carmel Beach (Ocean Avenue and Scenic Road, Carmel) parking lot at the very end of Ocean Avenue is closest to the water, but space is limited; additional parking along Scenic Road.

Playing with rocks near Cypress Point CASS KALINSKI

Alternate launch sites: Inside the harbor at Oliver Street; Breakwater Cove/San Carlos Beach Park just outside the harbor at the beginning of Cannery Row; the cove west of the parking lot at El Torito Restaurant (600 Cannery Row) and others along Ocean View Drive at Lovers Cove, Otter Cove, Coral Street, and a few others possible from pullouts at small, exposed, rocky beaches near Point Piños, or Asilomar Beach, depending on the sea conditions and your skill level. Alternate launch site for beginners: San Carlos Beach.

Miles and Directions

0.0 Paddle along the fishing pier from Monterey State Beach (N36 36.10 W121 53.32). Caution: Stay well away from pier, watching for fishing lines and for sea lions hauled out on pilings. Paddling below sea lions is dangerous as startled animals, some weighing 600 to 800 pounds, could fall on your lap.

0.3 Harbor mouth. Caution: Cross boat lanes carefully and quickly, staying out of the way of other vessels. Side trip: The loop through the harbor is interesting in its own right and an excellent option on rough days. There's good landing at Heritage Beach with access to snacks and public restrooms on Fisherman's Wharf. This is a great place to see harbor seals, but some have become so accustomed to kayakers that their curiosity can become a nuisance if they try to climb aboard. Discourage this by paddling quickly away.

0.75   Breakwater Cove (N36 36.60 W121 53.75) is at the beginning of Cannery Row and the kelp forests of the underwater park. Look for sea otters and marine birds, and watch out for divers in the water. The small beach at the end of the jetty is San Carlos Beach, a good landing possibility before Lovers Cove, with public restrooms.

1.5   Monterey Bay Aquarium at the end of Cannery Row (N36 37.15 W121 54.03) is a good turn-around place to avoid the rougher seas beyond Point Cabrillo. No landings are allowed because all beaches in this area are property of Hopkins Marine Lab. If rounding Point Cabrillo, the sandy beach at the far end of the next inlet (bearing 270° MN) is Lovers Cove.

2.5   Lovers Point is a good turn-around place because seas continue to build beyond the point. The beach at Lovers Cove (N36 37.50 W121 5.00), with public restroom and snack bar, makes a good lunch stop on calm days. Cautions: Stay right if landing to avoid submerged rocks on the left; watch out for swimmers.

3.5   The small beach at Coral Street (N36 38.15 W121 55.65) has a narrow channel that experienced rock garden paddlers can run to reach the beach even in fairly large swells.

4.0   Point Piños is the southern edge of Monterey Bay and has the full feel of the open sea complete with large swell and submerged rocks that cause "boomers." On calm days exploring rock gardens and landing on pocket beaches along the point may be possible for helmeted paddlers with strong skills. Caution: Extreme exposure. Continuing beyond Piños is recommended only for experienced coastal paddlers—on many days landings may be difficult or impossible for the next 8 miles.

6.0   Asilomar Beach (N36 37.10 W121 56.56) is a possible landing site, through the surf, if the waves are not too big on this northwest-facing beach. This is a good alternate launch to do the last (and most scenic) 8 miles to Carmel.

8.5   The sandy beach in the cove behind Bird Rock (N36 35.34 W121 57.86) is one of the more-protected landing options so far. Caution: Keep your distance from Bird Rock so you don't flush nesting birds.

10.0   Cypress Point, although the most exposed point on the route, has some great convolutions and channels you can explore on calm days, as well as several potential landing beaches in tiny coves, especially on the south side, which may be accessible even on rough days.

MONTEREY BAY NATIONAL MARINE SANCTUARY AND THE SUBMARINE CANYON

Spanning one-fifth of the California coast and reaching between 10 and 50 miles out to sea, the Monterey Bay National Marine Sanctuary, the largest federally protected area outside Alaska, is the crown jewel of the marine sanctuary program. Among the most productive marine habitats on Earth, the sanctuary encompasses a "geographic convergence zone," an area of overlapping habitats where cold-water species from the north coexist with warm-water species from the south. Within its boundaries thrives a bounty of marine life: some two dozen marine mammals, including seals, otters, whales, and dolphins; nearly one hundred species of seabirds; and more than three hundred species of fish. At the heart of the sanctuary, its raison d'être, is the Monterey Submarine Canyon, the deepest marine canyon on the West Coast of the Lower 48. Twice the depth of the Grand Canyon, more than 10,000 feet at its deepest point, the massive gorge cleaves Monterey Bay in two and reaches 60 miles into the Pacific. The sanctuary, with its access to abyssal depths so close to shore and its incredibly productive waters, offers unparalleled opportunity for marine research and a wildlife-rich environment for paddling.

10.5 Beach in the lee of Sunset Point (N36 34.60 W121 58.49) faces south and is well protected for landing in most conditions.

11.3 Famous postcard view of the Lone Cypress tree.

12.5 Pescadero Point is the start of Stillwater Cove, with several easy landing beaches.

14.0 Carmel Beach (N36 33.31 W121 55.86) may be crowded with swimmers by the time you arrive. Land carefully!

Where to Eat and Where to Stay

Restaurants: Grill on Lovers Point (831-649-6859) at Lovers Beach makes a good en route lunch stop for burgers and sandwiches. Cannery Row and Fisherman's Wharf are loaded with restaurants. **Lodging:** Accommodations also abound in this tourist mecca. Near the launch site are the Inn at Del Monte Beach (theinnatdelmontebeach.com; 831-655-0515) and Monterey Fireside Lodge (firesidemonterey.com; 831-373-4172). **Camping:** There are several private campgrounds in the area: Veterans' Memorial Park in Monterey (831-646-3865), Saddle Mountain in Carmel (saddlemountain-carmel.com; 831-624-1617), and Marina Dunes RV Park in Marina (marinadunesrv.com; 831-384-6914), but the closest state parks are Andrew Molera in Big Sur or Sunset Beach near Santa Cruz (reserveamerica.com; 800-444-7275).

Route 37
Stillwater Cove to Cypress Point

This scenic pocket of shoreline within the Carmel Bay Ecological Reserve lies at the southern end of 17-Mile Drive, the exclusive community adjacent the world-famous Pebble Beach Golf Links. A white sand beach surrounded by rocky outcrops within aptly named Stillwater Cove gives less-experienced paddlers an opportunity to meander in a generally protected area against a dramatic, open-coast backdrop. Longer, more challenging options are available to experienced kayakers, heading north along the famous postcard cliffs to Cypress Point.

Trip highlights: World-famous scenery and abundant wildlife: seals, otters, seabirds.

Trip rating:

Beginner: 1- to 2-mile round-trip meander within Stillwater Cove on days with no surf on the landing beach.

Intermediate: 7 miles round-trip for intermediates with previous coastal experience on days with swells below 4 feet and winds below 15 knots, especially if accompanied by an advanced leader. Good surfing at Carmel Beach in waves up to 3 feet. Protected rock gardens for skill building.

Advanced: 7+ miles round-trip to Cypress Point with many rock garden play spots, in swell to 8 feet and winds to 20 knots; often good on days when Point Lobos is too rough.

Trip duration: Part or full day.

Navigation aids: USGS Monterey (7.5 minute) and NOAA chart 18686 (charts .noaa.gov/OnLineViewer/18686.shtml).

Weather information: NWS zone forecast: "Coastal Waters from Pigeon Point to Point Piños" (forecast.weather.gov/MapClick.php?zoneid=PZZ560) and "Point Piños to Point Piedras Blancas" (forecast.weather.gov/MapClick .php?zoneid=PZZ565); buoys: Monterey Bay. Web cams: Looking south across Stillwater Cove from 18th hole at Pebble Beach (pebblebeach.com/golf/pebble-beach-golf-links/live-golf-cams/hole18); view of rock gardens in cove to the south of Stillwater (pebblebeach.com/golf/pebble-beach-golf-links/live-golf-cams/hole9).

Tidal information: Tide height has little effect.

Cautions: Submerged rocks and surge within cove; offshore winds, boomers, cliffs, few landing options, and confused seas outside protection of cove.

Trip planning: Kayakers are asked to check in at the Beach and Tennis Club before launching and to unload at the wharf but park back by the tennis courts,

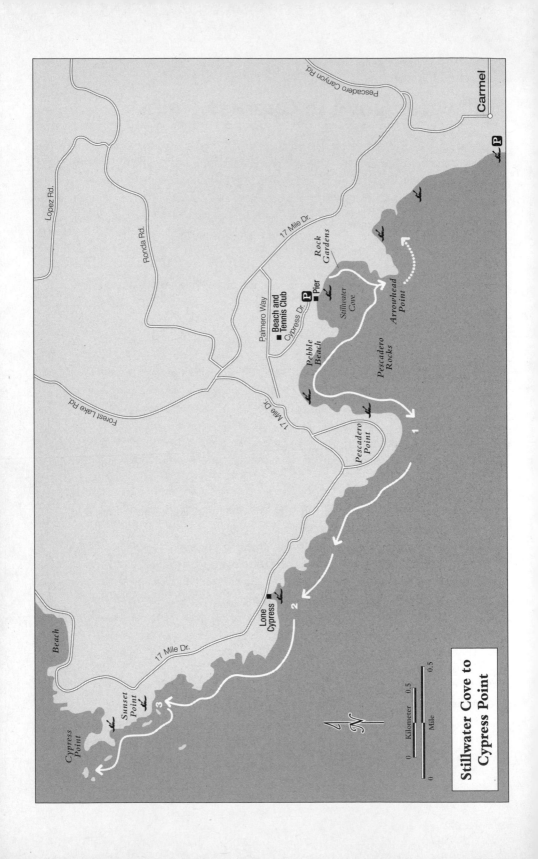

Stillwater Cove to Cypress Point

Kayaker contemplates the rocky coastline beyond Stillwater Cove. R. SCHUMANN

whose entrance is off Palmero Way. Note: From the parking lot you can follow the trail along the golf course back to the wharf, rather than walk all the way back around the way you drove.

Launch site: The beach behind the Beach and Tennis Club (1576 Cypress Dr., Pebble Beach) is well protected. From Highway 1 take the 17-Mile Drive/ Highway 68 exit and follow signs to the Lodge at Pebble Beach and the Beach and Tennis Club (turn left on Palmero Way, passing the lodge, and left again on Cypress Drive); pass the visitors' parking area at the 17th fairway and wind your way to the far end of the club's parking lot to the wharf. After unloading your gear, park back at the tennis courts. Facilities: Restrooms and water. Entrance fee to 17-Mile Drive is $10. Aerial photo: Wharf in Stillwater Cove behind Beach and Tennis Club (californiacoastline.org, image 200402266).

Alternate launch sites: The south end of Carmel Beach at the 8th Street stairs is more exposed and challenging.

Miles and Directions

0.0   Launch from white sand beach to left of pier (N36 33.98 W121 56.56) and head left along the shore.

0.4   Arrowhead Point makes a good turn-around spot, with good views of Carmel Bay. Side trips: On calm days the protected rock gardens inside the point make a good training area for intermediate paddlers, or you can round the point and access more rock gardens to the south or land though small surf on the north end of Carmel Beach.

0.75   Check out the harbor seals resting on Pescadero Rocks, the rocky islets in the middle of the cove, while keeping your distance from them and submerged rocks.

1.0   Make a loop into the far end of the cove and out to Pescadero Point. On calm days you might be able to land on a couple small, pocket beaches just inside the point. Caution: The cliffy coastline beyond the point is scenic but exposed and has few landing possibilities for the next 2 miles.

Other options: On calm days intermediates can launch through small surf on Carmel Beach and paddle north into Stillwater. Advanced paddlers can round Monterey Peninsula from Point Piños. (See Route 36.)

2.0   See the postcard-famous Lone Cypress tree if the waves aren't too big to approach the cliffs.

3.0   Beach in the lee of Sunset Point (N36 34.60 W121 58.49) faces south and is well protected for landing in most conditions.

3.5   Cypress Point, although the most exposed point on the route, has some great convolutions and channels you can explore on calm days, as well as several potential landing beaches in tiny coves, especially on the south side, which may be accessible even on rough days, depending on your skills. About 0.5 mile beyond Cypress Point is a sandy beach, but it's fully exposed to prevailing seas.

Where to Eat and Where to Stay

Restaurants: There are many great places to eat in Carmel, including R.G. Burgers (rgburgers.com; 831-626-8054), specializing in "Real Good" old-fashioned burgers and a wide variety of new-fangled recipes. **Lodging:** For a splurge try the Lodge at Pebble Beach or the Inn at Spanish Bay (both at pebblebeach.com/accommodations; 800-654-9300), where some suites cost as much as kayaks. For less extravagant digs, try Monterey Fireside Lodge (firesidemonterey.com; 831-373-4172). **Camping:** The closest state parks are Andrew Molera in Big Sur or Sunset Beach near Santa Cruz (reserveamerica .com; 800-444-7275); (or see Route 36 for private campgrounds in the area).

Route 38
Point Lobos State Marine Reserve to Mal Paso Creek

With its abundant wildlife and quintessential Monterey scenery—postcard vistas of wind-sculpted cypress trees clinging to craggy granite cliffs—Point Lobos is one of my favorite coastal day trips. Sea life thrives amid thick kelp beds, the rainforests of the sea, enhanced by proximity to deep, nutrient-rich water. Within 1 mile of shore, Carmel Canyon is 1,000 feet deep, dropping to 7,000 feet in just 6 miles where it joins the Monterey (submarine) Canyon off Point Piños. This sudden depth colors the seas an intense indigo and supports one of the richest ocean habitats in the world. Designated as the nation's first underwater reserve in 1960, the area is as sensitive as it is beautiful. It is a breeding area for harbor seals, sea lions, otters, and numerous seabird species, and unlike those in the well-traveled waters around Monterey, these animals remain wild and shy—requiring paddlers to maintain much greater distance to avoid disturbance. Named by early Spanish mariners for the constant barking of its *lobos del mar*, or "sea wolves," the point is home to a vociferous colony of California sea lions that flourishes to this day. The rock gardens around the park's southern boundary to Yankee Point, with a few small arches and caves mixed in, are some of the best in the area.

Trip highlights: World-class scenery and abundant wildlife, rock gardens, and caves.

Trip rating:

Beginner: 1 to 2 miles round-trip of safe harbor inside Whalers Cove on calm days if you stay well away from break zones at the cove edges and resist the urge to paddle out along the open coast unless accompanied by an experienced paddler.

Intermediate: 1 to 6 miles round-trip for adventurous intermediates with previous coastal experience or an experienced paddler leading on days with swells below 4 feet and winds below 15 knots.

Advanced: 6+ miles one-way for experienced coastal paddlers with strong water-reading skills and good sea sense. Excellent rock gardens, but swells above 8 feet limit access and make sightseeing difficult.

Trip duration: Part or full day.

Navigation aids: USGS Monterey (7.5 minute); NOAA chart 18686 (charts.noaa .gov/OnLineViewer/18686.shtml). The park map available at entrance station makes an excellent resource.

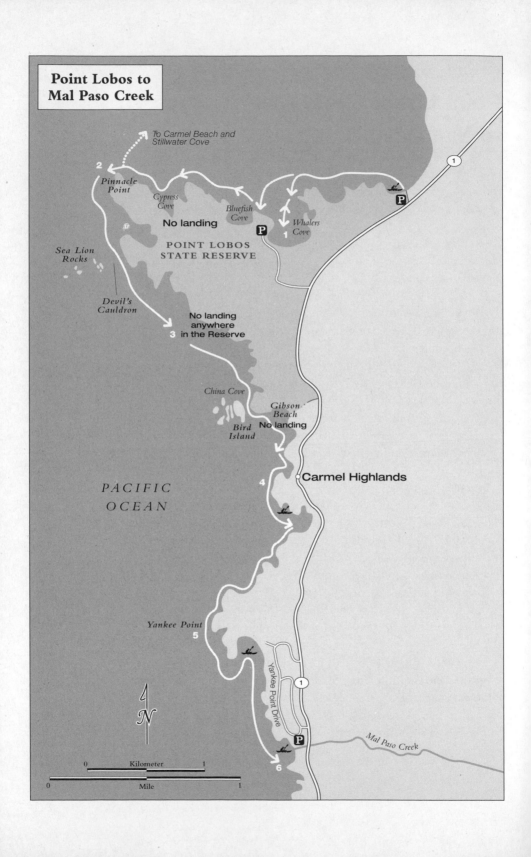

Point Lobos to Mal Paso Creek

To Carmel Beach and Stillwater Cove

2 Pinnacle Point

Cypress Cove

Bluefish Cove

No landing

Whalers Cove

1

P

P

1

Sea Lion Rocks

POINT LOBOS STATE RESERVE

Devil's Cauldron

No landing anywhere in the Reserve

3

China Cove

Gibson Beach

No landing

Bird Island

4

Carmel Highlands

PACIFIC OCEAN

Yankee Point

5

Yankee Point Drive

1

P

Mal Paso Creek

P

6

N

Kilometer

0   1

Mile

0   1

Exploring some back-channel options around Pinnacle Point R. SCHUMANN

Weather information: NWS zone forecast: "Coastal Waters from Pigeon Point to Point Piños" (forecast.weather.gov/MapClick.php?zoneid=PZZ560) and "Point Piños to Point Piedras Blancas" (forecast.weather.gov/MapClick.php ?zoneid=PZZ565); buoys: Monterey Bay. Web cams: Looking south across Carmel Cove to Point Lobos in the distance from 18th hole at Pebble Beach (pebblebeach.com/golf/pebble-beach-golf-links/live-golf-cams/hole18).

Tidal information: Tides have little effect except when extreme lows leave some rock gardens unrunnable.

Cautions: Strong winds and submerged rocks and boomers abound, and cliffs prevent landing and create confused seas from rebounding swells. Extremely sensitive habitat for birds and seals, so landing is absolutely prohibited anywhere within the reserve except at Whalers for those with permits. Dumping shore break at Monastery Beach has earned it a reputation as a challenging launch site. If doing a round-trip beyond Pinnacle Point from Monastery, save some energy to fight the northwest winds on your return.

Trip planning: Pick your day; conditions are more enjoyable in swell below 6 feet, the calmer the better. If you plan to launch from Whalers Cove inside the Reserve, you'll need a launch permit. Midweek you can usually pick up the permit at the front gate for $5, but only a limited number of boats, including kayaks, are allowed to launch each day, so you might want to make reservations ahead of time, especially on weekends. You can either call for a reservation (831-624-8413) or fill out the dive reservation form online (pointlobos.org/diving/reservations) at least a week in advance, even if you are only kayaking. Indicate in the "note" section that you are kayaking, not diving. They'll send e-mail confirmation and bill for $5 to launch each kayak, along with further instructions.

Launch site: Monastery Beach (27748 Hwy. 1, Carmel), just past the monastery at the southern end of Carmel River State Beach, is 1.5 miles south of the last traffic light at Rio Road in Carmel, 0.8 miles north of the entrance to Point Lobos Reserve. Facilities: Restroom and water. Aerial photo: Monastery Beach (californiacoastline.org, image 200402318).

Alternate launch site for beginners: Launching from Whalers Cove inside the park requires a $10 entrance fee and a $5 launch permit (see "Trip planning" above).

Landing site: Parking for Mal Paso Creek is in the neighborhood (112 Yankee Point Dr., Carmel) on the north side of the beach. From Highway 1 heading south, take the second of two right turns for Yankee Point Drive (which forms a big loop), bear left at the intersection with Carmel Riviera Drive, and look for the unmarked trail on the left, just past the fourth house from the corner. Facilities/fees: None. Caution: Take a moment to hike down the trail to scout wave conditions on the beach and to make sure you really want to carry your boat that far uphill after a long paddle (a 5- to 10-minute carry up a steep, overgrown trail).

Miles and Directions

0.0 Launch from the more protected area on far southwest (N36 31.37 W121 55.74) corner of Monastery Beach. Caution: This is a notoriously challenging launch off a steep beach with sometimes vicious, pounding shore break. Use teamwork to launch and if in doubt, don't go—the landing can be even worse, especially if the seas come up during the day as per usual. Stay outside the kelp beds, which get so thick and healthy that passing through them is like paddling through peanut butter.

1.0 Whalers Cove provides good protection for a rest break on calm water and is well worth exploring, but the entrance isn't obvious until you are directly in front of it. Caution: To enter, swing wide and stay midchannel to avoid rocks. Landing is prohibited without a permit.

Caves south of the park boundary **R. SCHUMANN**

1.25   If seas are calm, pick your way through the rocks into Bluefish Cove for an up-close look at some of the best scenery in the park. Keep a sharp eye out for seabirds, otters, and harbor seals, and keep your distance.

1.75   For skilled rock-garden paddlers, several narrow channels around Cypress Cove are navigable on very calm days, some ending in long slots between cliffs barely wide enough to turn a kayak around. Caution: Paddling into these coves can be dangerous; large sneaker waves breaking over numerous submerged rocks and smashing against the cliffs can turn these coves from dead calm to deadly in a heartbeat.

2.0   The west side of Pinnacle Point, which catches the full force of oceanic wind and swell, is a good turn-around point on rough days.

2.5   The infamous Devil's Cauldron (N36 31.08 W121 57.30) is the narrow passage where the namesake Sea Lion Rocks funnel and intensify any northwest swells into the steep cliffs on shore, often creating an exciting, sometimes frightening, 100- to 200-yard gauntlet of rebound waves and confused seas. The din of hundreds of barking sea lions only adds to the confusion. Once you pass through the Cauldron into the kelp beds beyond, the seas generally decrease noticeably. Caution: If it looks too rough to pass through, don't expect it to be any calmer if you try to take the half-mile detour to seaward of Sea Lion Rocks.

3.5   You can pass to shoreward of Bird Island if seas are calm enough, running the first of some interesting passageways and small arches in the bluffs next to shore. Caution: Stay well away from Bird Island, a sensitive breeding area for cormorants. Also, be aware that seemingly calm, protected channels here can turn nasty about as fast as someone can shout "Outside!"

3.7   Gibson Beach, the enticing, white sand beach in the cove south of Bird Island, marks the southern end of the reserve and is off-limits to landing. If it is calm, you can access a few small caves to the south, and the rock gardens from here to Yankee Point are the best in the area.

4.0   Small, rocky beach at the end of a narrow slot (N36 30.28 W121 56.27) is sometimes landable, especially for those with advanced seal-landing skills. There's a house on the bluffs above, so although beaches in the state are technically held in the public trust and access is permitted up to the mean high tide line, keep a low profile if landing.

5.0   Although there are some tight and technical rock gardens around Yankee Point, exposure increases dramatically in this area on rough days. Easy landings on small beaches below the cliffs of the protected cove on the point's south side, unless the tide is high. Caution: A minefield of boomers and breakers lines the shore from the point to Mal Paso.

6.0 Mal Paso Creek beach (N36 28.88 W121 56.31); be prepared for a long carry up
the overgrown trail along the creek—and to scout the beach before you paddle.
Caution: At low tide waves sometimes break on small boulders instead of sand.

Where to Eat and Where to Stay

Restaurants: Many possibilities nearby in Carmel's Crossroads Shopping Center at Rio
Road, including R.G. Burgers (rgburgers.com; 831-626-8054), specializing in "Real
Good" old-fashioned burgers and a wide variety of new-fangled recipes, milkshakes,
and vegetarian alternatives. **Lodging:** For a splurge try the Lodge at Pebble Beach or the
Inn at Spanish Bay (both at pebblebeach.com/accommodations; 800-654-9300), where
some suites cost as much as kayaks. For less extravagant digs, try Monterey Fireside
Lodge (firesidemonterey.com; 831-373-4172). **Camping:** The closest state parks are
Andrew Molera in Big Sur or Sunset Beach near Santa Cruz (reserveamerica.com; 800-
444-7275); (or see Route 36 for private campgrounds in the area).

Quick Trip Tips: Other Launch Sites in Monterey Bay Area

Pescadero Beach/Marsh (Beginner to Advanced)
The marsh is protected and full of birdlife, but reaching the water is a bit of a schlep. The
ocean launch here is sandy beach fully exposed to the northwest swell and tends to have
big surf. Pick your day and head north along the high bluffs.

Wadell Creek (Intermediate to Advanced)
A semi-protected surf launch on a rather exposed stretch of coast. The cliffs to the south
are tall and dramatic with few landings and a couple sketchy caves. The 7-mile trip
down to Davenport Landing (see Route 30) or 2 miles each way to a fair landing beach
at Greyhound Rock are great for very skilled coastal paddlers or very calm days. But get
back before the wind comes up; this is a busy kite-boarding spot most afternoons.

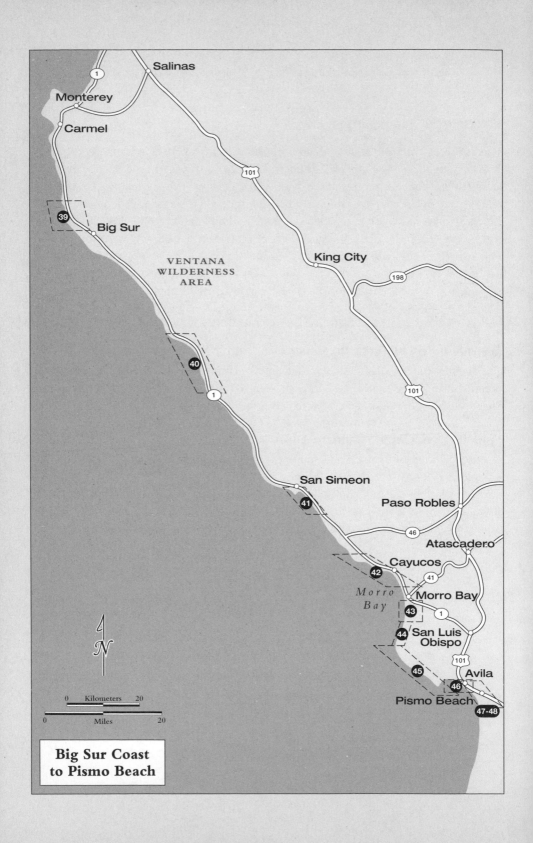

**Big Sur Coast
to Pismo Beach**

Big Sur Coast to Pismo Beach

Route 39

Andrew Molera State Park to Point Sur and Beyond

The very thing that makes paddling the Big Sur coast so difficult—its rugged inaccessibility—is precisely what makes it so appealing to some kayakers. If you can get your boat to the water, the paddling is excellent, but there are very few put ins—most of them are exposed to surf, rocky, and challenging. One exception is the sandy, protected beach at Andrew Molera. It is probably worth mentioning, however, that this exceptional beach is a full mile from the nearest parking lot. Anyone willing to carry a boat that far will be rewarded with the exceptional solitude and scenery this remote shoreline has to offer. Extensive kelp beds offshore are prime habitat for otters.

Trip highlights: Big Sur vistas, solitude, sea otters, rock gardens, and surfing.

Trip rating:

Intermediate: 1 to 6 miles round-trip for those with previous coastal paddling experience and an advanced paddler in the lead on a day with no fog, surf below 3 feet, and wind below 15 knots.

Advanced: 1 to 6+ miles round-trip requiring strong water-reading skills. Not recommended in swells above 6 feet, winds above 20 to 25 knots, or visibility less than 0.25 mile in fog.

Trip duration: Part to full day.

Navigation aids: USGS Point Sur Quadrangle (15 minute) and NOAA chart 18686 (charts.noaa.gov/OnLineViewer/18686.shtml).

Weather information: NWS zone forecast: "Coastal Waters from Point Piños to Point Piedras Blancas" (forecast.weather.gov/MapClick.php?zoneid=PZZ565); buoys: Point Sur and Cape San Martín. Web cam: Looking south from Nepenthe Restaurant, in hills high over Big Sur (nepenthebigsur.com/weather-cam.html).

Tidal information: More beaches available at low tide and more rocks exposed.

Cautions: Highly exposed and remote. Thick fog in the morning and strong winds in the afternoon are common. A shallow shelf between Molera and Point Sur extends 1 mile from shore, its countless submerged rocks and reefy areas creating a minefield of boomers that can be challenging and fun on clear days with a low swell, but difficult and dangerous on foggy days with large swell. Sea otters and seals are common here and quite shy, so give them plenty of space.

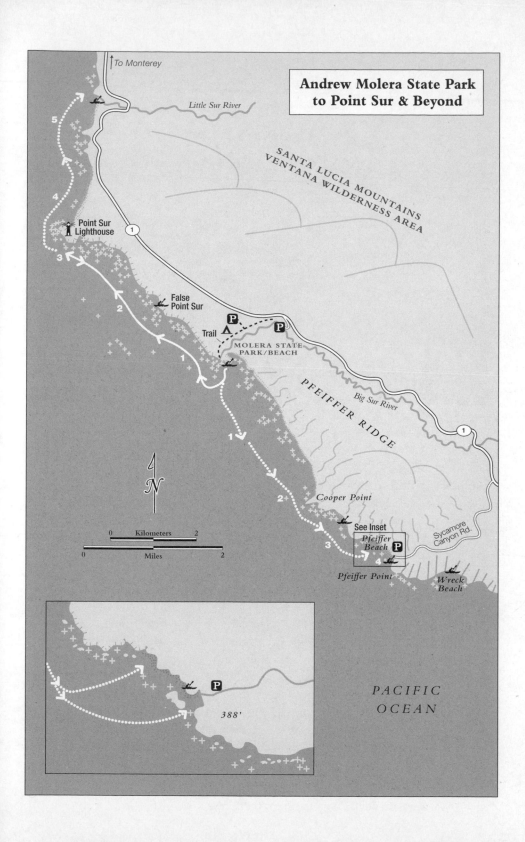

↑ To Monterey

Little Sur River

SANTA LUCIA MOUNTAINS
VENTANA WILDERNESS AREA

5

4

3

Point Sur
Lighthouse

2

False
Point Sur

Trail

1

P

P

MOLERA STATE
PARK/BEACH

PFEIFFER RIDGE

Big Sur River

1

1

N

2

Cooper Point

See Inset

Pfeiffer
Beach

P

3

Sycamore
Canyon Rd.

0   Kilometers   2

0   Miles   2

4

Pfeiffer Point

*Wreck
Beach*

388'

*PACIFIC
OCEAN*

Pushing off from Middle-of-Nowhere beach somewhere along the Big Sur Coast
SANDY RINTOUL-SCHUMANN

Trip planning: Choose your day carefully: the calmer and clearer, the better for access to isolated beaches. Check your weather radio in Monterey or the Morro Bay area before the Santa Lucia Mountains block the signal. Bring kayak wheels for the 1-mile carry to the beach. Off the water, supplies and services are somewhat limited and pricey. Because the drive and carry are so far for a day trip, plan to spend the night (or two) at Molera. Its first-come, first-served campground can get crowded on summer weekends, so get there early to get a spot.

Launch site: The main parking lot for Andrew Molera State Park is 3 miles south of Point Sur Lighthouse, on Highway 1. Walk-in trail camp is 0.5 mile down the trail toward the beach. From the campground it's another 0.5 mile to the beach. Slightly shorter carries from either of two roadside trailheads: one is 0.2 mile north of the main turn off, and other is 0.5 mile north; both are a little easier than the trail from the parking lot and avoid a tricky section of narrow trail. Facilities: Outhouses; day-use fee. Aerial photo: Mouth of the Big Sur River behind Molera Point (californiacoastline.org, image 200508713).

BIG SUR SEA OTTER REFUGE

By the beginning of the twentieth century, after years of intense hunting, sea otters were believed to be extinct on the California coast. Their soft, luxurious pelts, which have more hairs per square inch than any other animal (up to a half million or more), fetched hundreds of dollars apiece in the 1800s. Ironically, one of the most efficient ways to hunt otters on the open coast was by kayak, so greedy Russian fur traders enslaved Aleutian Islanders, among the world's best ocean kayakers, and systematically worked their way south. Eventually joined by local Mexican and American hunters, fur traders scoured the otters' West Coast range from Alaska to Baja, finally "harvesting" every otter south of the Canadian border. Or so they thought. During the construction of Highway 1 to Big Sur in the 1930s, a raft of otters was spotted. Apparently fifty or so had survived among the massive kelp forests on this inaccessible stretch of coast, and the area was designated a Sea Otter Game Refuge. The current population of southern sea otter—now hovering between two thousand and three thousand animals and ranging from San Luis Obispo County to north of San Francisco—all descends from those wary few who had disappeared into rugged folds of the Big Sur coast.

Alternate launch site: Pfeiffer Beach, 5 miles south, is more exposed with a shorter (although not short) carry. Facilities: Restrooms; day-use fees.

Miles and Directions

0.0 From Molera Beach (N36 16.86 W121 51.55) paddle well around the rocks off the point and head north up the coast. Caution: There are submerged rocks and shallow reefs scattered along the entire stretch. Side trip: Head south around Cooper Point 5 miles to Pfeiffer Beach. Caution: Scout carefully from Pfeiffer when you drop off the shuttle vehicle; this beach is rough and rocky and conditions won't get any better as the day goes on.

2.0 In the vicinity of False Point Sur are numerous isolated sandy beaches that will be yours alone if you can work your way to shore through the rocks. Caution: Private property on uplands, so stay on the beach.

3.0 The distinctive, 360-foot dome of Point Sur, among the more prominent landmarks on the California coast, makes a good turn-around point most days. Side trip: On a calm day, more-experienced paddlers may be able to round the point and continue another 2 miles to the beach at the mouth of the Little Sur River for possible landing. Caution: North side of Point Sur is extremely exposed, as are the beaches beyond. It is private property above high tide. Watch for steep shore break.

Other options: On calm days it's possible to launch from Pfeiffer Beach and paddle 4 miles up to Molera and back, avoiding the shuttle. There are also some nice beaches to the south of Pfeiffer Point, but if wind or fog comes up, getting back to Pfeiffer Beach can be extremely difficult or dangerous, and the next take out to the south at Limekiln Beach is nearly 30 miles away.

Where to Eat and Where to Stay

Restaurants: River Inn (bigsurriverinn.com; 831-667-2700) at the north end of Big Sur has outdoor tables along the Big Sur River and live music on Sunday afternoons. **Lodging:** River Inn (bigsurriverinn.com; 831-667-2700) is the closest, but other options exist in Big Sur. **Camping:** Andrew Molera State Park at the launch site has outhouses and drinking water but no showers and no reservations. Pfeiffer Big Sur State Park has restrooms with hot showers (reserveamerica.com; 800-444-7275), and books months in advance.

Packing the boats at the mouth of the Big Sur River, Andew Molera Beach **CASS KALINSKI**

Route 40
Lopez Point to Cape San Martín

The best thing about this stretch of the Big Sur coast is that it has four put ins within 9 miles—and one of the sites has hot showers. This may not seem like that big a deal, but in Big Sur this is a phenomenal statement. The shoreline is rugged and wild as tectonic plates grind together, smashing pure rock straight up from the sea. Directly behind the launch sites towers Cone Peak, whose 5,155-foot summit plummets to the sea in just over 3 miles, making it the steepest coastal gradient in the Lower 48. As Highway 1 clings tentatively to the cliffs along the entire 90-mile sweep of the Big Sur coast, there are barely a half dozen places where you can actually get your kayak to the water, short of hucking it off a ledge. The next launch sites to the north are an hour's drive distant: One is a mile from the parking lot down a rough dirt trail; the other, rocky and exposed. The next option to the south is another half hour until you are essentially off the Big Sur coast. And here, in the lee of Lopez Point, lies access to the beach—not once, but *four times*—and one even has a shower.

Trip highlights: Access to the beach (with shower), Big Sur cliff-hanging scenery, rock gardens, surf, sea otters, seals, seabirds, and solitude.

Trip rating:
Intermediate: 1 to 10 miles for those with previous coastal paddling experience in waves below 3 feet and winds below 15 knots; helmets and surf zone skills required; advanced trip leader recommended.
Advanced: 1 to 16+ miles for experienced coastal kayakers; not recommended in seas above 6 feet and winds above 20 knots.

Trip duration: Part to full day.

Navigation aids: USGS Lopez Point and Cape San Martín (7.5 minute) and Forest Service map, Los Padres National Forest.

Weather information: NWS zone forecast: "Coastal Waters from Point Piños to Point Piedras Blancas" (forecast.weather.gov/MapClick.php?zoneid=PZZ565); buoys: Point Sur and Cape San Martín.

Tidal information: Best selection of beaches at low tide. Beach access at Mill Creek can be hampered by tides above 4 feet if there is much swell.

Cautions: Steep beaches with high degree of exposure, rocks, cliffs, boomers, morning fog, and afternoon wind.

Trip planning: Pick a day with midday low tide so beaches along the cliffs will be uncovered; scout carefully from the road for conditions on landing beaches en route. Check weather radio in Monterey or Morro Bay area before the mountains block the signal. Campgrounds and lodgings are filled well in

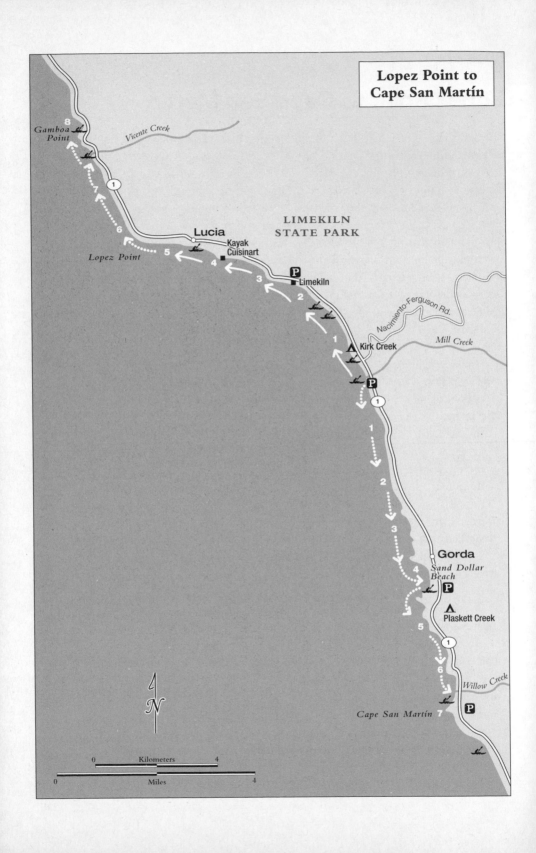

*Gamboa
Point*

8

Vicente Creek

1

7

6

Lucia

5

Lopez Point

**Kayak
Cuisinart**

4

3

2

P

Limekiln

**LIMEKILN
STATE PARK**

Nacimiento-Ferguson Rd.

Mill Creek

1

Kirk Creek

P

1

1

2

3

Gorda

*Sand Dollar
Beach*

4

P

Plaskett Creek

5

1

6

Willow Creek

Cape San Martín

7

P

N

0   Kilometers   4

0   Miles   4

Cruising the cliffs toward Lopez Point CASS KALINSKI

advance in summer. Hot showers are available at Limekiln even if you're not camping there ($3).

Launch site: Mill Creek Day Use area (Highway 1 and Nacimiento-Fergusson Road, Big Sur) is 25 miles south of Big Sur on Highway 1, just past Kirk Creek Campground (4 miles south of Lucia). Facilities: Vault toilet; no fee. Aerial photo: Mill Creek beach (californiacoastline.org, image 201005918).

Alternate launch sites: Limekiln State Park (3 miles north of Mill Creek). Facilities: Restrooms, water, and hot showers; day-use fee. Sand Dollar Beach (4 miles south of Mill Creek). Facilities: Vault toilets; $5 day use. Willow Creek (7 miles south of Mill Creek). Facilities: Vault toilets; no fee.

Miles and Directions

0.0   From Mill Creek (N35 59.05 W121 29.54) paddle out of the cove beyond rocks and kelp before heading north up the coast. Caution: Moderately protected but steep and dumpy, this beach can get hammered, especially on a south swell.

A GLIMPSE OF THE REAL BIG SUR

Much more than the scattering of restaurants, art galleries, and inns that hugs Highway 1 in "town," Big Sur is like the name given it by the original Spanish settlers in Monterey—*el Sur Grande*—that big place to the south, which stretches from Carmel to San Simeon, encompassing the coastal mountains and all of the Ventana Wilderness Area. More than anything, perhaps, it is these mountains, the Santa Lucia Range, and their proximity to the sea, that make Big Sur. The range is not particularly high, topping out at just under 6,000 feet, but what it lacks in stature is made up for in steepness.

Driven by a collision of tectonic plates, the main ridge of the Santa Lucias surges straight from the sea like a monster wave to over 3,000 feet. This relatively young range, which was near sea level just two million years ago (a quick tick on the geologic clock), is still on the rise at an average of a foot or two every thousand years. When the ocean gets rough, the full force of Pacific swells batter the seawall cliffs, sculpting them into craggy coves, carving out sea caves, and scattering the debris of rock gardens at their feet. This dynamic blend of water and rock creates some of the most celebrated coastal scenery on Earth, with some three million visitors overlooking these grand vistas each year. Yet very few get the chance to see this famous meeting of land and sea from water level, and there's nothing quite like a seal's eye view, with salt spray light on your skin and the rumble of waves against cliffs echoing in your ears.

1.0   Interspersed between rocky points are several small, sandy beaches along this stretch that make good rest stops at lower tide. Caution: Watch for submerged rocks in surf zone.

2.5   The sandy beach beneath the Highway 1 bridge at Limekiln State Park (N36 00.50 W121 31.20) is a good place to take a break; it offers restrooms, picnic tables, and the best alternative launch site. Caution: This is a steep beach with dumping shore break; scout from shore first. Side trip: On very calm days, advanced paddlers can run the arch at the south end of Limekiln Beach. Caution: This arch can be extremely dangerous even in a moderate swell.

3.8   The steep, distinctive cliff of this minor headland has many seabird nests above and resembles Swiss cheese below with wave-carved caves, crannies, and holes—none of them navigable. We nicknamed this cliff "the kayak Cuisinart" because of the curious way that waves washing into one opening sometimes spray, pour, and frappe out several other openings. Several postage-stamp beaches are scattered among the many rocks at the base of the cliffs along this stretch, and are landable with a low tide and swell.

4.5   The handful of buildings on the cliff above is Lucia.

5.5   Lopez Point makes a good turn-around point most days, with outstanding views up the coast, but no real beaches along the cliffs for another 2 miles near Vicente Creek unless seas are uncommonly calm.

Other options: The paddling south of Kirk Creek is as good as it gets, but beach access is not. The Sand Dollar Beach area, 4 miles south, has great sea stacks and a long sandy beach. However, only fanatics will deem the carry worth the effort: scaling the cliffs via stairway and switch-backing trail 0.5 mile to the parking lot. Willow Creek, 7 miles south, is accessible only on calm days at low tide. The shoreline in front of the parking lot is boulder strewn. A sandy launch/landing beach is 0.25 mile over the slippery rocks to the north along a cliff face that is awash at high tide. The beach itself is steep with dumping shore break. Both Sand Dollar and Willow Creek are popular board surfing areas, which should tell you something of their exposure to waves. I've had as many "adventures" and close calls here as I'd care to recall. It's no place for the timid or inexperienced. The next access is beyond Ragged Point, some 12 miles to the south.

Where to Eat and Where to Stay

Restaurants: Few options in this remote area: Lucia Lodge (lucialodge.com; 831-667-2391) has a cafe with great views and small store; the new Treebones Resort (treebonesresort.com; 877-424-4787) a unique, family-run eco-resort serves local food, some of it from their garden; or try the tired old Whale Watcher's Cafe (801-927-1590) in Gorda. **Lodging:** Lucia Lodge (above) has rustic cliff-side cottages; Treebones (above) offers unique yurts with stellar views. **Camping:** Limekiln State Park has restrooms and showers and is first-come, first-served, but may change to reservations (check at reserveamerica.com; 800-444-7275); Kirk Creek and Plaskett Creek have vault toilets and running water but no showers, and both now take reservations (recreation.gov, 877-444-6777) for about half their sites, all of which fill quickly within the six-month reservation window. The other half remain first-come, first-served.

Route 41
San Simeon Bay and Beyond

It was no mistake when William Randolph Hearst chose this picturesque cove as the site for his "beach bungalow" below Hearst Castle. This beautiful and protected white sand beach makes a classic scene and a fine backdrop for coastal touring. On calm days beginners can explore along the cliffs within San Simeon Bay, and more experienced kayakers have excellent access to open-coast rock gardens and isolated beaches beyond the point. Sea otters and seals are common in the area, as are fine coastal vistas. At the base of the Big Sur coast, this area retains a similar "wild" feel without the same exposure.

Trip highlights: Scenery, protected coastal paddling, access to isolated beaches, otters, seals, and seabirds.

Trip rating:

Beginner: 1 to 2 miles round-trip in lee of San Simeon Point on days with less than 1 foot surf on beach and winds below 10 to 15 knots; company of experienced partner suggested.

Intermediate: 1 to 7 miles round-trip on days with less than 3-foot surf and 15-knot wind; best to go on a fogless day, and advanced partner recommended beyond San Simeon Point.

Advanced: 7+ miles one-way, from Point Piedras Blancas or south to San Simeon Beach State Park with access to rock gardens and surf.

Trip duration: Part to full day.

Kayak rentals: Sea for Yourself Kayak Outfitters (kayakcambria.com; 805-927-1787) rents single and double sit-on-tops from William Randolph Hearst State Beach.

Navigation aids: USGS San Simeon (7.5 minute).

Weather information: NWS zone forecast: "Point Piedras Blancas to Point Arguello" (forecast.weather.gov/MapClick.php?zoneid=PZZ670); buoys: Cape San Martín.

Tidal information: More beaches but more rocks at lower tides.

Cautions: Surf, rocks, wind, and fog.

Trip planning: Better beach access at tides below 4 feet. Paddle early before wind, especially if rounding San Simeon Point; surf landings difficult beyond the protection of San Simeon Bay in swells above 6 feet. Links: William Randolph Hearst Memorial Beach (parks.ca.gov/?page_id=589).

Launch site: William Randolph Hearst State Beach (750 Hearst Castle Rd., San Simeon) is directly across Highway 1 from the turnoff to Hearst Castle. Park in

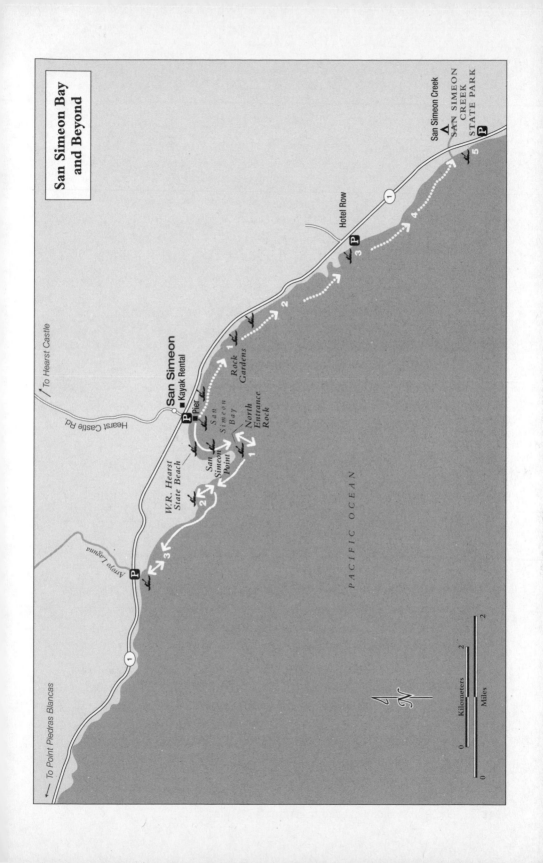

San Simeon Bay and Beyond

To Hearst Castle

To Point Piedras Blancas

Hearst Castle Rd.

Arroyo Laguna

San Simeon

Kayak Rental

Pier

W.R. Hearst State Beach

San Simeon Point

San Simeon Bay

North Entrance Rock

Rock Gardens

Hotel Row

San Simeon Creek

SAN SIMEON CREEK STATE PARK

PACIFIC OCEAN

N

Kilometers

Miles

0   2

Hidden cove somewhere north of San Simeon **KIM GRANDFIELD**

lower lot to right of fishing pier. Facilities: Restrooms and cold showers. Day-use fee. Aerial photo: San Simeon Cove looking north toward Point Piedras Blancas (californiacoastline.org, image 1799).

Alternate launch sites: The beach 3 miles north at Arroyo Laguna has fairly easy access when there are no elephant seals on the beach; Pico Avenue on Hotel Row, 3 miles south; and beach near San Simeon Creek campground. Facilities/fees: None.

Miles and Directions

0.0   Launch from the sandy beach north of the pier (N35 38.59 W121 11.30) and head right, paralleling the curve of shore. Side trip: Head left around pier to fine rock gardens beginning 0.5 mile to south. Caution: Avoid harbor seals hauled out on offshore rocks.

0.5   Bluffs begin at end of sandy beach. This is the most protected end of the beach and a nice place for a picnic or to practice surf landings.

1.0 Continue contouring along the bluffs to scenic San Simeon Point, thickly forested in cypress and eucalyptus. A small beach just inside the point makes a great private lunch stop if tide and swell permit (at low tide rocks choke the narrow entrance, and at high tide the beach may be awash). Caution: Submerged rocks extend well out beyond the point. Swing wide if you continue along the exposed, rocky shoreline beyond.

2.0 Follow the cliffs past several rocky, exposed pocket beaches (accessible only at low tide and swell) to the protected cove in the lee of the next point. The best landing is in the far left corner on steep but protected beach (N35 38.50 W121 12.30) that may be awash during higher tides and swells. Caution: Elephant seals sometimes haul out on these beaches, especially as you continue farther north.

3.3 Arroyo Laguna beach (N35 39.12 W121 13.30) is an alternative launch site unless there are elephant seals on the beach (generally from December through April). Side trip: If you continue north toward Piedras Blancas, you'll be passing the main part of the elephant seal rookery and should not land.

Other options: Run a shuttle and paddle south 3.5 miles from Arroyo Laguna to San Simeon, or continue another 5 miles down to San Simeon Creek State Park campground. Many small beaches and coves front the bluffs along this section, so landing is often possible for those with surf skills; however, it's fairly exposed so not recommended in swells much above 6 feet. Scout landings carefully from the shore first.

Where to Eat and Where to Stay

Restaurants: Sebastian's Store (805-927-3307) 0.5 mile north from the beach entrance has decent food (fish and chips, burgers, etc.), or head 3 miles south to "hotel row" in San Simeon. **Lodging:** Cavalier Oceanfront Resort (cavalierresort.com; 805-927-4688) on the bluffs in San Simeon; many other options are found along "hotel row" in San Simeon or 7 miles south in Cambria. **Camping:** San Simeon Creek State Park, 5 miles south on Highway 1 (reserveamerica.com; 800-444-7275).

Route 42
Cayucos State Beach to Point Estero

In the lee of Point Estero, the shoreline faces south for half a dozen miles, forming good shelter from prevailing wind and swell. The point's steep cliffs give way to low bluffs, backed by a coastal bench or marine terrace (see below). In front of this terrace, a second shallow platform extends well out to sea, forming an outer reef that absorbs the brunt of the waves and leaves a jigsaw puzzle of rocks scattered across the more-protected inner waters. This coincidence of southern exposure and shallow, rocky shelf creates one of the more extensive and most accessible rock garden areas in Central California. On calm days this area provides an excellent introduction to the fun of rock garden exploration, but there's still more to recommend it. Sea otters and seals frequent these waters. Along shore, many pocket beaches dot the bluffs. Because the grassy pasture behind the bluffs is private property, these beaches feel quite remote and isolated, despite the proximity of Highway 1. The highway cannot be seen from the beach, but it is nonetheless accessible in case of emergency, adding a margin of safety.

Trip highlights: Excellent introductory rock gardens, secluded beaches, scenery, and an excellent place to see otters and seals.

Trip rating:

Beginner: 1 to 2 miles on days with 1-foot surf or less on the beach, less than 10 knots of wind; going beyond immediate beach area is not recommended without an experienced paddler leading (tours available through Good Clean Fun; see "Kayak rentals" below).

Intermediate: 1 to 4 miles on days with less than 3-foot surf on beach and 15-knot wind for those with previous coastal paddling experience or with an experienced trip leader.

Advanced: 1 to 11+ miles of excellent rock garden and surf play in waves to 6 feet and winds to 20 knots.

Trip duration: Part to full day.

Kayak rentals: Good Clean Fun (goodcleanfunusa.com, 805-995-1993) near the pier in Cayucos rents single and double sit-on-tops.

Navigation aids: USGS Cayucos (7.5 minute) and NOAA chart 18703 (charts .noaa.gov/OnLineViewer/18703.shtml).

Weather information: NWS zone forecast: "Point Piedras Blancas to Point Arguello" (forecast.weather.gov/MapClick.php?zoneid=PZZ670); buoys: Cape San Martín and Diablo Canyon. Web cams: Cayucos Pier live cam (goodcleanfunusa.com/gcf-story/gcf-beach-live-cam-view) and not-so-live cam (cayucosshorelineinn.com/beach.php).

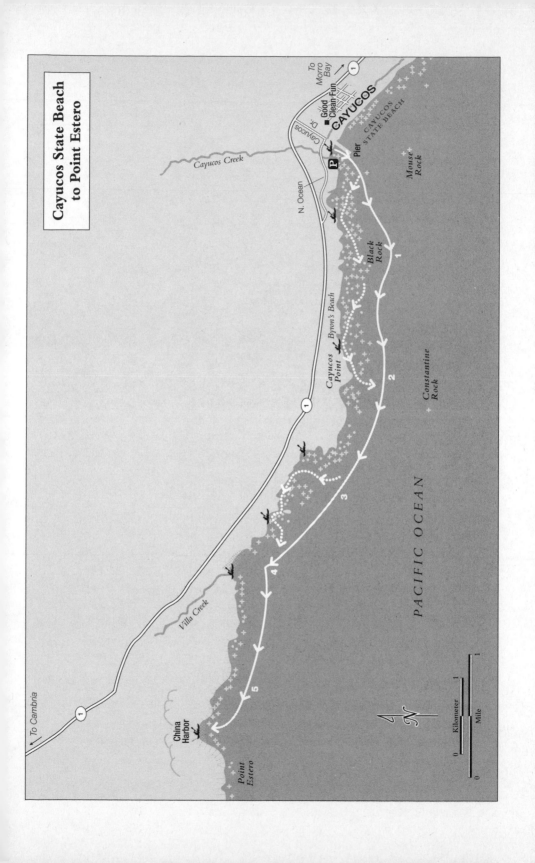

Cayucos State Beach
to Point Estero

View of Morro Rock from Cayucos R. SCHUMANN

Tidal information: Better beach access and better protection in rock gardens during lower tides.

Cautions: Surf, rocks, boomers, wind, fog, seal haul outs, and private property above beaches.

Trip planning: Paddle early before wind, especially if rounding Cayucos Point. A day with low tide in late morning would give best protection from both wind and swell in the rock gardens. Avoid paddling in thick fog; rocks and shore will be difficult to spot.

Launch site: Cayucos State Beach (282 N. Ocean Ave., Cayucos), sandy and gently sloping, provides a fairly well-protected launch through small to moderate surf. Take Cayucos Drive off Highway 1, turn right on North Ocean Avenue, then an immediate left into the parking lot on the north side of the pier. Facilities: Restrooms, water, and cold showers. Aerial photo: Cayucos Pier and State Beach (californiacoastline.org, image 200509699).

Alternate launch sites: Beach on north end of Studio Drive, 2 miles south, has less protection but is a more scenic spot to launch on calm days. Facilities/fees: None.

Miles and Directions

0.0   Launch on the northwest side of the pier (N35 26.93 W120 54.43) near the mouth of Cayucos Creek, swinging wide to avoid the submerged rocks around the point to the right. Side trip: In the cove just beyond the point is the beginning of the "inside passage": an excellent rock garden playground for the next 2 miles with good protection during low tide and swell. There are many small, private beaches if you can work your way through the rocks. Caution: Boomers, waves breaking into rocks, seal haul outs, and private property above beaches.

2.0   As you approach Cayucos Point exposure gradually increases, but a protected landing at Byron's Beach (N35 26.86 W120 56.06) makes a good turn-around spot for many paddlers on most days. Look for some big oak trees by a windmill on the otherwise treeless bluffs at San Geronimo Road. Caution: Experienced paddlers (or trip leaders) are recommended beyond Cayucos Point if there are any waves. Numerous reefs and seal haul outs force you well out to sea for an exposed rounding of the outer reef, where waves may break 0.5 mile or more offshore.

3.0   Sandy beach in the cove just north of the point gets good protection from the reef. Side trip: Although more exposed here, the "inside passage" continues with more advanced rock garden play for the next 1 mile and more small beaches.

4.0   The wide beach where the bluffs end at the mouth of Villa Creek (N35 27.61 W120 58.17) makes a better landmark (it's the only beach that big) than a landing. Not that anything's wrong with this beach, but it's not as pretty or private as the "pocket" beaches you've been passing, and there are no bluffs for wind protection. Wide, sandy, and gently sloping, it is a good beach for surf practice when tide and swell are right.

5.5   On the final 1.5 miles to the well-protected beach at China Harbor (N35 27.82 W120 59.59), the cliffs steepen and rock gardens and landing beaches give out. This beach is very remote and private and makes a great lunch spot and turn-around point. Beyond Point Estero the coast turns hard to the northwest, dramatically increasing exposure. Although remote and dramatic, steep cliffs with only occasional small rocky beaches make landings next to impossible in all but the calmest of seas for most of the 10 miles to Cambria.

Other options: The 6-mile, one-way trip from Cayucos to Morro Bay makes a dramatic entrance to the harbor with great views of Morro Rock (see Route 43).

The exposed 15-mile stretch to Cayucos from Leffingwell Landing in Cambria passes some remote and rugged shoreline, but plan on little access to landings for the first 10 miles until China Cove, unless it is relatively calm.

Where to Eat and Where to Stay

Restaurants: Several restaurants along the beachfront have take-out menus featuring fresh local fish and chips, or try Schooner's Wharf (schoonerswharf.com; 805-995-3883), which serves fancier fare and ocean views. **Lodging:** Shoreline Inn (cayucosshorelineinn .com; 805-995-6381) is one of several beachfront hotels on North Ocean Street. **Camping:** Morro Bay State Park has camping with hookups and hot showers. Morro Strand State Beach 2 miles north on Highway 1 has beachfront camping but only cold, outdoor showers; Montaña de Oro State Park south of Los Osos is more scenic and primitive with outhouses and water, but no showers or hookups (reserveamerica.com; 800-444-7275).

Route 43
Morro Bay Estuary

One of the more prominent coastal landmarks in the state, 578-foot Morro Rock is the last of the Seven Sisters, a series of dramatic outcrops (there are nine, actually), stretching over 10 miles inland in a line to San Luis Obispo. The word *morro,* Spanish for a dome-shaped promontory, reflects the distinctive shape of this peak, which has for centuries provided an important landmark for mariners. The sheltered estuary at Morro Bay, bordered by nature preserves, is prime habitat for beginning paddlers, as few areas provide such sea life, scenery, and solitude so close at hand. The largest coastal wetlands in the area south of Elkhorn Slough, the bay, which encompasses the fertile salt marsh of Morro Estuary Natural Preserve, is among the West Coast's better birding spots. More than 250 species have been recorded in the area with winter migrants flocking in by the tens of thousands. Paddlers also see harbor seals, sea lions, and otters, and, after a short crossing to the sandspit in Morro Dunes Natural Preserve, they are treated to remote beach hiking with great ocean views. Options abound for beginners, and the bay is also a good spot to build intermediate skills in a fairly protected setting.

Trip highlights: Excellent birding, scenery, and hiking.

Trip rating:

Beginner: 4- to 5-mile loop to mouth and back. Basic knowledge of tides and boat traffic rules a must. For shorter trips of 2 to 3 miles, cross to the sandspit for a hike or explore the marsh at the mouth of Osos Creek.

Intermediate: 5+ miles round-trip, with good places to practice ferrying in currents at the end of the sandspit or try surfing inside the jetty on days when waves are less than 3 feet.

Advanced: 5+ miles with good surf and rough-water practice possibilities around the mouth or heading down to Montaña de Oro (see Route 44).

Trip duration: Part or full day.

Kayak rentals: There are several rental shops on the Embarcadero: Kayak Horizons (kayakhorizons.com; 805-772-6444) rents single and double recreational kayaks as well as a few short touring models; Rock Kayak Co. (rockkayak.com; 805-772-2906) has sit-on-tops only; the Kayak Shack (morrobaykayakshack.com; 805-772-8796) rents rec boats; and Sub Sea Tours (centralcoastthingstodo.com; 805-772-9463) rents both sit-ons and rec boats. So Kayak Horizons is your best bet if you're looking for anything approaching an actual touring kayak.

Navigation aids: USGS Morro Bay South (7.5 minute) and NOAA chart 18703 (charts.noaa.gov/OnLineViewer/18703.shtml).

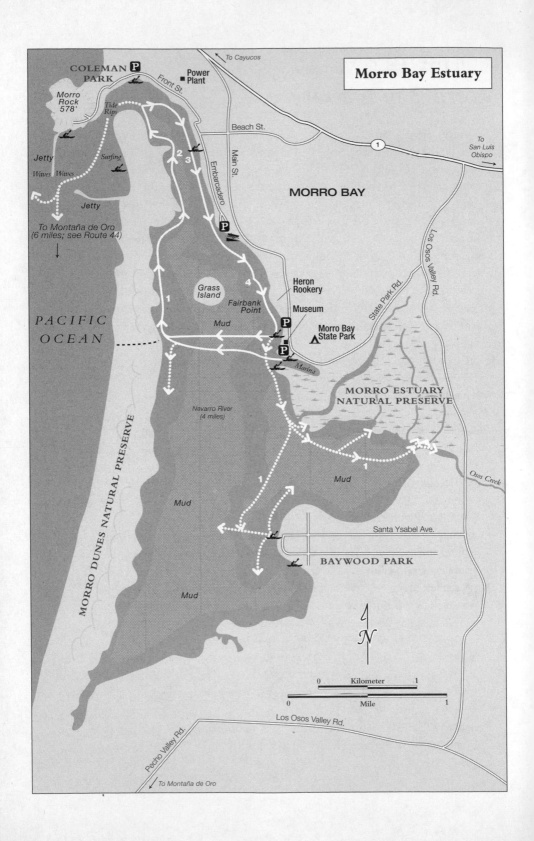

Morro Bay Estuary

COLEMAN PARK

P

Power Plant

To Cayucos

Morro Rock 578'

Tide Rips

Front St.

Beach St.

Jetty

Surfing

Waves Waves

Jetty

2
3

Main St.

Embarcadero

1

MORRO BAY

To San Luis Obispo

PACIFIC OCEAN

To Montaña de Oro (6 miles; see Route 44)

Grass Island

4

Fairbank Point

Mud

Heron Rookery

Museum

P

P

Marina

Morro Bay State Park

State Park Rd.

Los Osos Valley Rd.

MORRO ESTUARY NATURAL PRESERVE

Navarro River (4 miles)

1

1

Mud

Osos Creek

MORRO DUNES NATURAL PRESERVE

Mud

1

Mud

Santa Ysabel Ave.

BAYWOOD PARK

N

Mud

0 Kilometer 1

0 Mile 1

Los Osos Valley Rd.

Pecho Valley Rd.

To Montaña de Oro

Weather information: NWS zone forecast: "Point Piedras Blancas to Point Arguello" (forecast.weather.gov/MapClick.php?zoneid=PZZ670); buoys: Cape San Martín and Diablo Canyon. Web cam: View of Morro Rock (morrobaywebcam.com).

Tidal information: Extensive mudflats begin to uncover at tides below 2 or 3 feet, but a boat channel along the near (eastern) shore keeps the bay navigable to Baywood Park at any water level.

Cautions: Mudflats, afternoon winds, boat traffic around main harbor area, tidal currents and rips at the mouth of the bay, and breaking waves at ocean jetties.

Trip planning: If crossing to the sandspit, novices should paddle early before the wind kicks up; if you want to hike over to the ocean, land where red flags mark hiking corridors, as much of the area is fenced off to protect snowy plover nesting areas. Pick a day with a rising tide to avoid getting stuck in the muck. More than one kayaker has been stranded on the sandspit waiting until after dark for the tide to return. When returning from the mouth, the longer you wait after high tide, the more mud and opposing current you'll have to fight.

Did anyone remember to check the tide book? Pulling out on the mud in Morro Bay. **R. SCHUMANN**

Launch site: State Park Marina (10 State Park Rd., Morro Bay) has a small launch beach at the west end of the parking lot by the Bayside Cafe that can get muddy at low tide. Then you can launch off the Kayak Shack dock for $2. From Highway 1 take the Los Osos/Baywood exit onto South Bay Boulevard. Following the signs to Morro Bay State Park, turn right on State Park Road. Facilities: Restrooms and water; no fee. Aerial photo: State Park Marina (californiacoastline.org, image 2131).

Alternate launch sites: Tidelands Park (300 Embarcadero, Morro Bay) has a launch ramp and docks. Facilities: Restrooms and water; no fee. The beach north of the Museum of Natural History (on State Park Drive just north of the marina) provides easy access, but is very muddy at low tide. No facilities/fees. Coleman Park (Embarcadero and Colman, Morro Bay) is good for paddling near the mouth (see Route 44); Pasadena Park (Pasadena Drive at Santa Ysabel Avenue, Baywood Park) in Baywood Park—try the end of Santa Ysabel Road. Free parking at both sites.

Miles and Directions

0.0 From the marina (N35 20.77 W120 50.61), head straight across the bay staying left of Grass Island and its seal haul out. To hike across the sandspit, look for the trail across the dunes marked with red flags. Side trips: The eucalyptus grove on Fairbank Point, 0.25 mile north of the harbor, shelters one of California's largest great blue heron rookeries. Several other species of herons and egrets roost here year-round. Interested birders can swing by the rookery before crossing the bay, or they can avoid crossing the bay and follow the shoreline south at high tide for 2 miles into the narrowing channels of Morro Estuary Natural Preserve for some of the area's best birding.

0.8 On reaching the sandspit, paddle north along it. Side trip: Head south into the back bay for more solitude (if you've considered the effects of wind and tides on your return).

1.5 As the dunes recede the hike across for an ocean view gets slightly shorter.

2.5 Great view of Morro Rock from the end of the spit and a good spot for a rest before heading back along the waterfront. Caution: Currents, waves, and boat traffic can cause hazardous conditions in the channel at the end of the spit, especially on an outgoing tide. Side trips: On calm days, experienced paddlers can head out to the surf beach inside the jetty or paddle out on the sea for views of the steep backside of Morro Rock, or continue 6 miles to Montaña de Oro (see Route 44).

3.0 Head back along the sandspit, or cross the channel to where landings are permitted on two small, public dinghy docks, one across from the "12" channel marker on the north side of the Galley Restaurant and the other farther down. Morro Bay's Embarcadero is a picturesque, New England–style waterfront replete with a working fishing fleet and a plethora of small gift shops and restaurants. Caution: Avoid boat traffic by skirting the right (west) side of the boat lane outside the channel markers.

3.7 Tidelands Park, alternate launch site.

4.2 Fairbank Point Heron Rookery Natural Preserve.

4.7 Return to marina.

Other options: Continue into the pickleweed marsh at the mouth of Osos Creek, another 1.2 miles, and explore the maze of channels there, or head another mile or more up Osos Creek; this assumes you have a rising tide and a good 3 to 4 feet or more of water. On a rising tide you can also explore another 2 miles farther to the very end of the bay.

Where to Eat and Where to Stay

Restaurants: Options abound along the Embarcadero, from fresh local seafood at the Galley (galleymorrobay.com; 805-772-7777) to stands selling cappuccino, ice cream, and salt water taffy. Or try the Bayside Cafe (baysidecafe.com; 805-772-1465) at the launch. **Lodging:** Lodging is plentiful; contact Morro Bay Chamber of Commerce (morrobay .org, 805-772-4467). The Back Bay Inn (backbayinn.com; 805-528-1233) bed-and-breakfast in Baywood Park has a quiet, waterfront location with launching access for guests. **Camping:** Morro Bay State Park has camping with hookups and hot showers. Morro Strand State Beach 2 miles north on Highway 1 has beachfront camping but only cold, outdoor showers; Montaña de Oro State Park south of Los Osos is more scenic and primitive with outhouses and water, but no showers or hookups (reserveamerica.com; 800-444-7275).

Route 44

Morro Rock to Spooner's Cove in Montaña de Oro

The dynamic stretch of uninhabited coastline south of Morro Rock offers some of the more dramatic scenery and challenging conditions in the area. Leaving the protection of Morro Bay reveals spectacular views of Morro Rock's steep ocean side and the cliffs along Montaña de Oro State Park—the "Mountain of Gold" coined by Spanish explorers for the California poppies and other wildflowers that blanket its bluffs each spring.

Trip highlights: Outstanding coastal vistas, surfing, and solitude.

Trip rating:

Intermediate: 7 miles one-way, this trip is recommended only to intermediates with previous open-coast experience (because of its exposure) preferably led by an experienced paddler on a day with waves below 4 feet and winds to 15 knots. Good surf zone practice between south jetties, but beware of getting swept out to sea during strong ebb tides.

Advanced: The 7-mile, one-way trip suggested here requires a shuttle; to avoid shuttling (or to shorten or lengthen the mileage), launch from Spooner's and paddle north toward Morro Bay for whatever distance, then return with the afternoon wind for a round-trip of up to 14 miles. Good surfing can be found all along the sandspit in waves to 6 feet or so, and I've even managed to pull off this trip in swells over 12 feet (not recommended) by staying well out to sea, as the landing site at Spooner's Cove is protected enough to make landing possible, if somewhat sketchy, even in big seas.

Trip duration: Part to full day.

Kayak rentals: Central Coast Kayaks (centralcoastkayaks.com; 805-773-3500) in Shell Beach will rent closed-deck kayaks on calm days to experienced paddlers and will also provide a shuttle service for those with their own boats.

Navigation aids: USGS Morro Bay South (7.5 minute) and NOAA chart 18703 (charts.noaa.gov/OnLineViewer/18703.shtml).

Weather information: NWS zone forecast: "Point Piedras Blancas to Point Arguello" (forecast.weather.gov/MapClick.php?zoneid=PZZ670); buoys: Cape San Martín and Diablo Canyon.

Tidal information: Tide height makes little difference along most of this stretch, but more landing beaches and more rocks are exposed along the cliffs during lower tides.

Cautions: Conditions can change quickly here as the warning sign at the harbor mouth would suggest: it reads HAZARDOUS WATER AHEAD—OFTEN UNSAFE FOR SMALL

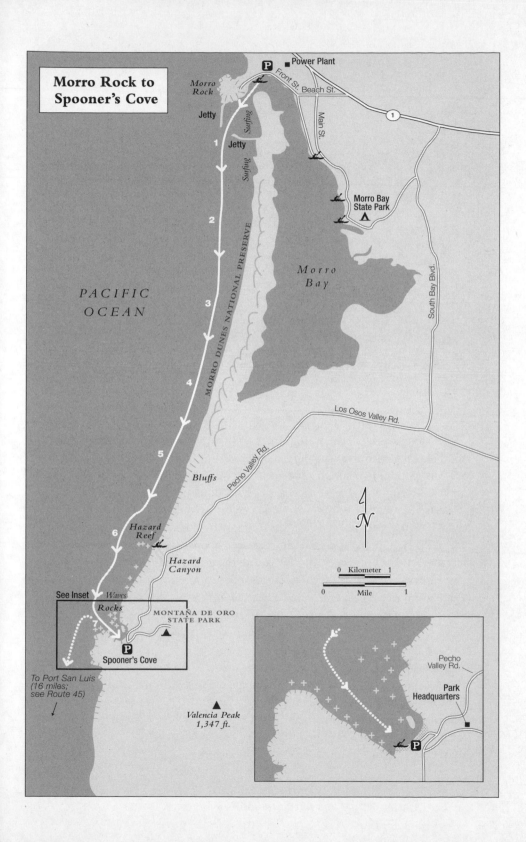

Morro Rock to Spooner's Cove

Power Plant

P

Morro Rock

Front St. Beach St.

Jetty

Surfing

1

Main St.

Jetty

Surfing

Morro Bay State Park

2

MORRO DUNES NATIONAL PRESERVE

Morro Bay

3

PACIFIC OCEAN

4

South Bay Blvd.

5

Los Osos Valley Rd.

Bluffs

Pecho Valley Rd.

6

Hazard Reef

N

Hazard Canyon

0 Kilometer 1

0 Mile 1

See Inset

Waves

Rocks

7

MONTAÑA DE ORO STATE PARK

P

Spooner's Cove

Pecho Valley Rd.

Park Headquarters

To Port San Luis (16 miles; see Route 45)

▲ *Valencia Peak 1,347 ft.*

P

Bumpy water inside the reef at Spooner's Cove KEN CROY

CRAFT. This trip runs the gamut of coastal hazards: boat traffic, tide rips, breaking waves, strong afternoon winds, fog, and surf—and that's just leaving the harbor mouth. On the open coast submerged rocks and sneaker waves can appear up to 0.5 mile from shore during a big swell. The steep, gravel beach at Spooner's can look deceptively calm between sets of hard-dumping shore break.

Trip planning: Scout first to assess conditions before leaving the shelter of Morro Bay. Where the road dead-ends at Morro Rock provides a good place to get a look at sea conditions, as do the bluffs above Spooner's Cove at the take out.

Launch site: To reach Colman Park (Embarcadero and Colman, Morro Bay) from Highway 1 take the Main Street exit into Morro Bay, turn right on Beach Street, right again onto Front Street, and then follow the waterfront past the power plant to Coleman Park, where Coleman Drive heads out to Morro Rock. Launch from the small access beach across from park entrance. Facilities: Restroom and water; no fee.

Alternate launch site: Launch through the surf from the beach on the other side of Colman Park. Aerial photo: Looking south over Morro Bay (californiacoastline.org, image 2108).

Landing site: Spooner's Cove at Montaña de Oro State Park (end of Pecho Valley Road, Los Osos): From Highway 1 south of Morro Bay, take the Los Osos/Baywood exit onto South Bay Boulevard, following the signs to Montaña de

Oro. Turn right on Los Osos Valley Road and follow it into the park (where it becomes Pecho Valley Road). The dirt lot at Spooner's is on the right just before park headquarters. Aerial photo: Spooner's Cove (californiacoastline .org, image 2171).

Miles and Directions

0.0   From the beach at Coleman Park (N35 22.33 W120 51.61), head out the mouth past Morro Rock. Caution: tide rips, breaking waves, and boat traffic.

1.0   When you reach the open sea, reassess conditions because it won't get any calmer as the day progresses. Caution: Stay well beyond the breakers and head south along shore; when a big swell is running, sneaker waves can break well out to sea. Side trips: Good surfing can often be had at the semiprotected beach between the south jetties. This makes a fun day trip for paddlers who are crunched for time or feeling less ambitious about running a shuttle to Montaña de Oro. Or you can paddle north along the back side of Morro Rock for dramatic views of the cliffs, often with pounding surf and nesting seabirds. Expect confused seas with lots of rebound and chop.

2.0   If you have strong surf zone skills and a calm day, you may land anywhere along the sandspit from here to Hazard Canyon.

6.0   Hazard Canyon (N35 17.32 W120 52.96) is the narrow gully at the first obvious rock reef to break the long, sandy beach. Landing may be possible or just use it as a landmark. The shoreline from here to Spooner's is reefy and rocky, so landing is difficult.

7.2   The first obvious point along this fairly straight shoreline marks the far side of Spooner's Cove (N35 16.47 W120 53.30). Look for cars parked along the bluffs, hikers, and, if it's not foggy, the distinctive cone shape of Valencia Peak, which dominates the ridgeline behind the take out. Caution: Don't cut the corner when landing; swing wide, staying to the deep water midchannel to avoid submerged rocks on the left (north) side. The landing itself is fairly well protected but steep, so there can be a strong surge or dumping shore break.

Where to Eat and Where to Stay

Restaurants: Options abound along the Embarcadero, from fresh local seafood at the Galley (galleymorrobay.com; 805-772-7777) to stands selling cappuccino, ice cream, and salt water taffy. **Lodging:** Lodging is plentiful; contact Morro Bay Chamber of Commerce (morrobay.org; 805-772-4467). The Back Bay Inn (backbayinn.com; 805-528-1233) bed-and-breakfast in Baywood Park has a quiet, waterfront location with launching access for guests. **Camping:** Montaña de Oro State Park is remote and primitive with outhouses and water, but no showers or hookups (reserveamerica.com; 800-444-7275).

Route 45

Spooner's Cove to Point Buchon
and Port San Luis

The coastline from Montaña de Oro around Point Buchon to Port San Luis is remote, rugged, and essentially roadless for 15 miles, making it a mini Lost Coast. With landing beaches few and far between—and likely nonexistent in big seas—it is as exposed as any stretch of seashore in the state. Not only does this trip promise just about every coastal hazard in the book, you also have to detour a mile out to sea around a nuclear power plant guarded by Homeland Security. Scattered with caves, arches, and sea stacks, however, it is an advanced kayakers' playground, and a great challenge for serious coastal paddlers.

Trip highlights: Outstanding coastal vistas, rock gardens, caves, arches, and challenge.

Trip rating:

Intermediate: 4 to 10 miles round-trip out to Point Buchon and back or north up the coast from Port San Luis for those with previous coastal experience or an experienced paddler leading in swells in the 4- to 6-foot range, winds to 15 knots, and no fog.

Advanced: The 16-mile, one-way trip suggested here requires a shuttle; once around Point Buchon, 2 miles into the trip, if the wind comes up, you are committed to completing another 12 miles before reaching the shelter of the Port San Luis jetty. While it is certainly possible to complete the journey in bigger seas by staying far from shore, conditions with swells in the 4- to 6-foot range or less, with winds below 10 to 15 knots, allow safer access to explore the endless jigsaw puzzle of rocks and chutes and arches that make this section especially worth the effort.

Trip duration: Full day.

Kayak rentals: Central Coast Kayaks (centralcoastkayaks.com; 805-773-3500) in Shell Beach will rent closed-deck kayaks on calm days to experienced paddlers and will also provide a shuttle service for those with their own boats who want to tackle the Spooner's to Port San Luis downwind run.

Navigation aids: USGS Morro Bay South (7.5 minute) and NOAA chart 18703 (charts.noaa.gov/OnLineViewer/18703.shtml).

Weather information: NWS zone forecast: "Point Piedras Blancas to Point Arguello" (forecast.weather.gov/MapClick.php?zoneid=PZZ670); buoys: Cape San Martín and Diablo Canyon.

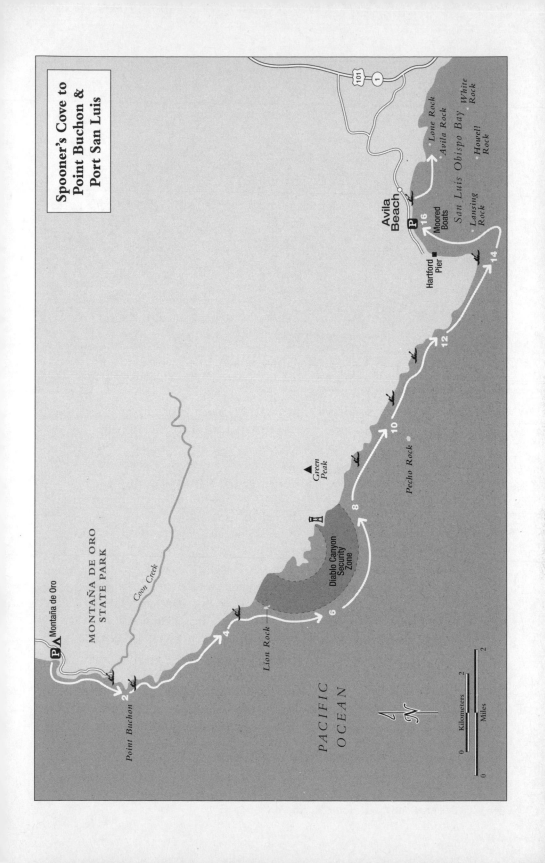

Rocks and fog beyond Point Buchon BUCK JOHNSON

Tidal information: More landing beaches and more rocks are exposed along the
cliffs during lower tides.

Cautions: Extreme exposure, strong afternoon winds, fog, submerged rocks,
sneaker waves, and boat traffic. You need to observe the 1 nautical mile
boating exclusion zone as you pass El Diablo.

Trip planning: Scout from the trail overlooking the bluffs south of Spooner's
Cove to get a better idea of conditions along the cliffs. Get a good weather
report and choose your day wisely. Carry a VHF radio, as cell coverage
is nonexistent. In an emergency you could bail out in the cove at Diablo
Canyon, but plan on being seriously hassled if you do. It is fairly certain that
they won't look kindly on unexpected visitors.

Launch site: Spooner's Cove at Montaña de Oro State Park (end of Pecho Valley
Road, Los Osos) has free parking for your shuttle vehicle. From Highway
1 south of Morro Bay, take the Los Osos/Baywood exit onto South Bay
Boulevard, following the signs to Montaña de Oro. Turn right on Los Osos
Valley Road and follow it into the park (where it becomes Pecho Valley Road).
The dirt lot at Spooner's is on the right just before park headquarters. Aerial
photo: Spooner's Cove (californiacoastline.org, image 2171).

Landing site: Olde Port Beach launching access ramp (6520 Avila Beach Dr., Avila
Beach); from Highway 101, take Avila Beach exit west and follow signs toward
Port San Luis on Avila Beach Drive. Pass Avila Beach and look for launch ramp
down to the sand on left just beyond the long, white pier. Facilities: Restrooms
and water; no fee.

Miles and Directions

0.0   From Spooner's Cove (N35 16.47 W120 53.30) head south toward Point Buchon. Caution: Keep an eye out for boomers breaking on submerged rocks, and try to resist too much playing in the rocks along the way. You've still got miles and miles ahead of you, and the play spots only get better around the point.

1.5   Take a long look at the beach at the mouth of Coon Creek. It might be the last landing spot you see for awhile. Caution: Stay well beyond the breakers when a big swell is running; sneaker waves can break well out to sea.

2.0   Point Buchon (N35 15.30 W120 54.00) can be difficult to pick out among the many rocky points on this wide cape, but it's the one with the longest arc of rocks and reef, and you might see a navigational buoy about a mile to the southwest or hear its whistle. Ideally seas will be calm enough for you to cut inside the reef and begin exploring for caves, which riddle the cliffs around the point. Caution: This is a good turn-around point if you have any doubts about the conditions.

5.0   The barking from the Lion Rock (N35 13.08 W120 52.35) sea lion colony will alert you to start your detour a mile out to sea around the power plant security zone.

6.5   When you are adjacent to the twin domes of the power plant, look for Green Peak, the tallest peak on the ridge to the south, and start angling back toward shore, looking also for a radio tower on the bluffs. Stay to the south of the cove beyond the tower and you should still be outside the security zone.

10.0   Pecho Rock, another sea lion colony 0.5 mile from shore, is a good landmark. From here on, a number of small, semiprotected coves may provide landing opportunities on small, low-tide beaches at the base of the cliffs.

14.4   The end of Port San Luis breakwater (N35 09.36 W120 44.98) provides well-earned shelter.

16.0   Old Port Beach (N35 10.69 W120 44.78), the landing spot, on the right side of the beach between the first two piers.

Where to Eat and Where to Stay

Restaurants: Several restaurants along Avila's quaint 3-block-long beachfront feature locally caught seafood, chowder, and fish and chips, including the Old Custom House (oldcustomhouse.com; 805-595-7555), which has ocean views and a patio sun deck. **Lodging:** The Inn at Avila Beach (hotelsavilabeach.com; 805-595-2300) overlooks the ocean at the east end of the beach. A few miles inland, Sycamore Mineral Springs Resort (sycamoresprings.com; 805-595-7302) has rooms with private outdoor hot tubs. Tub rentals also available by the hour for an après-paddle soak. **Camping:** Montaña de Oro State Park is remote and primitive with outhouses and water, but no showers or hookups (reserveamerica.com; 800-444-7275).

Route 46
Port San Luis, Avila Beach, and Beyond

Tucked in the substantial lee of Point San Luis, the sheltered arc of San Luis Obispo Bay provides the most protected coastal touring for 100 miles in either direction. To augment the bay's excellent natural shelter, a 0.5-mile breakwater was constructed around the turn of the twentieth century from materials quarried from Morro Rock in Morro Bay (before it became a nature preserve). Port San Luis provided safe harbor for a thriving shipping industry during the last 150 years or so, and it is now a refuge for the local fishing fleet and a handful of kayakers. Beginners will generally enjoy flat water all the way from the launch beach to the point; more experienced paddlers can access the secluded beaches and rock gardens along the cliffs to the east or to the north of the jetty. Sea otters, harbor seals, and sea lions frequent the area.

Trip highlights: Good marine mammal viewing, ocean birding, and excellent protection; access to remote and challenging coastlines nearby.

Trip rating:

Beginner: 1 to 3 miles round-trip to Point San Luis on days with less than 1-foot surf on beach and winds below 10 to 15 knots. On calm days, you could head south toward Fossil Point, being careful to return before the wind comes up, especially with an experienced paddler leading (see Route 47).

Intermediate: 1 to 5+ miles on days with surf to 3 feet, winds below 15 knots; those with some previous coastal experience or an advanced paddler in the lead can leave the protection of the breakwater and head north along a suddenly remote stretch of shoreline (see Route 44).

Advanced: 1 to 5+ miles in surf to 6 feet, winds to 20 knots; with calmer seas there is great access to rock gardens and isolated beaches in both directions (see Routes 45 and 47).

Trip duration: Part to full day.

Kayak rentals: Central Coast Kayaks (centralcoastkayaks.com; 805-773-3500) in Shell Beach rents both sit-on-top and closed-deck touring kayaks from their shop in Shell Beach and will deliver kayaks to Port San Luis or Avila Beach; they'll also provide a shuttle service to or from Avila Beach (or even Montaña de Oro; see Route 45) if you want to do a one-way trip. SLO Coast Kayaks (slocoastkayaks.com; 805-704-6902) rents sit-on-top singles and doubles in Port San Luis and Avila Beach.

Navigation aids: USGS Port San Luis (7.5 minute) and NOAA chart 18704 (charts .noaa.gov/OnLineViewer/18704.shtml).

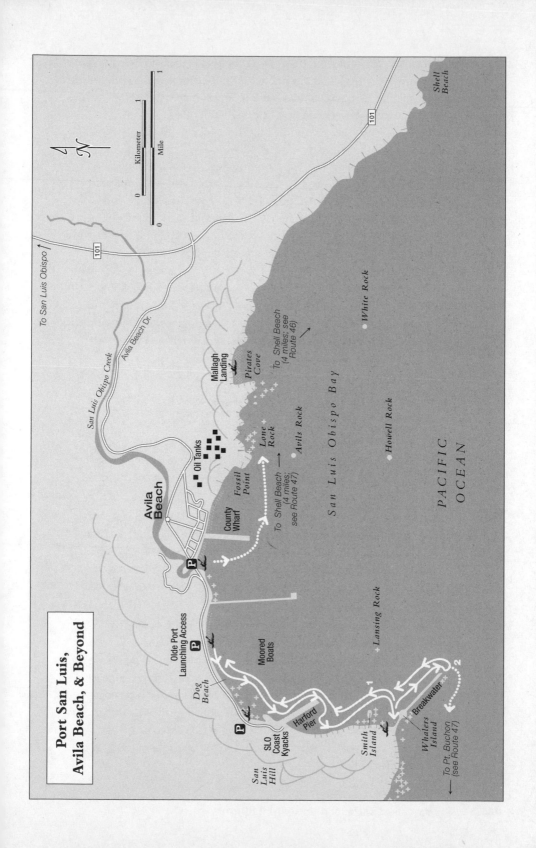

Port San Luis, Avila Beach, & Beyond

To San Luis Obispo

101

San Luis Obispo Creek

Avila Beach Dr.

Avila Beach

■ Oil Tanks

County Wharf

Fossil Point

To Shell Beach
(4 miles;
see Route 47)

Lone Rock

Mallagh Landing

Pirates Cove

To Shell Beach (4 miles; see Route 46)

Avils Rock

White Rock

Howell Rock

San Luis Obispo Bay

PACIFIC OCEAN

Shell Beach

101

Olde Port Launching Access

P

Dog Beach

Moored Boats

SLO Coast Kyacks

P

Harford Pier

Breakwater

Whalers Island

Smith Island

Lansing Rock

San Luis Hill

To Pt. Buchon
(see Route 47)

1

2

Kilometer

Mile

0   1

N

Weather information: NWS zone forecast: "Point Piedras Blancas to Point Arguello" (forecast.weather.gov/MapClick.php?zoneid=PZZ670); buoys: Diablo Canyon.

Tidal information: Little effect except extreme high tides may cover some beaches.

Cautions: Offshore wind, boat traffic, fog, and seal haul outs.

Trip planning: Paddle early before wind or hug shore to stay in wind shadow of San Luis Hill.

Launch site: To reach Olde Port Beach Launching Access (6520 Avila Beach Dr., Avila Beach) from Highway 101, take Avila Beach exit west and follow signs toward Port San Luis on Avila Beach Drive. Pass Avila Beach and look for launch ramp down to the sand on left just beyond the long, white pier. Facilities: Restrooms and water; no fee. Aerial photo: Port San Luis Pier with launch beach on left (californiacoastline.org, image 200510070).

Alternate launch sites: Fisherman's "Dog" Beach 0.5 mile farther on Avila Beach Drive is even more protected, but not quite as easy to get your boat to the sand, since there is no ramp to drive down. Facilities: Restrooms and water; no fee. Far west end of Avila's Main Beach near creek and away from swimmers. Facilities: Restrooms, water, showers; metered parking.

Miles and Directions

0.0   Launch from sandy beach at Olde Port Launching Access (N35 10.68 W120 44.87) and head right, contouring along bluffs.

0.5   Dog Beach, alternate launch site.

0.7   Once you reach the steeper terrain behind Harford Pier, the last canopied pier in the state, you should enjoy excellent wind protection. Round the pier or paddle carefully under it, avoiding any fishing lines.

1.5   The beach at the base of the jetty (N35 09.67 W120 45.37) just past Smith Island is fairly isolated, offering good views up the coast. It is well protected and should make an easy landing in all but the highest tides. This is a good place to turn around, especially if it's windy. Caution: Stay close to shore if the wind has come up. The farther you stray from the wind shadow of San Luis Hill, the harder the wind blows offshore.

2.0   For more experienced paddlers, paddling to the end of the breakwater provides a good view of sea lions hauled out on the jetty and excellent vistas of the wild coastline to the north. Side trip: On calm days paddlers with ocean experience or an experienced paddler in the lead can head around the jetty and up the coast to access remote beaches and rock gardens. Caution: If the wind is blowing, the return along the jetty can be difficult. Wind blows offshore, and if you aren't strong enough to fight it, your next landfall is somewhere around Pismo Beach, across 5 miles or so of open ocean. Extreme exposure and few landing beaches for several miles north of Point San Luis.

Offshore rock south of Avila Beach R. SCHUMANN

Other options: On calm days more-experienced paddlers can explore the cliffs, coves, and rock gardens around Fossil Point and Pirates Cove (see Route 47). Caution: Returning to Avila against the afternoon wind can be difficult. Also, note that the pretty, secluded beach at Pirates Cove is "clothing optional."

Where to Eat and Where to Stay

Restaurants: Several restaurants along Avila's quaint 3-block-long beachfront feature locally caught seafood, chowder, and fish and chips, including the Old Custom House (oldcustomhouse.com; 805-595-7555), which has ocean views and a patio sun deck. **Lodging:** The Inn at Avila Beach (hotelsavilabeach.com; 805-595-2300) overlooks the ocean at the east end of the beach. A few miles inland, Sycamore Mineral Springs Resort (sycamoresprings.com; 805-595-7302) has rooms with private outdoor hot tubs. Tub rentals also available by the hour for an après-paddle soak. **Camping:** Pismo State Beach has tent sites near the beach 10 miles south (reserveamerica.com; 800-444-7275).

Route 47
Avila Beach to Shell Beach

Within a mile of Avila's gentle, sandy-beach launch, the cliffs, coves, and caves begin. While such features are often reserved for more advanced paddlers, those around Fossil Point are tucked in a relatively protected location, and it is not very far back to Avila if the wind comes up in your face. In calm conditions this is a great stretch for intermediates looking to gain some coastal paddling experience and for beginners with an experienced paddler in the lead to get an introduction to the sometimes challenging realities that make coastal touring so interesting. Beyond Pirates Cove, not quite the halfway point, exposure increases, along with your level of commitment. If the fog rolls in or the wind comes up and seas get rough, returning to Avila could be just as difficult as continuing to Shell Beach. In this case, neither direction is very far, and a bailout at Pirates Cove provides a safety valve if needed, although the long, steep carry up to the parking lot will not be easy. Such are the decisions that keep one-way coastal adventures like this exciting.

Trip highlights: Great access to some cool cliffs, coves, caves, and rock gardens in a relatively protected area. Enough exposure to keep things interesting without being too far from a safe bailout option.

Trip rating:

Beginner: 1 to 3 miles round-trip to explore the coves around Fossil Point on days with less than 1-foot surf on beach and winds below 10 knots. May head south to Pirates Cove with experienced paddler (with tow rope) leading, or could continue to Shell Beach if no surf on the beach.

Intermediate: 1 to 4+ miles one-way on days with surf to 3 feet, winds to 15 knots. Continuing south of Pirates Cove recommended only for those with previous coastal touring experience or an experienced paddler in the lead, as exposure increases.

Advanced: 1 to 4+ miles one-way with great access to rock gardens and isolated beaches in swells to 6 feet and winds to 20 knots.

Trip duration: Part to full day.

Kayak rentals: Central Coast Kayaks (centralcoastkayaks.com; 805-773-3500) in Shell Beach rents both sit-on-top and closed-deck touring kayaks from their shop in Shell Beach and will deliver kayaks to Port San Luis or Avila Beach; they'll also provide a shuttle service to or from Avila Beach (or even Montaña de Oro; see Route 45) if you want to do a one-way trip. SLO Coast Kayaks (slocoastkayaks.com; 805-704-6902) rents sit-on-top singles and doubles in Port San Luis and Avila Beach.

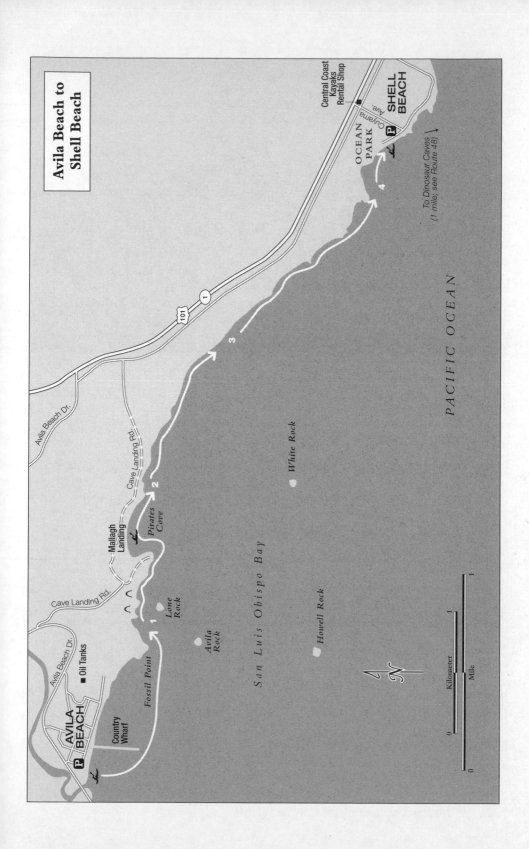

Avila Beach to Shell Beach

Avila Beach Dr.

Oil Tanks

AVILA BEACH

Country Wharf

Cave Landing Rd.

Avila Beach Dr.

Fossil Point

1

Lone Rock

Avila Rock

San Luis Obispo Bay

Howell Rock

Mallagh Landing

Cave Landing Rd.

Pirates Cove

2

White Rock

3

101

Avila Beach Dr.

Ocean Park Ave.

Cuyama Ave.

Central Coast Kayaks Rental Shop

SHELL BEACH

P

OCEAN PARK

4

To Dinosaur Caves (1 mile; see Route 48)

PACIFIC OCEAN

N

Kilometer
0   1

Mile
0   1

Into the maze, north of Pirates Cove, Buck Johnson **R. SCHUMANN**

Navigation aids: USGS Port San Luis and Pismo Beach (7.5 minute) and NOAA chart 18704 (charts.noaa.gov/OnLineViewer/18704.shtml), which cuts off in the south less than 0.1 mile north of the landing cove.

Weather information: NWS zone forecast: "Point Piedras Blancas to Point Arguello" (forecast.weather.gov/MapClick.php?zoneid=PZZ670); buoys: Diablo Canyon and Santa Maria. Web cam: Several views around Fossil Point and Port San Luis (shellbeachwebcam.com).

Tidal information: More beach landing possibilities at low tide.

Cautions: Offshore wind, surf, rocks, fog, and seal haul outs. This is a downwind trip with ever-increasing exposure, so turning around may not be possible if the wind comes up.

Trip planning: Check the marine weather report and paddle early if you want to avoid the wind. Be mentally primed to turn around at Pirates Cove or before if conditions seem to be deteriorating, or be ready to hike your boat (a good 10-15 minutes!) up the trail at Pirates if need be. Parking can be tough on weekends, so arrive early or expect to drop your kayak off by the beach and then go look for parking farther inland.

Launch site: To reach the launch site at the end of San Juan Street (San Juan and Front Street, Avila Beach) from Highway 101, take Avila Beach exit west and follow signs toward Port San Luis on Avila Beach Drive. Turn left on San Juan Street. Launch from the north end of the beach by the mouth of San Luis

Creek, staying outside the marked swim area and avoiding swimmers (and lifeguards) on the main beach. Facilities: Restrooms, water, and cold showers; metered parking. Aerial photo: Launch beach near the mouth of San Luis Creek (californiacoastline.org, image 201007145).

Alternate launch site: You might find easier (and free) parking by the beaches on the other side of the creek, beyond the long, white Unocal Pier, another 0.5 mile farther on Avila Beach Drive (see Route 46).

Landing site: Ocean Park beach in Shell Beach on Ocean Boulevard at either the Cuyama Avenue "straight stairway" or the "crooked stairs" a block north at the end of Vista Del Mar (see Route 48). Facilities/fees: None.

Miles and Directions

0.0   Head south from the north end of Avila Beach (N35 10.74 W120 44.25) toward Fossil Point. Caution: Stay outside the white buoys marking the swim area to avoid getting scolded by the lifeguards.

1.0   Fossil Point (N35 10.45 W120 43.54) marks the beginning of the fun zone for the next 0.5 mile in the cove between here and Pirates Cove. In calm conditions you can contour along the cliffs to explore the caves, channels, and little beaches of this scenic and convoluted shoreline. Caution: Keep an eye out for sneaker waves and submerged rocks, and avoid disturbing any resting seals or seabirds.

1.7   Pirates Cove beach is generally an easy landing, although it is steep and can get dumpy. The left side is generally less exposed, both in terms of easier landing and in terms of it being a clothing-optional beach.

Beyond Pirates Cove you begin to lose some of the protection Port San Luis gives from swell and wind, so it might be a good turn-around point. Otherwise the coastline for the next 2.5 miles becomes cliffy again, with more rock gardens and a few caves and small, low-tide beaches that you may be able to land on.

4.1   Ocean Park landing site at Cuyama Avenue stairs (N35 09.35 W120 40.67).

Where to Eat and Where to Stay

Restaurants: Options abound in nearby Pismo, but Ventana Grill (ventanagrill.com; 805-773-0000) is perched on the cliffs with views of the Dinosaur Caves; Zorro's Cafe and Cantina (805-773-9676) a few blocks from the put in is a favorite locals' hangout. **Lodging:** Several oceanfront options along the bluffs include Best Western Plus Shelter Cove Lodge (bwsheltercove1-px.rtrk.com; 805-351-4539) overlooking Dinosaur Caves, and Cottage Inn by the sea (cottage-inn.com; 888-440-8400), and SeaCrest Oceanfront Hotel (seacrestpismo.com; 866-939-9358), both overlooking the surf break at the end of Pismo Beach. **Camping:** Pismo State Beach has tent sites near the beach a few miles south (reserveamerica.com; 800-444-7275).

Route 48

Shell Beach Dinosaur Caves to Pismo Beach

If you live on the south Central Coast and don't want to bother with the long drive to Mendocino, the Dinosaur Caves in Shell Beach is a handy alternative. With a launch site that's easy to access and a generally protected shoreline, this mini-Mendo features the opportunity for SLO-county paddlers to sample a brief slice of sea-caving heaven within a mile of the launch. On calm days, even novice paddlers can safely explore the alluring recesses of a number of tunnels and caves.

Trip highlights: Sea caves, hidden beaches, sea life.

Trip rating:

Beginner: 1 to 3 miles to the Dinosaur Caves and back on days with less than 1-foot surf and winds below 10 knots. Because of numerous submerged rocks and sneaker waves, it is suggested that you paddle here accompanied by an experienced coastal paddler, especially if launching or landing through surf.

Intermediate: 1 to 4+ miles on days with surf to 3 feet, winds to 15 knots, for those with surf zone experience.

Advanced: 1 to 4+ miles in surf from 4 to 6 feet or so and wind to 15 to 20 knots. Strong coastal paddling experience and helmets required.

Trip duration: Part to full day.

Kayak rentals: Central Coast Kayaks (centralcoastkayaks.com; 805-773-3500) in Shell Beach rents both sit-on-top and closed-deck touring kayaks from their shop just up the street from the launch, and will also provide a shuttle service to or from Avila Beach (see Route 47).

Navigation aids: USGS Port San Luis and Pismo Beach (7.5 minute).

Weather information: NWS zone forecast: "Point Piedras Blancas to Point Arguello" (forecast.weather.gov/MapClick.php?zoneid=PZZ670); buoys: Cape San Martín, Diablo Canyon, and Santa Maria. Web cam: Looking north over Pismo Beach toward Port San Luis (classiccalifornia.com/cam.htm).

Tidal information: Extreme lows make the launch beach rocky, but there is a channel through the reef; extreme high tides may cover some beaches, especially if the swell is up.

Cautions: Offshore wind, surf, rocks, fog, and seal haul outs. Wear a helmet if paddling around rocks and caves.

Trip planning: Finish paddling by early afternoon if trying to avoid wind. The "straight stairs" off Cuyama Avenue are easier to carry your kayak down than

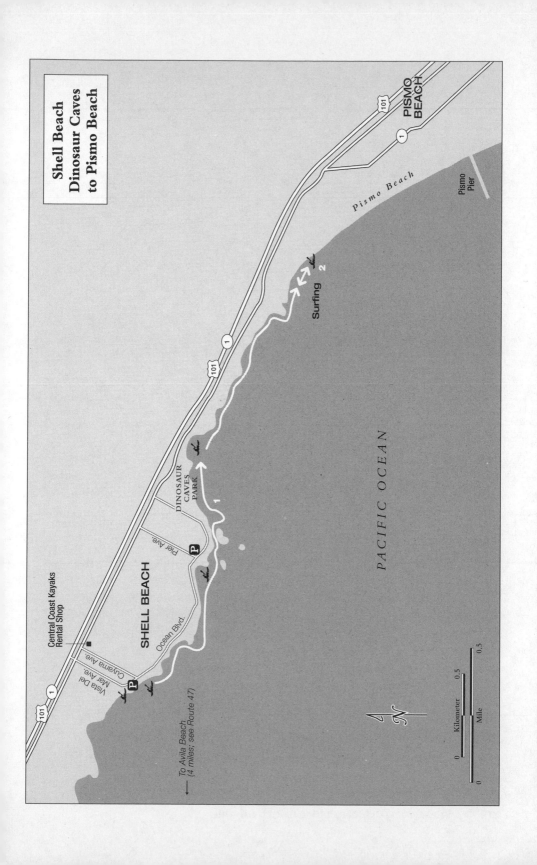

Shell Beach
Dinosaur Caves
to Pismo Beach

PISMO BEACH

101

1

Pismo Beach

Pismo Pier

Surfing

2

1

101

1

DINOSAUR CAVES PARK

Pier Ave.

P

SHELL BEACH

Ocean Blvd.

Central Coast Kayaks
Rental Shop

Vista Del Mar Ave.
Cuyama Ave.

P

To Avila Beach
(4 miles; see Route 47)

PACIFIC OCEAN

101

1

N

Kilometer   0   0.5

Mile   0   0.5

Bluffs and coves north of Pismo **R. SCHUMANN**

the "crooked stairs" at Vista Del Mar; however, the beach by the "crooked stairs" is more protected. While the Cuyama launch is fine in most conditions, during low tide, the surf zone gets rocky, and during bigger swells you'll have to deal with breaking waves. To access the calmer, "crooked stairs" cove, your options are to use the easier "straight stairs" to get your kayak to the beach and then drag your boat 100 yards across the sand to the "crooked stairs" or else to navigate the more challenging switchbacks on the "crooked stairs" with your kayak and save yourself having to drag down the beach.

Launch site: Access the Ocean Park beach from Ocean Boulevard at either the Cuyama Avenue "straight stairway" (Cuyama Avenue and Ocean Boulevard, Shell Beach) or the "crooked stairs" a block north at the end of Vista Del Mar.

From Highway 101 (north or south) take the Shell Beach Road exit. Turn toward the ocean when you get off the highway, then onto the frontage road, which will be Shell Beach/Price Road, and continue in whichever direction (north or south) you had been originally heading on the highway. From either direction, in about a mile you'll turn toward the ocean on Cuyama Avenue. Facilities/fees: None. Aerial photo: The launch beach on Ocean Boulevard (californiacoastline.org, image 200510170).

Alternate launch site: Stairs at the end of Pier Avenue (Pier and Ocean Boulevard, Shell Beach), 0.5 mile closer to the caves, are long, but the cove is more protected.

Miles and Directions

0.0　Head south from the beach (N35 09.34 W120 40.66), swinging wide to avoid the shallow reef. Caution: Watch for submerged rocks and sneaker waves, and be careful not to disturb resting seals and seabirds.

0.75　The protected cove and stairs at the end of Pier Avenue (N35 09.17 W120 40.22) is a possible landing beach. Look for the gazebo on the bluff of the southern point at Margo Dodd Park. From here south the fun begins as the coastline quickly gets more interesting, with offshore rocks, channels, caves, and coves with tiny, hidden beaches.

1.0　As you round the point and enter the next cove, the Dinosaur Caves proper begin. Caution: As you approach or enter the caves, don't get so enthralled with how cool they are that you forget to keep an eye out behind you for approaching waves.

1.25　The larger beach past the end of the caves (N35 09.20 W120 39.79) is generally the easiest landing site in this area.

2.0　More cool caves, coves, and beaches along this stretch down to the far north end of Pismo Beach, where experienced surf paddlers will find a nice surf break and possible landing beach (N35 08.77 W120 38.98). Caution: On busy beach days, landing any closer to the Pismo Pier through the crowds of swimmers and surfers would not be a wise idea.

Where to Eat and Where to Stay

Restaurants: Options abound in nearby Pismo, but Ventana Grill (ventanagrill.com; 805-773-0000) is perched on the cliffs with views of the Dinosaur Caves; Zorro's Cafe and Cantina (805-773-9676) a few blocks from the put in is a favorite locals' hangout. **Lodging:** Several oceanfront options along the bluffs include Best Western Plus Shelter Cove Lodge (bwsheltercove1-px.rtrk.com; 805-351-4539) overlooking Dinosaur Caves, and Cottage Inn by the sea (cottage-inn.com; 888-440-8400), and SeaCrest Oceanfront

Hotel (seacrestpismo.com; 866-939-9358), both overlooking the surf break at the end of Pismo Beach. **Camping:** Pismo State Beach has tent sites near the beach a few miles south (reserveamerica.com; 800-444-7275).

Quick Trip Tips: Other Launch Sites Along the Big Sur Coast

Garrapata Beach (Advanced)

Exposed to the northwest, with often steep and dumpy surf, and a tricky, single-track trail down the bluffs—the launch from Garrapata is not for the timid. What recommends it is that it exists at all along the mostly inaccessible Big Sur coastline.

Partington Creek (Very Advanced)

Theoretically possible launching from Partington is rather improbable except in uncommonly calm seas. Following a long, steep carry down a narrow trail from Highway 1, the "beach" is a pile of hay bale–sized boulders. I've paddled past and scouted from the road, but have rarely seen it calm enough to actually land.

Appendix
Lessons, Tours, Rentals, and Clubs

The following companies offer kayak tours, rentals, and/or classes.

The Lost Coast and Mendocino

Adventure Rents (adventurerents.com; 707-884-4386), Gualala River.
Albion River Campground (albionrivercampground.com; 707-937-0606), Albion.
Catch a Canoe and Bicycles, Too! (catchacanoe.com; 707-937-0273), Big River, Mendocino.
Force 10 Ocean Kayak Tours (force10tours.com; 707-877-3505), Elk.
Kayak Mendocino (kayakmendocino.com; 707-937-0700), mobile tour operation at Van Damme State Beach, Mendocino.
Liquid Fusion Kayaking (liquidfusionkayak.com; 707-962-1623), Fort Bragg.
Lost Coast Shuttle (lostcoastshuttle.com; 707-986-7437), Shelter Cove area.

Point Reyes National Seashore and Vicinity

Blue Waters Kayaking (bwkayak.com; 415-669-2600), Inverness and Marshall on Tomales Bay.
Bodega Bay Kayak (bodegabaykayak.com; 707-875-8899), Bodega Bay.
Point Reyes Outdoors (pointreyesoutdoors.com; 415-663-8192), Point Reyes Station.
Stinson Beach Surf and Kayak (stinsonbeachsurfandkayak.com; 415-868-2739), Stinson Beach.
Water Treks (watertreks.com; 707-865-2249), Jenner.

San Francisco Bay Area

Aquan Sports (aquansports.com; 650-593-6060), San Carlos.
Cal Adventures (recsports.berkeley.edu; 510-642-4000), Berkeley.
California Canoe and Kayak (calkayak.com; 510-893-7833), Oakland and Pillar Point Harbor; (650-728-1803), Half Moon Bay.
City Kayak (citykayak.com; 415-294-1050), San Francisco.
Current Adventures (currentadventures.com; 530-333-9115), Lotus.
Half Moon Bay Kayak Co. (hmbkayak.com; 650-773-6101), Pillar Point Harbor, Half Moon Bay.
Outback Adventures (outbackadventures.com; 510-440-8888), Freemont, Stevens Creek Reservoir, and Larkspur.

Outdoors Unlimited (campuslifeservices.ucsf.edu/fitnessrecreation/outdoor_programs; 415-514-4581), San Francisco.

Sea Trek (seatrek.com; 415-332-8494), Sausalito.

Bay Area Lakes

Sunrise Mountain Sports (sunrisemountainsports.com; 925-447-8330), Livermore/ Lake Del Valle.

Outback Adventures (outbackadventures.com; 510-440-8888), Stevens Creek Reservoir, Freemont, and Larkspur.

Monterey Bay Marine Sanctuary and Vicinity

Adventure Sports Unlimited (asudoit.com; 831-458-3648), Santa Cruz.

Adventures by the Sea (adventuresbythesea.com; 831-372-1807), Monterey.

Capitola Boat and Bait (capitolaboatandbait.com; 831-462-2208), Capitola.

Eskape Sea Kayaking (eskapekayak.com; 831-566-5385), Santa Cruz.

Kayak Connection (kayakconnection.com; 831-479-1121), Santa Cruz and Moss Landing.

Monterey Bay Kayaks (montereybaykayaks.com; 831-373-5357), Monterey and Moss Landing.

Venture Quest (kayaksantacruz.com; 831-427-2267), Santa Cruz.

Big Sur Coast to Morro Bay

Central Coast Kayaks (centralcoastkayaks.com; 805-773-3500), Shell Beach.

Good Clean Fun (goodcleanfunusa.com; 805-995-1993) near the pier in Cayucos.

Kayak Horizons (kayakhorizons.com; 805-772-6444), Morro Bay.

The Kayak Shack (morrobaykayakshack.com; 805-772-8796), Morro Bay.

Rock Kayak Co. (rockkayak.com; 805-772-2906), Morro Bay.

Sea for Yourself Kayak Outfitters (kayakcambria.com; 805-927-1787), Hearst Beach,. San Simeon.

SLO Coast Kayaks (slocoastkayaks.com; 805-704-6902), Port San Luis.

Sub Sea Tours (centralcoastthingstodo.com; 805-772-9463), Morro Bay.

Kayak Clubs

Bay Area Sea Kayakers (bask.org), San Francisco and North Bay.

Kayak clubs (no rentals or tours):

Western Sea Kayakers (westernseakayakers.org), San Jose and South Bay.

Route Index

About the Author

Roger Schumann has been leading kayak trips and teaching classes along the California coastline since 1992 as owner of Eskape Sea Kayaking. He is certified as a Level 5 Instructor Trainer Educator in Advanced Open Water by the American Canoe Association. He lives in Santa Cruz, California.